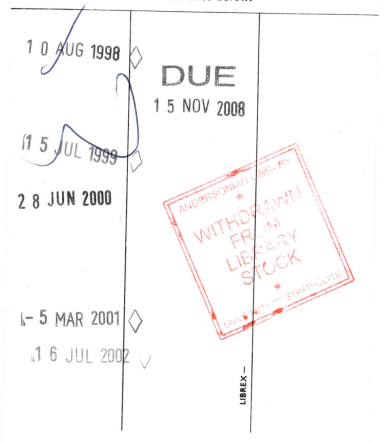

THE LEARNING ORGANIZATION IN THE PUBLIC SERVICES

For my sister, Carol, and her struggle with Multiple Sclerosis
Janice A Cook

To all those who have helped us learn
and continue to inspire us
Derek Staniforth

To my late father, Jack, who helped me elicit my
insatiable thirst for learning as a child
Jack Stewart

THE LEARNING ORGANIZATION IN THE PUBLIC SERVICES

EDITED BY

Janice A Cook
Derek Staniforth
Jack Stewart

Gower

Published by
Gower Publishing Limited
Gower House
Croft Road
Aldershot
Hampshire GU11 3HR
England

Gower
Old Post Road
Brookfield
Vermont 05036
USA

British Library Cataloguing in Publication Data

The learning organization in the public services
  1. Organizational learning 2. Human services 3. Public administration
I. Cook, Janice A. II. Staniforth, Derek III. Stewart, Jack
361'.0068

ISBN 0 566 07773 6

Library of Congress Cataloging-in-Publication Data

The learning organization in the public services / edited by Janice A.
  Cook, Derek Staniforth and Jack Stewart.
      p.   cm.
  Includes bibliographical references and index.
  ISBN 0-566-07773-6 (cloth)
  1. Organizational learning.   2. Public administration—Great
Britain. I. Cook, Janice A. II. Staniforth, Derek. III. Stewart,
Jack, 1952– .
HD58.82.L395 1997
352.3'9'0941—dc21   96-45185
                                               CIP

Typeset in Cheltenham by Raven Typesetters, Chester
and printed in Great Britain by Biddles Ltd., Guildford

Contents

List of figures and tables

LIST OF FIGURES

LIST OF TABLES

List of abbreviations

BPR	Business Process Re-engineering
CCT	Compulsory Competitive Tendering
CFBAC	Central Fire Brigades Advisory Council
DMS	Diploma in Management Studies
EC	European Community
FMI	Financial Management Initiative
GNP	Gross National Product
HMSO	Her Majesty's Stationery Office
HRD	Human Resource Development
HURMIS	Human Resource Management Information System
IFAL	International Foundation for Action Learning
IIP	Investors in People
INLOGOV	Institute of Local Government Studies
IT	Information Technology
LGTB	Local Government Training Board, now the LGM (Management) Board
LO	Learning Organization
MBO	Management by Objectives
MCI	Management Charter Initiative
NALGO	National and Local Government Officers Association
NEBSM	National Examining Board for Supervisory Management
NGO	Non-Government Organization
NHS	National Health Service
NJC	National Joint Council
NLP	Neuro-Linguistic Programming
NVQ	National Vocational Qualification
OD	Organizational Development
PDP	Personal Development Plan
PRP	Performance-Related Pay

PSO	Public Service Organization
QAWG	Quality Assurance Working Group
QC	Quality Circle
RAT	Racism Awareness Training
SAUS	School for Advanced Urban Studies
SCC	Surrey County Council
SCF	Save the Children Fund
SSI	Social Services Inspectorate
TEC	Training and Enterprise Council
TEED	(The Department of Employment's) Training, Enterprise and Education Directorate
TQM	Total Quality Management
UNICEF	United Nations (International) Children's (Emergency) Fund
VFM	Value For Money
VSO	Voluntary Service Overseas

Notes on contributors

Mike Aiken is responsible for policy support and staff development as Assistant Divisional Director for the London Division of the Save the Children Fund. Since 1982 he has worked in the voluntary sector in training and development roles and his current interests are in the fields of homelessness, urban regeneration and voluntary organizations in the context of European social policy. He can be contacted in Brighton on 01273 504527.

Cliff Allen MA, BEd, Cert. Ed. is Training and Development Manager with Portsmouth City Council, and has won local, regional and national awards for excellence in training, including a National Training Award. He is a programme director, management assessor and internal verifier of National Vocational Qualifications in Management. He is a visiting lecturer to Diploma in Management Studies courses, the Institute of Management, Institute of Industrial Relations and Local Government Personnel and the Management Services Society. Cliff is an Organizational Development Consultant and a Leading Officer for OD approaches to Unitary Status. He is now researching measuring effectiveness, leading to a Ph.D.

Chris Blantern and Anne Murphy are partners in Re-view and associates of the Learning Company Project. In times characterized by diversity, fragmentation, and the growth of internal and external partnerships organizational learning means finding ways of achieving mutually satisfactory working across functional, institutional and cultural boundaries. Through Re-view and in association with other consultancies such as the Learning Company Project and AT Kearney, the main focus of their work is to provide methods, tools and structures for working across the space between groups and organizations in both face-to-face and virtual settings. In situations where ownership and leverage are dispersed this approach provides a framework for action where traditional methods are dissatisfying or failing.

John Bolton is the Chief Social Services Inspector at the London Borough of Camden. He has 25 years of experience of working in Social Services. He completed his Certification of Qualification in Social Work in 1974. He has been managing in Social Services since 1976.

Bruce Britton is a Consultant in Management and Organization Development, working in the UK and Asia. He works part-time as Training and Staff Development Manager for the Save the Children Fund in Scotland. He can be reached on 0131 527 8200, or by e-mail at bb002@post.almac.co.uk.

Janice A Cook is the Social Services Head of Human Resource Group at the London Borough of Camden. Her career began by working for a national government organization, then she moved into the private sector, and has spent the last six years in Camden Social Services. Janice is a qualified personnel professional. She is a National Trustee of the Multiple Sclerosis Society, and cares for her sister who has Multiple Sclerosis. She is also a National Trustee of the Association for Management Education and Development (AMED).

Kenneth Franklin is an Education and Training Consultant. He had a lengthy career in government service as a policy maker and senior manager and worked on the development of the Youth Training Scheme into a two-year programme. Subsequently, responsibility for the former Department of Employment's Further and Higher Education Portfolios followed [including the Enterprise in Education initiative]. He was the Manpower Services Commission's Regional Director for vocational education and training, East Midlands/ Eastern region, 1986–90.

Ray Mahoney is the Learning and Development Manager for the Corporation of London. He left school and served an apprenticeship in the tele-communications industry. He became a sound-system and closed-circuit television engineer before moving into local government. His experience ranges from apprentice and manual worker training to management training. He also served five years in various trade union posts, at the London Borough of Newham. He is an Executive Member of the International Foundation of Action Learning, a Trustee of the Women Returners Network, and Board Member of the City University Management MBA Consortium.

Bianka Mensah has been a Human Resource specialist for over 13 years. She gained her first degree in social sciences and went on to do a post-graduate Diploma in Personnel at the London School of Economics and Political Science. A Corporate Member of the Institute of Personnel and Development, she has practised her profession mainly in the public services sector. Her experience spans health, housing, local government and, currently, media.

Anne Murphy (see entry for **Chris Blantern**)

Brian Reddy BSc (Hons), MIFireE is a professional Fire Officer and is a Member of the Institution of Fire Engineers. He studied Fire Engineering and progressed to Senior Personnel Officer in a large local authority Fire Brigade. He has a keen interest in Human Resource Management, organizational structures and culture. He believes that changing workforce attitudes and flexibility by becoming a Learning Organization is the key to success.

Jo Somerset has worked for Manchester City Council since 1985 and is currently Team Leader of the Corporate Training and Development Team. Previously a printer, Housing Association worker and peace activist, she has been inside many organizations in the public and voluntary sectors. She is convinced that organizations must embrace human values in order to effect change that benefits everyone.

Derek Staniforth, BA (Hons), DMS is Principal Management Training Officer at Leicestershire County Council. He spent 21 years in management services and production management in industry before taking a year out to complete a degree. He joined Leicestershire County Council in 1978 as an Organization and Methods Officer, moved into training eight years later, and was subsequently promoted to his current post. He is responsible for the development and delivery of the authority's management training programme, and has particular interests in team building, change management and the development of organizational learning.

Jack Stewart is a psychotherapist, Managing Director of Organisational Healing Ltd, and a Certified Trainer of Neuro-Linguistic Programming. He is currently engaged on researching, developing and applying the concepts and practice of healing people, organizations and communities. By synthesizing the tools and techniques of Neuro-Linguistic Programming and the healing arts of Reiki, Tai Chi and Spiritual Healing, he shares with others the belief that the future of organizations lies not only in their ability to learn, but to heal.

Liz Wallace trained as a teacher and careers advisor, and began her working life in a local authority Careers Service. Changing employers and progressing into management posts, Liz then altered her career path and joined the National Health Service in a training and development role. A move back into local government followed, still within training and development, along with an MA in Management Learning (computer-mediated), undertaken through Lancaster University. Finding this an enriching experience, Liz has found herself tantalized by the notion of the Learning Organization ever since. She currently works as a Project Manager within North Warwickshire NHS Trust.

Richard Wells graduated as an Exhibitioner in Modern Languages from St Peter's College, Oxford. He spent the following 28 years in the Metropolitan Police, building his interest in operational command, training, community relations and media affairs. From 1986 to 1990 he commanded North-West *xv*

London, then accepted his current appointment of Chief Constable with the South Yorkshire Police. He was awarded the Queen's Police Medal in 1987; elected a companion of the Institute of Management in 1991; made a Freeman of the City of London in 1992; and has been an Officer Brother of the Order of St John since 1994.

Preface

The Learning Organization in the Public Services is the result of a suggestion made at a meeting of a group of people working in the public sector, who have a passionate interest in the Learning Organization. This group, which was originally supported by the Local Government Management Board, continues to meet and provides a forum for anyone in the Public Services with an interest in this topic. This now includes both the statutory and voluntary sectors.

The objective in both writing and compiling this book was to explore the concepts that underpin the Learning Organization and then to show how these have been used and developed in this sector of the economy. The chapters which illustrate practice have been written as a series of case studies by a number of practitioners in both Organization and Management Development. They stand alone and enable the reader to dip into them in an order that suits them.

Part I is concerned with concepts and provides a background to the case studies. Chapter 1 explores the underpinning writings of the acknowledged experts and the various ways in which they have approached the theory. Chapter 2 then addresses the issues of whether the Learning Organization is relevant to these services. This is followed in Chapter 3 by consideration of concepts of Organizational Development, other than learning, that may have taken root. Chapter 4 visits the problems of sector transferability – an area about which there is much debate in the Public Services at present. This chapter looks at the differences and similarities across the public/private divide. Finally in this section of concepts, Chapter 5 considers Community Learning, which is based on the ideas of constructive stakeholder dialogue.

This theoretical introduction is then followed in Part II by a series of chapters which show how these concepts have been used. These have been linked in what we consider to be a logical order but it is up to you, the reader, to decide whether we have succeeded. In Chapter 6 the author looks at the impact of Action Learning sets upon managerial performance and illustrates his approach to this. This is followed by Chapter 7 which considers the issue of the evaluation of learning in an organization, which is an area we may all be guilty of not carrying out as well as we might. Chapter 8 looks at three different ways of introducing the concepts of organizational learning into a shire county and what lessons the developer learned from the experiences. In Chapter 9 a Social Services Department links the need to improve quality assurance with the use of learning at all levels to achieve the end result. This is followed in Chapter 10 with a discussion of the continuous challenge of change and a need to constantly transform the organization to cope with this, linking back to the definition of 'learning company' in Chapter 1 by Pedler, Burgoyne and Boydell, and examines the process of achieving this transformation. Chapter 11 illustrates a different approach to the same type of issues and describes a stakeholder community approach and how this aided city-wide learning. This series of local government case studies finishes with a contribution that asks if a politically controlled organization can develop into a Learning Organization.

The other chapters in this section illustrate the use of the concepts in other public services. It starts in Chapter 13 by exploring the relationships between Investors in People and the Learning Organization and links this back to some of the work on single- and double-loop learning discussed in the first chapter. The next chapter, 14, illustrates a voluntary sector approach and concludes that there is a place for its ideals in a value-driven organization which is high on concern of equality and quality delivery of services. Chapters 15 and 16 are concerned with two types of organization, Fire and Rescue and the Police, that are usually seen as hierarchical and modelled on the military. Both these chapters illustrate how the principles can be applied to improve the service quality and morale of organizations. Chapter 17 shows how a committed management team can use the underpinning ideas to assist in implementing radical changes. Our final chapter gazes into the future of the Public Services and how they might deliver better services if everyone in them actually feels valued.

This book has been written to have a wider appeal than the Public Services and is for anyone with an interest in the subject. It was also our intention to illustrate that the idea of the Learning Organization is not solely rooted in the private sector. It is our belief that we can and should learn from each other. It is not a set of rules but an *aide-mémoire* on a journey. We believe it will appeal to an audience ranging from senior managers to developers, both in organizations and management, to all who believe that learning will lead to more effective and rewarding places to work in. We have not set out to answer that intriguing question as to whether public service organizations can develop into Learning Organizations. We leave it to the readers to form their own views on this complex and challenging question.

The Learning Organization Network

The Learning Organization in the Public Services has been coordinated by the remaining core members of the Learning Organization Network, which has been in existence for over five years. This group has produced two interest papers which were aimed primarily at local government, but which did find their way into other public sector organizations. As well as following on from these in a wider Public Services context, we hope that it may help to widen membership of our network.

As members of this network, we have often been accused of displaying missionary zeal – we believe this is a compliment to the concept. We hope that this book will inspire more people to look at what the concept and practice of organizational learning can do for them in this ever-changing and developing world of work. We believe it will influence senior managers and change agents to consider the Learning Organization as a viable way forward.

It is our experience that too many managers underestimate the power of learning in enabling organizations to change. We have, however, come across managers with the vision to see that these ideas will enable their organizations to compete, survive and grow in the current competitive climate, with a workforce that then has a belief in their ability to influence the future direction of their place of work. It is a number of those enlightened managers, who have contributed to this book, who emphasize the power of learning in their organizations.

We would like to thank Malcolm Stern and his colleagues for all their help and support in encouraging us to take an idea and turn it into reality. We must also thank all our contributors. They coped with our pressure, responded to our queries and delivered their chapters. Without them this book would not have been completed. Last, but by no means least, we are indebted to our families for putting up with the many, often fraught, hours we all spent on this project. Without their support this would never have moved beyond being a nice idea.

Janice A. Cook
Derek Staniforth
and Jack Stewart

Part I
CONCEPTS

1 The development of the theory of the Learning Organization

Derek Staniforth, Leicestershire County Council

Since the early 1980s an interest and belief in the value of organizational learning had been growing within a number of people who worked for several different local authorities. In 1991 this led to the formation of an interest group at the inaugural meeting of the Management Development Networkshop sponsored by the Local Government Management Board. All its members believed that learning was a whole life process and that organizations would progress and improve as a result of encouraging learning to take place. On the other hand, experience had shown this group that, in many instances, learning was considered to be a senior management activity while the rest of the staff were trained, and thus the potential contributions of all members of any organization were ignored. The group considered that most people were treated as mere numbers once they entered the workplace, had left their brains outside and needed to be controlled by rules, procedures and manuals. Similarly, our research and discussion showed that few attempts were made in any organization to find out what skills and knowledge employees had and used outside the workplace in a variety of voluntary or charitable organizations. In many instances, the only time this became of any real interest was if these extra-mural activities interfered with their ability to carry out their paid duties. It seemed to the members of the group that a large pool of talent and experience was being wasted that, if harnessed, would enhance the ability of the employer to deliver first-class and improved services to its customer. The outcome of this shared feeling was that the Learning Organization Network should research the background to organizational learning and then see how it could be encouraged in the public sector. The result of this research into the background and theory is the subject of this chapter.

HISTORY

The concept of the Learning Organization seemed to the Learning Organization Network to be of fairly recent origin, but is this the case? A review of the literature on the subject (or even looking at the many books of quotations under the subject heading of learning) shows that it is a concept, even if it is somewhat loosely defined, that can be traced back for many centuries. Throughout the centuries it has been seen as a concept that was, and is, available to enable people to cope with the pressures of change. The pace and intensity of the change process may have altered over time but in each case it would have appeared to those affected to be as threatening as it is to many organizations today. Plotinus, a Greek philosopher, said, 'All things are filled full of signs, and it is a wise man who can learn about one thing from another'.[1] Was this type of view the extremely early forerunner of some of the current thinking on the Learning Organization? Similarly, to bring the background more up-to-date, the following (attributed to Winston Churchill) has been seen on an office wall, 'To look is one thing. To see what you look at is another. To understand what you see is another. To learn from what you understand is something else. But to act on what you learn is all that really matters.' Perhaps these two quotations, which are some 1 700 years apart, indicate that the concept of learning is not new.

CONTEMPORARY DEVELOPMENTS

The development and acceptance of the concept of the Learning Organization has been accelerating over the last 15–20 years, and judging by the number of references and articles relating to the topic, it is still growing in significance. At a recent seminar given to the London Chapter of the Institute of Management Studies in London, Beverley Kaye said, 'The Learning Organization should not be a fad but a long-term reality'.[2] To discover where the concept of the Learning Organization is now it is necessary to follow the development of thinking about organizational learning through the works of those who have written about it.

The book that is regarded by many people as being the seminal text on the subject is *Organizational Learning: A Theory of Action Perspective* by Argyris and Schön.[3] It is in this book, particularly its early chapters, that the theories that have underpinned further developments of organizational learning are articulated. First, the authors differentiate between what a person says he or she would do in a hypothetical situation and what they actually do if that situation becomes reality. This gives a clue to one of the major problems of learning at senior levels, in particular, in most organizations: senior managers will pay lip service to phrases such as 'empowerment', 'learning from mistakes', etc., and, if challenged, will illustrate their commitment to these principles, but in reality it is not usual for them to act in the way they say when confronted with the actual situation. Therefore, it is often necessary to spend time with people encouraging them to change their mind sets. This is not easy as the instinctive reaction to a situation is the outcome of the strength of the culture of the organization in which a person works, and the norms and behaviour that are acceptable in that particular work situation. However, unless this mind-set change occurs meaningful organizational learning will not take place.

Second, the authors define what they regard as the real crux of effective organizational learning: that it cannot take place without individual learning. However, individual learning may not be enough to enable the organization to learn. It is here that they define single- and double-loop learning and highlight the essential differences between them. In their view, which is backed up by their research both prior to and since the book was written, this is what differentiates a Learning Organization from any other. Single-loop learning, in their opinion, is the way most organizations deal with problems. It means that if there are changes internally or externally affecting the organization it will respond to these in such a way as to maintain its organizational norms and values; it will stay within its natural response to any problem that enables its service to continue without having to change its culture. This approach does not solve the issue but merely prolongs the arrival of the time when this type of quick acceptable fix will no longer work.

In contrast, they developed the idea of double-loop learning. This is the name given to that form of organizational learning that occurs when the response to either external or internal problems leads to a shift in the organizational norms, strategies and assumptions. In other words, the problem is such that the organization has to amend its basic assumptions or else it will not be possible to resolve the issues raised. It is this type of learning that actually moves organizations forward by requiring managers and others to rethink their current mind sets. It is, of course, not as simple as the above would indicate because the more usual result is a compromise that buries the problem for the time being. Compromise occurs because the type of shift of behaviour that this method of learning requires more often than not results in conflict. Most of us will do our very best to avoid conflict and will revert to trusted methods – that is, single-loop learning – to resolve the issue. Double-loop learning will also challenge the way managers react to situations and, hopefully, move them towards actually acting as they say they would in the hypothetical situation.

Finally, the authors talk about the realization that has come about in the last 40 years, that learning is not a one-off occurrence but an on-going process and they call this process second-order learning. Second-order learning is about learning to learn and often about new strategies of learning. The original work in this area was done by Bateson.[4] The rest of this book develops and illustrates these themes, using case studies where the authors were used to facilitate the process. The book itself is well worth reading to enable those interested to have a starting point for understanding how organizations learn and establishing a base point.

Further important texts on Learning Organizations have been published by Bob Garratt. Two in the 'Association for Management Education and Development Series' will be considered here. These are *The Learning*

Organization[5] and *Creating a Learning Organisation*.[6] Bob Garratt has worked with organizations in the United Kingdom, Europe and the Far East, but came to the Learning Organization Network's attention when Richard Penn, Chief Executive of Bradford Metropolitan Council, spoke to the group on the work that had been carried out there in conjunction with him, providing a valuable insight into the similarities as well as the differences of the public and private sectors.

The approach in both of these relatively slim volumes (in size but certainly not in content) is different from others. Garratt concentrates directly on those who are at the top of organizations and how they learn to lead. He considers there are two key skills that senior managers require: (a) to be able to learn continuously; (b) to be able to be direction-givers. In his argument for these skills he articulates a situation that will be familiar to many who work in Training and Development, that as people move up organizations they are not given the tools to carry out the next level of job. Therefore, under increased pressure, they tend to regress to the last job they had in which they felt really comfortable. This regression is a result of specialization rather than the development of generic managerial skills. The regression causes resentment and other problems such as higher staff turnover, increased absence, etc., among those whose role they have reverted to. He, therefore, sees as essential a need to clarify the role of top management so there is encouragement for a climate and system of learning in organizations. This shift will not occur if the senior management group returns, however temporarily, to their former specialist roles. Once the regression process has been addressed an organization can start to involve the group of staff that has greatest knowledge about how the organization actually works or where the changes can be made to improve its performance. What is this group? It is the employees usually at the front-line who have the smallest voice and the least influence in the organization. As a result of this analysis the following way forward was suggested:

1 There needs to be a clarification and publication of the role of the director within the organization.
2 The organization's structure must have learning at its core.
3 There needs to be a development process in place so that each and every member of the organization can understand and accept their rights and duties.

These steps are easy to outline but less easy to achieve. It will take time to arrive at a climate where people are ready to learn. It is important to acknowledge that learning is good for the organization as well as the individual and accept that mistakes are to be learned from, not punished. It is in the latter area that performance very often does not equate to rhetoric but if it does not the organization will switch off. Garratt then goes on to look at what he calls first- and second-order change, which equates to single- and double-loop learning.[7] The conclusion of this analysis is that there has to be a dynamic in organizations which allows for feedback throughout it but particularly to the top and which leads to strategic re-adjustments. Consequent upon this, he characterizes the Learning Organization as follows:

1 It will have a three-level hierarchy of Policy, Strategy and Operations.
2 It will have a double loop of learning that allows for multiple feedback.
3 It will have a means of processing and integrating all these information flows. This will be accomplished by siting the direction-giving at the centre of the organization's learning.

These concepts led to two models which are at the core of his thinking and which he has used extensively with organizations and particularly with directors and senior managers. It is important to remember here that the thrust of his work is about developing directors to carry out their functions.

Garratt has found Figure 1.1, 'The Business Brain', to have uses throughout organizations enabling people at all levels to understand what their contribution means to the development of the business that is striving to learn more so it can grow and survive. His second model, Figure 1.2, was

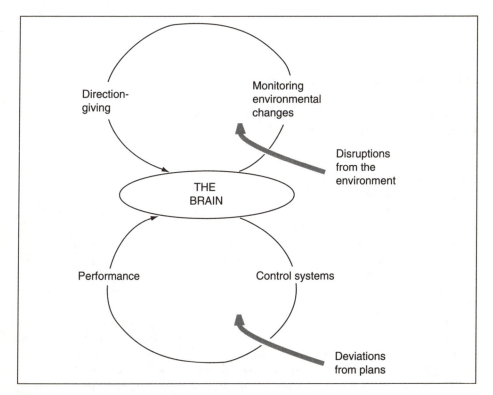

Figure 1.1   The Business Brain

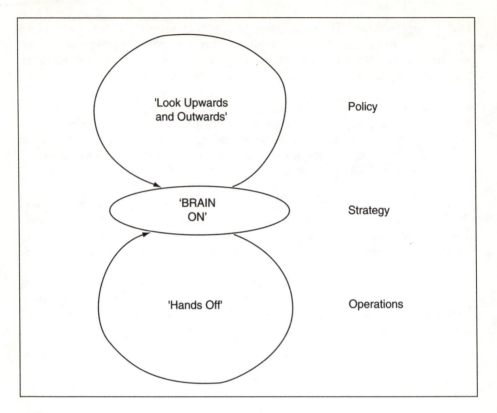

Figure 1.2   Manifesto for directors

developed as a result of work with directors. It came out of discussions of a variety of issues, for example how the boundaries in an organization should be managed. Most of these issues are studiously ignored in many businesses as they cause friction. This model, which was entitled jokingly as the 'Manifesto for directors', indicates the need for the top management to keep itself away from operational issues.

The clarification of responsibility for supervision of different areas of an organization causes many problems, especially in the public sector. In local government, in particular, divorcing the policy level from operations is fraught, given the role of the elected member, who is not only a policy maker but also a representative of his or her electorate. The latter role often involves them in operational matters. I suspect similar issues arise in other areas of the Public Services.

In both these models there must be information flows both up and down and those who work within the business must be fully in touch with these. It is this part of the process that enables them to feel they are listened to and involved in the future of the organization. None of this will work unless there is a radical shift in mind sets at the top of the organization and this will require continuing reinforcement. Garratt points out that he considers Reg Revans' dictum which is expressed as 'Learning is equal to or greater than Change' is true. His work, as described in *The Learning Organization*, is based on this being an essential to survival.

In *Creating a Learning Organisation*, published in 1990, Garratt looks at how individuals learn to lead organizations. The major principle behind this volume is that learning is essential to the survival and growth of any organization. He agrees with the view expressed by Ray Stata: 'The rate at which individuals and organizations learn might become the only sustainable competitive advantage, especially in the knowledge-intensive industries'.[8] There is also an opinion expressed that in the twenty-first century the learning of many organizations will become their major tradable asset.

However, he returns to a theme from his previous book which is that without commitment at the top this may never occur. It is his view that all the learning invested in and accumulated within the many parts of the organization will be of no use unless there is a mind-set change. Those at the top, and possibly even more so in the middle of an organization, must be able to value learning and turn it to the use of that organization. Possibly the middle of organizations is even more a blockage to such progress than the top. This is as a result of employees feeling a need to protect specialization and division, and to keep out of controversy to preserve their promotion prospects. *Creating a Learning Organisation* suggests that there are certain blockages to creating a Learning Organization and these can be summarized as:

1 a lack of strategic awareness – most directors are still too concerned with day-to-day routine;
2 a lack of personal development for directors so they can learn how to develop themselves further;
3 the fixation of top management on action rather than Action Learning.

It is how these are to be overcome that is the major issue discussed. The problem is not one of complexity but of doing what most directors believe they are already carrying out, but in the eyes of their subordinates are not.

Garratt believes that the detailed learning in organizations is done at its lower levels because it is here that the needs of the customer are expressed and met. The question that is to be addressed is: how do we get the senior management to understand this? As a result of rising through the organization and acquiring a specialism senior management often see themselves as the fountain of knowledge and they need to become willing to learn from others. This means that they will have to accept that those words that appear regularly in statements by Chief Executives and others that staff are an organization's most valuable resource are actually true. Garratt, in a paper given to an Association for Management Education and Development and Institute of Directors Conference in 1991, stated that he thought this phrase was a requirement of Company Law as it was so often said but so little followed. The learning ability will be enhanced by becoming more humble and actually seeking help from all levels of the organization.

The next work in this review is that of Pedler, Burgoyne and Boydell entitled *The Learning Company: A Strategy for Sustainable Development.*[9] This book was the result of research that focused their efforts on to the 'learning company'. The concept was inspired by a speech by Geoffrey Holland, who at the time was Director of the Manpower Services Commission. The key part of that speech was: 'If we are to survive – individually or as companies, or as a country – we must create a tradition of "learning companies". Every company must be a learning company'.[10] The authors define what they mean by a learning company: that it is a vision of what might be possible as a result of learning at the whole organization level. Their definition has been seen and heard in many settings but bears repeating: 'A Learning Company is an organization that facilitates the learning of all its members and continuously transforms itself'.

Following this definition, the authors believe the book is for all those people who understand that every organization has a massive amount of under-developed potential within it and want to be able to release it for the good of all its members. Members, in their terms, covers a broad church from employees, owners and customers to, probably, even competitors. Another term, in vogue today, could be stakeholders. This perception accords with the view that was behind the original research for the Learning Organization Network being started, which was that improvements in service delivery would come about by involving everyone in deciding how to improve their own jobs. They also believe that a learning company does not come about as a result of Training and Development but by a change of a mind set in the company. While admitting that the concept has a very long history, perhaps as far back as Moses, they acknowledge that the current interest in it starts with Argyris and Schön.[11] In fact their history lesson covers one paragraph but does give any interested reader references that can be followed up.

Their basic concept is that action alone is not enough. One must act and learn from those actions. There are two objectives that must result from any such action: (a) to resolve the immediate problem; (b) to learn from that action. The authors stress that the concept is not a 'quick fix' nor an instant solution, or even the right answer, but is experimental. They do look at the previous 'right' answers which many in Training and Development now realize were nothing but fads. They believe only by learning and engaging all the members/stakeholders in the process will organizations survive and gain advantage over their competitors. From their research, which is still continuing, through the Learning Company Project, an organization based in Sheffield, they arrived at eleven features for the learning company which can be put into five clusters and these are given in Figure 1.3.

The detailed description of what is meant by each of the features is in *The Learning Company* but, briefly, the clarification of a climate whereby the organization as a whole is more important to all its members than any individual unit. Figure 1.3 demonstrates free flows (up, down and across) of ideas, information, etc., which enables people to feel they can access the help they need and are also valued for their knowledge and skills. This framework is

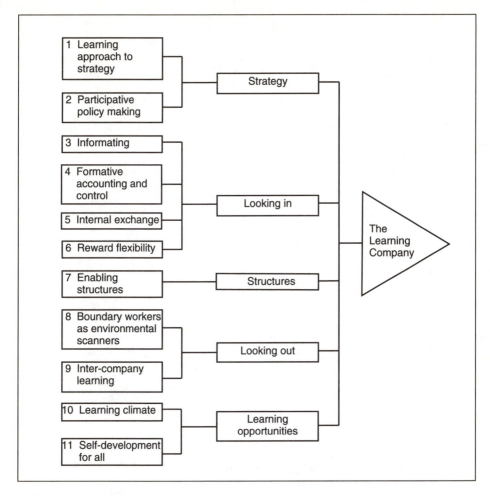

Figure 1.3   Eleven characteristics of the Learning Company

now being used as an analytical tool. These concepts underwent a further refinement as the authors felt there was a dynamic about a learning company and that energy flowed within it. They moved their eleven-point, five-cluster model through an interlocking profile which was considered to be too rigid and mechanistic. The next development was to form a classic fishbone diagram, which will be familiar to many as a tool for problem solving, but which, again, suffered from being static. They stood this on end and produced from it what they called a 'fountain tree' which started to show energy and life but it still did not fully represent what they were striving to illustrate. Finally, they arrived at a model of four double loops or figures of eight which represented the interconnection and flows of energy within the company (see Figure 1.4).

As Figure 1.4 illustrates, it is not possible to say where to begin or end as people and organizations never stop learning and developing. Pedler, Burgoyne and Boydell continue to research, develop and refine this model so   *11*

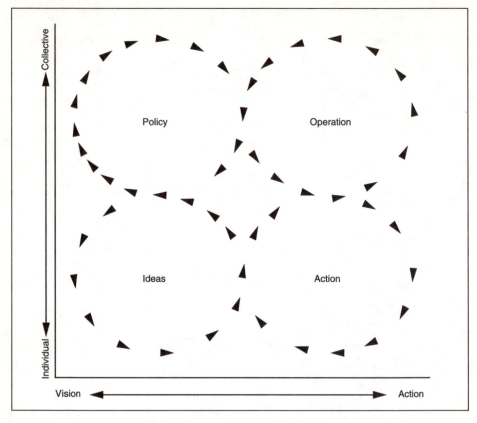

Figure 1.4   The Energy Flow Model

that they and, in the end, their readers and listeners, can better understand how a learning company works.

These authors go on to look at how to start the process and how to analyse where an organization is at present. Finally, the book contains one hundred glimpses from a variety of sources which can be related to the eleven points of a learning company and may trigger thoughts within the reader. Glimpse fourteen, which is the learning company 'litmus test', is concerned with how the organization deals with errors, breakdowns or failures. It asks one to consider the three occurrences and then to answer the following three questions.

1   Did people talk openly about them or did they hide them away and avoid the subject?;
2   What was learnt from the mistakes?
3   Did people get blamed or did they feel empowered as a result of the post-mortem?

12   It is called the litmus test because the non-learning company just does not talk about mistakes but the learning company will seek to understand and learn from them.

At a recent Association for Management Education and Development Conference[12] Tom Boydell and two of their researchers gave some insights into recent developments. Boydell talked about how further refinements are being undertaken on the eleven-point, five-cluster model to enable it to be used even more as a diagnostic tool. Research is also being carried out into company partnership working, and this research is looking at both reasons behind why it is occurring, and what learning has resulted from this from these inter-company relationships. This is possibly something that public service organizations have had an understanding of for some time. However they have never really developed this idea fully. Finally, the authors have a network experiment on IT and learning that is about four months old. They expect to be able to make some judgements about both of these last two areas within the next twelve months. They are following their own definition and transforming themselves in facilitating the learning of all their members.

Another researcher was working in America at the same time as Pedler, Burgoyne and Boydell and this was Peter Senge. He originally published his work in the USA in 1990 and it was published in paperback in the UK in 1993.[13] He also stresses that as the world of business becomes more complex and dynamic it will no longer be possible to have one person, or even a small group, learning for the whole of the organization at its pinnacle. The excellent organizations will be those who are able to use the capacity and capability of *everyone* in the organization to learn. He believes this is possible because, as human beings, we are all learners and actually love to learn. While admitting that, in the past, organizations have groped in the dark to find a way forward he believes that the future is going to be based upon the mastery of five basic disciplines. These he describes briefly in his early chapters and goes on to develop throughout the book. The five are:

1 *Systems Thinking*: Senge believes that we have to understand that business is a system and that we must stop focusing on snapshots and learn to look at the interrelated whole. He believes the tools and body of knowledge built up over the last 50 years will enable us to look at the whole rather than the bits.
2 *Personal Mastery*: This discipline is not, in his terms, related to dominance or control over other people but about an ability to constantly realize results that matter to the person. It is about a commitment to one's own lifetime learning. Senge emphasizes that this is a discipline of clarifying our personal vision and enabling us to see reality objectively. He feels this is the essential cornerstone of the Learning Organization – it is its spiritual foundation.

   Unfortunately, he believes that far too few organizations do anything about encouraging this in their people. The result is that bright young entrants move into a mind set that is about survival to retirement in many cases. This is, in his view, the greatest waste of ability to learn and move organizations forward today. His interest is in the relationship between the committed personal learner and the learning of the organization.

3 *Mental Models*: Mental models are those ingrained assumptions and beliefs that we all have and use to help us to understand our environment and determine how we take action. These are as powerful in organizations as they are in people because they often prevent action being taken for the benefit of the organization as it cuts across deeply held organizational mental models. Others may consider what is being talked about here is organizational culture, which is very strong especially if you subscribe to a vernacular definition of culture as being 'the way things are done around here'.

Perhaps the organization that tackled this problem with a great deal of success was Royal Dutch Shell. Under Arie de Geus, the Co-ordinator of Group Planning, it challenged these mental models by the use of Scenario Planning, the outcome of which changed the mental models existing within the company. De Geus thought of planning as learning and of corporate planning as institutional learning.[14]

To tackle these mental models people and organizations must start to unlearn them by bringing them to the conscious surface and subjecting them to scrutiny.

4 *Building Shared Vision*: This discipline is the one idea, in Senge's view, that has inspired organizations since the earliest days – it is the capacity to have a view of the future of the organization to which all its members subscribe. There does not spring readily to mind any organization that could be described as great that does not have shared values and goals within it. This may be reduced to a mission statement, which many people outside the organization may see as banal, that encapsulates this. One local authority has as its mission 'to be the best'.

The problem with this area is that the values are too often those arrived at by the top echelons of management without any input or commitment from the members of that body in total. If it is going to move to a Learning Organization concept an organization must enable this process to be company wide so that there is a genuine commitment to the values espoused. Organizations are now learning that it is counter-productive for senior management to spend an away day arriving at their vision and then mentally ticking it off as done. Once there is a vision which is corporately accepted, constant work will need to be done to ensure that it is maintained.

5 *Team Learning*: Senge illustrates the problem of team learning by the use of a metaphor of the team of managers all with a high IQ individually, but behaving collectively with a very low IQ. This paradox is confronted by team learning. This will be done by a dialogue whereby team members suspend their individual assumptions or mental model and start to think together. Dialogue is, in his terms, different from discussion, which he views as a winner-take-all competition. Dialogue consists of learning how to recognize the patterns of behaviour that inhibit learning, surfacing

these, and dealing with them to the benefit of the team. It is his view that team learning is vital because it is teams, not individuals, that have now become the basic unit within the corporate body.

Why does he call the book *The Fifth Discipline*? It is because he sees discipline as a body of theory and techniques, to be studied, mastered and then put into practice, and that it is necessary to be a lifetime learner. He does not believe any organization will ever be able to say we are a Learning Organization because everything that is learnt will reveal further learning opportunities. After this introductory overview of his topic, Senge goes on to outline some of the disabilities that have to be overcome before learning can start. Most of these will be familiar to those who work in Training and Development. In brief these are:

1. 'I am my position' – the mind set that is about people being their job and not being able to realize their potential.
2. 'The enemy is out there' – the ability to blame others for organizational or personal failure.
3. 'The illusion of taking charge' – senior management often say that employees must be proactive, that is, to be seen to be doing something. This is often pursued without thought for the eventual outcome.
4. 'A fixation on events' – a belief in a cause-and-effect system and dealing with these on an *ad hoc* basis, rather than realizing it is the slow long-term processes that really affect organizations.
5. 'Boiled frogs' – a lack of understanding that it is gradual change that threatens the existence of any corporate entity. Senge illustrates this with the lack of realization of the threat in the USA to its motor industry that the Japanese posed until the time came when they had 21 per cent of the market. An organization must learn to slow down and look at the evolving picture.
6. 'Delusion of learning from experience' – the paradox here is that we learn best from experiences, but many times in organizational life we cannot directly learn in this way since the decisions we have taken are long term and we may not even be there when the outcome becomes evident.
7. 'The myth of the management team' – a major dilemma and must be examined again. Are management teams corporate and dedicated to organization learning or do they act as turf guards? Senge believes that many management teams are full of people who are extremely proficient in preventing themselves from learning anything.

The Fifth Discipline then goes on to explore these disciplines and disabilities in greater depth. There is not room to go into this in great detail but it is a book well worth reading.

Peter Senge published a further work in 1994, in conjunction with a number of colleagues, called *The Fifth Discipline Fieldbook*.[15] This is a book for dipping in and out of rather than reading straight through. It deals with how to start, *15* readings and comments on the five disciplines and some visions of the future. It is partly written by the authors and partly uses extracts from other writers on organizational learning. Particularly useful sections to anyone who is just starting on this journey or who wishes to see how they are doing in relation to others are those about core concepts and defining your Learning Organization. There is yet another definition in this section of what it is: 'Learning in organizations means the continuous testing of experience and the transformation of that experience into knowledge – accessible to the whole organization, and relevant to its core purpose'. This definition can be used as a checklist of your own progress. In the same section of the book is a series of self-analysis questionnaires on defining your Learning Organization. The purpose of these is to enable the readers to create their own vision of what a Learning Organization is. This is followed by a set of exercises to be carried out within an organization that wants to develop a new way of working. It is followed by a description of how one organization used the exercise to move itself forward.

The book continues in a way that is similar to the glimpses in *The Learning Company* and explores the five disciplines that were dealt with in the original work. At the end of the book is a section headed 'Arenas of Practice'. This covers a number of organizational activities. These cover a variety of issues and organization types where it is felt that learning disciplines have made a difference. The scenarios illustrated include both successful and less successful strategies and are mainly from North America. Finally, this volume looks at some of the areas of practice that fall outside the five disciplines but which may yet develop further, particularly organizations as communities and learning laboratories. The latter looks at how computer-based models could assist in this development and bears some relationship to the IT network being researched by the Learning Company Project.

This has been a resumé of a research that has been carried out since the publication of Argyris and Schön's work in the late 1970s. It is of necessity an overview that has attempted to highlight the major areas of progress. All the works referred to are worth a visit if only to add further gloss to this narrative or to enable your own ideas to be explored. In addition, a constant stream of articles in management journals, personnel journals and newspapers on this topic are well worth examining. The question must be asked: is it another fad? The answer appears to be that this is a concept that is growing in credibility and is not, therefore, just another developmental fad.

REFERENCES

1   Plotinus *Enneads*, Book II, treatise iii, sec. 7.

2   Kaye, Beverley, *IMS Seminar*, London, August 1995.

3   Argyris, C. and Schön, D.A. (1978), *Organizational Learning: A Theory of Action Perspective*, Harlow: Addison-Wesley.

4   Bateson, G. (1973), *Steps to an Ecology of Mind*, Boulder: Paladin.

5   Garratt, Bob (1988), *The Learning Organization*, London: Fontana.

6   Garratt, Bob (1990), *Creating a Learning Organization*, Hemel Hempstead: Director Books.

7   *Ibid.*

8   Stata, Ray (1989), 'Organizational Learning: The Key to Management Innovation', *Sloan Management Review*, **30**, (3), Spring.

9   Pedler, M., Burgoyne, J. and Boydell, T. (1991), *The Learning Company: A Strategy for Sustainable Development*, Maidenhead: McGraw-Hill.

10 Holland, G. (1986), 'Excellence in Industry: Developing Managers – A New Approach', *Speech*, Dorchester Hotel, London.

11 Argyris and Schön, *Organizational Learning*.

12 Association for Management Education and Sundridge Park Management Centre (1995). Research and Development Conference.

13 Senge, Peter M. (1993), *The Fifth Discipline: The Art and Practice of the Learning Organization*, London: Century Business.

14 De Geus, A.P. (1988), 'Planning as Learning', *Harvard Business Review*, March/April.

15 Senge, Peter M. (1994), *The Fifth Discipline Fieldbook*, London: Nicholas Brealey.

2 Why look at the Learning Organization in the public services?

Janice A Cook, Camden Social Services

Why should the profit-making private sector make use of this good idea, and not organizations which deliver public services? No reason whatsoever!

One of the main reasons why every organization, no matter their size or their type, should explore the concept of the Learning Organization is the society in which we live. Today, we have an even greater responsibility than in years past to individuals in our organizations to achieve the highest level of job satisfaction for all of them (not just some of them). This is because our organizations will never achieve high-quality, highly competitive services unless we try to meet employees' high expectations in terms of job satisfaction and keep them highly motivated. This is the same for all organizations, whether they are in the public or the private sector.

ORGANIZATIONAL DEVELOPMENT

The concept of the Learning Organization (like many theories of organizational development) should be explored and analysed for its relevance and helpfulness for your organization. It is irresponsible of any organization which services our community not to ensure that it is developing its organization in the best possible way to meet its customers' needs. Therefore, looking at theories of organizational development and applying them in an appropriate way is one way of living up to this responsibility. There are of course many others. Once this exploration and analysis of the Learning Organization concept begins, some of the negativities will disappear and the true value of learning to an organization's survival will be unfolded.

One of the regularly discussed negative opinions is the insular nature of learning. Some people believe that developing a Learning Organization is pandering to the whims of individuals in organizations and has nothing to do with high-level customer care. These people have failed to see the inextricable link between an individual's learning and the delivery of high-quality services to users. For example, District Nurses (professionally qualified) are now expected to encourage independent living in patients in the community. This was not part of their original professional training. One District Nurse reads up on the subject, asks their own personal network about ways of achieving this new responsibility, and makes continual attempts to implement what they have learnt. During this new way of working the Nurse asks for feedback from the patients being nursed about whether this new approach is supporting the patient to live independently, and learns from the responses, changing behaviour as necessary. Another District Nurse labels the new instruction as 'rubbish' and no learning occurs. Which Nurse is delivering the highest quality service to the patients? The Nurse who has taken responsibility for their own learning by reading, asking questions and requesting feedback from service users is the sort of person every organization wants to nurture. Developing a Learning Organization is one way of doing this, maybe the only effective way for organizations who wish to either maintain or improve their competitive edge.

Historically, the emphasis in the public services has not been on beating competitors, nor on customer care, but on getting good press. Customer care and competition are relatively recent in the long history of the public services. Now that there is such a high-profile focus on these two areas, the Learning Organization also takes on more significant importance.

SOME THINGS TO TRY

There are various approaches to developing a Learning Organization. Following are some ideas which any organization can develop effectively.

Identifying key objectives and evaluating progress

It is essential that customers are involved in both the development of key objectives and the evaluation of their progress. Attempts to set key objectives within an organization without this input will lead to the opinions of the professionals being more influential. It is this view that has predominated in the past, but with some recent improvements in many areas. Customer suspicions that public service organizations exist for their employees and not the public they serve are entrenched but need to be changed. The learning process must in some way address this issue.

It may be relatively easy to think of examples of good practice, but these examples need to be carefully examined. Are they simply skimming the surface, or are they really addressing the customers' needs? It is very easy for organizations to play the game of listening to the customer, without any effective consultation. Analyse your own organization to see if it really listens.

Learning as part of the total philosophy

If an organization is going to move towards learning as a part of the total   *19* philosophy, then it has to consider the equal opportunities dimension. Learning cannot be seen as the prerogative of senior managers who then impose or sell their wisdom on to the rest of the organization. Effective Learning Organizations will involve everyone at all levels to enable them to feel they are part of the process. It is undoubtedly true that if you want to know what is actually happening in the organization then you need to talk and listen to those in direct contact with the customer, and therefore gain a more realistic picture of the service.

However, how do you enable these staff to contribute and be heard? Not easy. The sense of hierarchy and the inability to feel free to express views will have to be overcome if there is to be forward movement towards the involvement of everyone. A Learning Organization is one whereby the whole organization recognizes the need to involve staff irrespective of their personal circumstances or their level in the organization.

Networking

Networking is an important process for all organizations striving to develop a learning approach. The initial problem is that too many people in organizations regard it as simply 'talking to each other'; it is, of course, much more than that.

For the Learning Organization, networking is perceived to take place at a number of different levels. One important level is the networking that takes place within the organization, so that employees know which people in the organization have specific skills, abilities, knowledge and know-how relevant to emergent issues, projects and subjects. Having an understanding of people who have talents which are used outside the framework of their current job expands the available resources which can be brought to bear while engaged in a transformation process.

If you are a manager, do you manage the whole person or just the individual at work? When you talk to the people you manage do you find out about skills, abilities and knowledge they are developing outside of work? Maybe they are a School Governor, a Scout Leader, a Volunteer in their local community, have several children to manage and organize, etc., etc. If you don't know, you will never tap all of these resources and the transformation process will be slowed down. Cross-professional and cross-departmental networking also establishes contacts which may be accessed to contribute to a novel or new situation occurring in the organization's field of activity. However, networking is not just a list of contacts locally, nationally and internationally. The concept of networking goes much deeper. To network effectively a professional with knowledge and expertise in one area needs to be aware of other professions, their systems, procedures and technology as well as knowing a contact name.

Networking may require a process of work shadowing and/or investigation of other professions to enable a learning experience to occur outside the narrow boundaries of one's own professional expertise.

NATIONALLY ORGANIZED INITIATIVES

Investors in People and National Vocational Qualifications are nationally orga-nized initiatives which can help organizations in their journey towards becom-ing a Learning Organization. The mistake which can be made is in thinking that these alone can develop a Learning Organization.

Investors in People

Investors in People sets out various criteria to be achieved in the areas of training and communication with employees. Working towards meeting these criteria is a very important part of achieving quality of service provision, through supporting and developing staff.

However, Investors in People has its limitations with regard to developing the whole culture of an organization towards learning. Its focus on training as opposed to learning (quite correct in itself) is not the total approach needed to develop organizational learning. Investors in People has an approach whereby training must be set in the context of organizational objectives, and the investment in training measured in this context. How is learning (outside of formal training) measured in this same way? For example, you could have an organization which has achieved an Investors in People Award, and in which the theory of internal/external customer has been applied so that the quality of care customers receive is now of a much higher standard. Alternatively, you could have an organization which has no Investors in People Award but which encourages learning rather than training. The result of this process of learning is that there is full user involvement in the development of organizational objectives, champions of change are nurtured, the organization builds piece-meal and thinks holistic, effective networking is developed, and facilitators are used to support employees in the process of change. Or, ideally, you have an organization which has both: the Investors in People Award and an acceptance of the importance of learning, thereby achieving a structured and correct approach to training and communication as part of the total focus of developing a Learning Organization.

National Vocational Qualifications

National Vocational Qualifications are only part of developing a Learning Organization. Organizing competency-based training and work-based assessment would certainly instil a sense of learning from experience as being important; however, the journey to achieve a Qualification is labour intensive (and all labour costs money). An important consideration is whether this approach encourages a total organizational learning culture. I would argue that it does not, but that it certainly helps in the development process. For example, a manager could implement National Vocational Qualifications in their area and, at the same time, develop a punitive culture based on management by fear. This culture is not a Learning Organization approach – *21* which is based on enablement and empowerment at the local level where skills, abilities and knowledge (whatever their source) are valued, where teamwork and any working in partnership models are also respected – but one where employees are scared to take initiatives for fear of reprisal. A manager who uses National Vocational Qualifications to help them build a Learning Organization is the wise manager, looking to the survival of their service.

Copies of the Investors in People criteria and associated information, as well as information on the Management Charter Initiative can be obtained from your local TEC (Training and Enterprise Council).

CONCLUSION

It is not easy to develop an organization towards becoming a Learning Organization if the existing culture in that organization is doing everything to work against it. All employees, from senior management down, must be dedicated to the ideal for the journey to be as swift and successful as possible.

How do you get people on board? Research the subject thoroughly through reading and networking, find systems and approaches that will be easy to implement in your organization and start with those. Pass your learning from the research on to other people in the organization, and be ready to answer any questions at any time as to why learning is so important. Maybe it would be better not to tell anyone you are trying to develop a Learning Organization; introduce new ways of working, linking them to initiatives which already have the commitment of the organization. Think of the future and what it should hold for public services.

3 Why the Learning Organization?

Jack Stewart, Organisational Healing Ltd

Chapter 1 has already described something of the origins and subsequent development of the Learning Organization, both as a concept and application. Subscribers to the Learning Organization ideal hold it up as an exemplar of managing, anticipating and sustaining planned change. This chapter considers alternative change strategies and explores the context of change processes and tools. Most creators of new change theories, fads or panaceas would like to regard their creation as having a significant and lasting impact. 'Disposable' theories abound, yet some have enough appeal to enter our daily conversational language.[1] Some fade and become popular again occasionally in a new guise after a lengthy absence.

Several questions arise regarding the Learning Organization. What appeals about it (surely an idea whose time has come)? Is it because it is endorsed by influential people? Because it utilizes a natural and inevitable human process (learning)? Because it is a 'softer' version of Total Quality Management, an advance on Investors in People (IIP) and a less risky strategy than Business Process Re-engineering (BPR)? But, do you have to embrace the whole concept to gain from it? Whose approach will you use? Is one better than another? Having decided on Learning Organization inspired change and begun to implement your grand plan how can it be sustained?

CHAOS THEORY

There is a case put forward most persuasively by a small group of physicists (chaos theory) which is that *all change* is unpredictable and random, there is no certainty, and no discernible patterns.[2] Applied to organizations, chaos theory suggests we can best spend our time discovering the underlying orderliness in order to provide temporary reassurance, before the order collapses triggering a new search. This has profound implications for all change theorists, managers and agents. However, a recent article (Stacey 1993) suggests it is possible to approach change from this perspective and he offers eight steps to 'create order out of chaos'. One step draws directly on Learning Organization technology (group learning), and it could be argued that so do the other seven. If there is true chaos rendering Stacey's formula ineffective, then this may have a bearing on the search for the holy grail of change prescriptions. It could be argued that in many ways (ironically sharing consistency with the above) to allow organizations to evolve might make more sense. So is it reasonable to assume that every organization, whether explicit or implicit, will have a strategy (of varying degrees of sophistication) or plan or plan of sorts?

INTENDED AND REALIZED STRATEGIES

Three reasons are usually given when the question is posed, 'Why don't our plans turn out the way we intended?' It was Mintzberg and Waters who first appraised these ideas in 1985.

Strategists come together to design a plan which captures their intentions for the organization. This is the intended strategy. What actually happens is called the realized strategy. Deliberate strategies are those which are realized as intended. Figure 3.1 shows that some of the intentions do not happen (are unrealized), and some emerge (not having been planned or anticipated) from the environment.

The intended strategy could only be realized in exactly the way it is planned if:

- the environment is either predictable, benign, or controllable by the organization, or all three
- clear intentions, at all levels, are articulated in precise, concrete detail
- the intentions are owned by the whole workforce, or accepted totally from the leaders

So the chances are that to be (relatively) successful in achieving strategies, first knowledge of, and skill in managing, the environment helps. Second, the plan is comprehensive, and third, there is either self-management, or trust in the leadership.

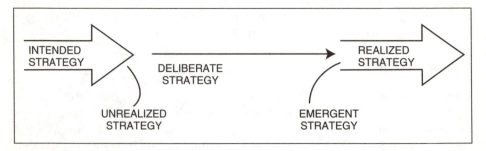

Figure 3.1   Types of strategy Source: Mintzberg, H. and Waters, J.A. (1985), 'Of Strategies, Deliberate and Emergent' in Asch, David and Bowman, Cliff (eds) *Readings in Strategic Management*, London: Macmillan Education Ltd.

What options exist for doing this?

GETTING YOUR INTERVENTION IN FIRST

A model of changing

There are clear differences between the public services and the private sector. This naturally depends on which aspect of the public services is under consideration. The debate is covered in greater depth in Chapter 4, but at this stage, in order for the most appropriate intervention to be chosen, the person(s) who champion(s) the process may examine the issues shown below in Figure 3.2.

Consider, first, why do you want to change, towards what ends, from a

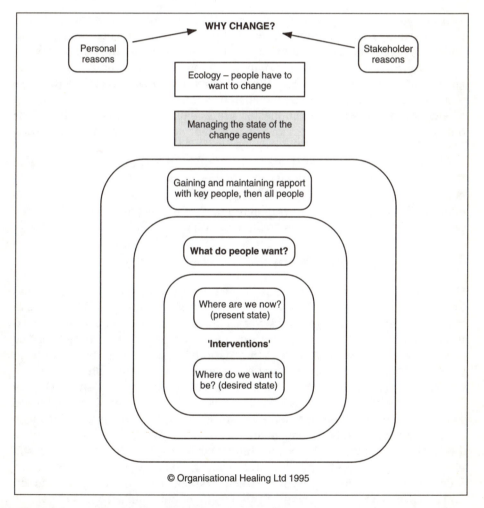

Figure 3.2   Taking the whole workforce with you

personal perspective? Then, why should stakeholders change, towards what ends? Next, how can you check out who wants to change? Importantly, how you can 'manage your state' (walk the talk, show congruence between what is espoused, and what happens),[3] and the 'state' of those implementing the change.[4] How do you establish and maintain a meaningful dialogue and effective communication (rapport) between those leading the change, and those affected by it? How do you establish exactly what those affected by the change want for themselves, and their staff/members/colleagues? How do you make explicit the journey between where you are now (again from a variety of perspectives) and where you want to be? Perhaps, once these questions have been addressed, you can start to think about your interventions.

What kind of intervention?

Throughout this book you will find explanations of why certain strategies were chosen against the competing claims of others. The author's personal quest to find organization-wide change strategies began with the discovery of 'Organization Development' (OD) in the 1980s, having found it had been around since the 60s in the USA.[5] When it emerged, OD was unique in having a step-by-step, organization-wide focus, underpinned by values, and comprising a selection of tools and techniques to bring about the desired results. OD is discussed in further detail below. It has had, and is having, an interesting history.

OD appealed to *me* (I was working in a local authority at the time), because the values were explicit, albeit threatening to some (Truth and Love). In comparison to Total Quality Management and Business Process Re-engineering, Organization Development must be unique, for it has produced a publication devoted exclusively to 'failure' (Mirvis and Berg 1977).

Total Quality Management

Over the last few years there has been a financial incentive (Training and Enterprise Council grants) to follow the Investors in People path. (Investors in People is effectively analysed by several contributors, and will not be included in any depth here.) In manufacturing, many companies have opted for the quality assurance (BS 5750, and its international equivalent ISO 9000) route. In the USA, Total Quality Management has been publicized through the Malcolm Baldridge Annual Quality Award, set up in 1987. In Japan, the Deming Quality Award has been running since 1951. The European equivalent of Baldridge and Japan's Japanese Union of Scientists and Engineers (JUSE) is the European Foundation for Quality Management Award. This award was established in 1991. All these awards share one thing, third party/external validation and accreditation. The author's doctoral research has led him to suggest the following distinctions may exist between a typical Total Quality Management and a Learning Organization approach, based on personal accounts of over 50 directors, managers and front-line staff in three organizations undergoing quality-driven or influenced initiatives (see Table 3.1).

Table 3.1   A comparison of TQM and LO approaches

A Total Quality Management Organization	A Learning Organization
Sets standards	Learning Organization looks for answers, adapts ideas
Process controls the work	People improve the process
Quality has to be learned	Everything is learned
Driven and led from the top, supports employee *training*	Supports employee *development* and empowerment
Internal (and external) benchmarking	Capturing, documenting (and now benchmarking)[6] learning
Focus on process output	Focus on internal culture and processes
Problem-solving, often single-loop learning	Questioning assumptions, double-loop learning

It is also possible that a Total Quality Management approach may incorporate many of the characteristics of the Learning Organization by design or default.

Business Process Re-engineering

Business Process Re-engineering has been described as revolutionary by its critics and admirers alike. One session with Dr Mike Hammer, the person who is recognized as having invented the term, would convince the sceptic of the accuracy of this label. The system promotes a total, organization-wide approach to achieving radical improvements to customer service and organizational efficiency. Like the treatment of Total Quality Management and other approaches, only a brief description, sufficient for the reader to want to investigate further, can be offered. Business Process Re-engineering, being the latest 'fad', now has a whole industry, producing up-dates and revisions, behind it.

Hammer suggests six principles of re-engineering:

1 organize around outcomes, not tasks;[7]
2 have those who use the output of the process, perform the process;
3 subsume information-processing work into the real work that produces the information;
4 treat geographically dispersed resources as though they were centralized;
5 link parallel activities instead of integrating their tasks;

27

6   put the decision point where the work is performed and build control into the process.

Does a Learning Organization approach compensate for weaknesses in the others? It all depends on what you want! If you wish to measure or benchmark the results of your interventions, can you:

- agree upon what measures you want?
- decide on how you are going to measure them?
- agree upon a process for interpretation?
- convince your stakeholders of the value of the measures?

Critics of the Management Charter Initiative (MCI) have argued that a good manager in one organization may not be so in another (how reliable and rigorous are the measures of competence?). Interestingly, returning to Investors in People briefly, this is an example of an organizational model which has demonstrated a high degree of reliability across organizations of different sizes, configurations and sectors. Total Quality Management, Business Process Re-engineering and Learning Organization approaches, despite the 'points, characteristics, disciplines, steps' of several authors and practitioners, are all less outwardly prescriptive than Investors in People's 24 'assessment indicators'. But what is common to those who adopt a Learning Organization line?

WHITHER THE LEARNING ORGANIZATION?

The author remembers an encounter with the Deputy Chief Executive of a Training and Enterprise Council a few years ago, when the subject of Learning Organizations came up. He appeared anxious not to show his ignorance in front of a person (myself) who, as an independent consultant, he was not sure how to relate to. 'Ah yes, we are a Learning Organization,' he said. 'We send a lot of our people on day-release.'[8] But, is it possible to be a Learning Organization if you *do not* send employees on day-release or its equivalent?

How far are we from having commonly agreed criteria to assess Learning Organizations?[9] We all know that there is no universal panacea. In the private sector, such a search has a further constraint: 'The search for generic strategies, for recipes for corporate success, is doomed to failure. There can be no such recipes, because their value would be destroyed by their very identification' (Kay 1993, 368).

Senge suffers from no such inhibitions, as he declares in his discussion of why bother?:

Because we want superior performance.
To improve quality.
For customers (satisfying, delighting).
For competitive advantage (sustaining achievement).[10]

For an energised, committed workforce.

To manage change.
For the truth (those damned Organization Development people are at it again !).
Because the times demand it (Learning Organization people are able to create the future).
Because we recognise our interdependence.
Because we want it.

(Senge 1994, 9–12)

So, unless Senge's prescriptions are followed blindly, it is always a question of what your own reasons are for changing. Are we back then to the question of realized strategies?

Panaceas - an ethnocentric phenomenon?

Current management concepts or fads, as articulated by management gurus, and accepted widely, if only superficially, by corporations, have played a major role in shaping the corporate cultural rhetoric of many American corporations.

(Humes 1993)

and:

The variety of concepts, and prescriptive models ('paradigms' to use the managerial hype), the profusion of gurus hawking them, and above all, the willingness of executives to seek and try out novel approaches, buzzwords and theories are unmatched by any other nation.

(Thackray 1993)

and further:

Is this merely an American phenomenon, or in this country (regardless of sector) do we read them as grist for thought, not as prescriptions to be acted upon?

(Pascale 1990, quoted in Humes 1993)

Problems

Thackray maintains that the problems that beset industry (below) are those problems these concepts are designed to tackle. How far do these problems influence the public services?:

● pace of change (been here before)
● failure of older ideas
● failure of computerized information systems to deliver lower costs and higher productivity
● the need to 'make leviathan companies less muscle-bound' (I assume this means leaner and fitter, or de-layering)
● failure of down-sizing and re-structuring (to deliver improved competitiveness).

29

Solutions

Pedler *et al.* (1991) look at the issue from a different perspective. To them, taking ideas from Ronnie Lessem, organizations pass through phases, or stages of development. But it is possible to stick at any point, with often very limiting consequences:

1 *Primal phase* – when the organization is formed. Movement to the second phase occurs when key people realize that informal and energetic ways of working are ineffective in managing large complex situations.
2 *Early rational phase* – when the organization needs to be differentiated, as specialist functions are necessary. Movement *within* this phase occurs because now the internal focus proves to be problematic. Customers/clients/stakeholders become increasingly isolated. Bureaucracy rules.
3 *Later rational phase* – actions in this phase may be of the 'quick-fix' or temporary mentality (ripe for fads and panaceas). Movement to the next phase may occur because the temporary solutions are just that, or people reject exhortations to develop themselves, not having been given encouragement or resources to do so.
4 *Developmental phase* – typified by integration, the phase during which Total Quality Management may be applied. It is also the phase in which there is the greatest potential for Learning Organization ideas.

According to Pedler *et al.*, each problem within the phase (informal working, bureaucracy, communication, etc.) is solved, but another emerges, the seeds of which are sown by the previous solution. So another problem emerges, requiring another solution. And so it goes on. Figure 3.3 shows this process.

Let us take the example of Departmental Development (DD), a term which described a prescription for local authority housing departments in the early 1980s, which emerged from collaboration between the Local Government Training Board and the School for Advanced Urban Studies. It was designed to address the problem of 'the failure of … conventional training to develop the

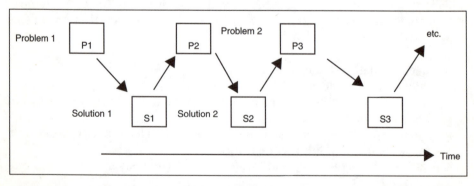

Figure 3.3   The problem-solving process Source: Pedler, M., Burgoyne, J. and Boydell, T. (1991), *The Learning Company*, Maidenhead: McGraw-Hill.

organization itself' (LGTB/SAUS 1983). However, much emphasis was placed on the Chief Housing Officer/Director of Housing to support development, not least their own.

The 'solution' to the failure to 'develop staff talents, create good working environments (and therefore) deliver a better, more effective service to the public and elected members' was to follow a series of recommendations:

- the chief officer embracing the central leadership task (inspiring staff, creating and maintaining good working relationships);
- the departmental management team taking ownership of development of the department;
- the chief officer examining his/her own role, delegating more, meeting more with elected members, informal meetings of the management team, etc.

There is much 'common sense' in this publication, and little to obviously challenge.[11] Yet the seeds of a further problem may come to mind. In the local authority, what if one department runs ahead too far of another? So the second problem may be a heightened sense of rivalry, from an internal perspective. From an external perspective, the public may object to closer links with elected members.

So solutions to these problems may have been 'public service orientation'. Public service orientation was a (reasonably successful, if judged on the way councils have adopted the jargon) way of ensuring the provision of a service *for*, rather than *to* the public. Again, a series of prescriptions followed. Stewart and Clarke, (1985) elaborate on this concept, should anyone outside local government wish to find out more.

These prescriptions were:

- detailed service analysis (what does the customer want?)
- rewarding employees for customer-orientation
- making the physical environment more welcoming and open
- designing working methods around the customer
- establishing service criteria
- carrying out progressive staff policies

Is it possible some more seeds were being sown? And what has followed since? Pedler *et al.*'s model, and it is all the more welcome for this, does not declare that the 'Learning Company'[12] is the final link in the chain. They state that the problem which their own prescriptions may not solve is that of morality and spirituality in organizations. At the time of writing (1991) no solutions had been offered, except in their 'glimpses' section, where some embryonic ideas were suggested.

An era of panaceas?

The final piece in Pedler *et al.*'s contribution is the notion of eras, or external time-frames, economic and cultural contexts. Tom Peters, at a lecture given in Liverpool in March 1994, described external time-frames as 'waves'.[13] The first wave being agriculture, then industrialization, then a time of intensification of information, then (something he has written extensively about), the fourth wave of creative intensification, the last being a time in which creativity at work is essential to prosper and (no doubt in his mind set) survive. Peters would not distinguish between public and private sectors here.

So, we have panaceas which appeal primarily to Americans, but are dependent on where the organization is at in terms of its own development, what has gone on before, and what problems they are brought in to solve. We can safely assume we are in the era of Learning Organizations.

In a recent article Gill and Whittle (1992) examine three 'consultant-driven approaches', Management by Objectives (MBO), Organization Development (OD), and Total Quality Management. They estimate that Organization Development has gone through birth, adolescence, maturity and decline, each stage of the 'panacea life-cycle' lasting ten years. *Birth* occurs when an author or 'charismatic leader' writes a seminal book. The idea may be slow in taking off, but is accelerated if consultants develop material attractive to managers (*adolescence*). Key features are three-letter acronyms (TLAs), brand names (for example, Blake's Grid), user manuals and instructional films. Gill and Whittle quote other authors who argue that management is essentially an oral tradition, in which meaning is given through talking. Interestingly, Senge, an American, describes his second and third 'disciplines' (mental models, shared visions) in primarily visual terms. *Maturity* occurs when the material is routinized and then mechanically reproduced. *Decline* sets in when the package becomes rigidly applied, costs exceed benefits, the novelty may have worn off, and substitutes appear (or reappear?).

What makes panaceas attractive?

Do any of these strike a chord or feel familiar?:

- pressures from above and below
- pressure for solutions requiring a minimum of effort and investment
- rewards for short-term innovation
- pressure from networks, peers outside the organization
- financial incentives from a variety of sources
- customer and supplier pressures
- the need to avoid detailed evaluation
- locked into procedures or contracts making it too late to turn back
- raised employee expectations

The above may be manifest *consciously* (being told to do things, previously expensive mistakes with other strategies, existence of grants), or un-consciously. The concept of paradigm describes an essentially unconscious set of beliefs in an organization of which those working in the organization are often unaware. One way to understand paradigms, and how they can be changed if they are no longer useful, is to use metaphors to describe organizational phenomena. Think now about your workforce, or certain members of it, your employees. What are they like?:

- busy bees (who is the queen?)
- sheep (who is the shepherd, or the sheepdog, or the wolf?)
- lifers (who are the warders?)
- associates (with whom or what do they associate?)
- burnt-outs (who or what lit the fire?)
- children (what kind of family do they belong to?)

Supposing someone came to you, and suggested an approach to solve your organizational difficulties which would develop your employees and encourage them to take more responsibility. It would stimulate their natural curiosity and creativity and, not only that, this change package could be easily understood by those using it, allowing people to be schooled in the disciplines it offered. It promised, and would virtually guarantee success, provided the principles were mastered by the person who was timetabling the changes. Are you interested? What does the above presuppose about your organization, and the way it is perceived?

Gill and Whittle close with some rather telling comments:

Perhaps some ways managers may be helped to understand what is really happening, and so become more aware of the pitfalls, is by a form of process consultancy which may enable managers, through feedback of interpretations, to be given insights into what is actually occurring . . . the 'truthsayer, or organizational fool' may be one way of providing a functional countervailing influence to the drift from reality induced by many consulting packages . . . finally we await a change in fashion with interest, and speculate that a culture change intervention in business ethics may well be the next consulting package to be offered as a panacea for organizational ills.

Can change be made piecemeal?

With the exception in recent years of Investors in People in the UK, much change is done piecemeal, episodically, or incrementally. Even BS 5750/ISO 9000 programmes, while covering the procedural side of the organization, do not guarantee wholesale scrutiny of policy, strategy, employee competence, customer relations, financial viability, etc. Indeed it is hard to imagine any approach which embraces all of these. If we subscribe to Senge's view that we (in this case he was referring to the whole planet) are interdependent parts of a whole, then change which does not address the whole organization is bound to have some limiting effects.

There are two principal metaphors in use in contemporary organization *33* theory, they are the organization as a machine, or as a biological organism. In both cases, there is a leaning towards wholeness. Neglect of parts of a machine, or parts of your body, may not lead to immediate breakdown or collapse. The machine may run on for a long time until eventual component (then possible total) failure, likewise the body.[14] Perhaps few organizations are like the euphemism often applied to football teams (a well-oiled machine), and is it either desirable or necessary to have every part of the organization 'healthy'? Perhaps it depends whether you are (in) that part.

Self-sustaining momentum

Is it possible to create a learning society?[15] Just suppose that the education system produced (or is it conceived?) people who had not only learning skills, but a hunger or thirst for knowledge and skills. And the 'raw material' or trainees were encouraged to learn more, in organizations which facilitated conversion into the finished article, or were self-motivated developers.

Definitions of Learning Organizations incorporate the idea of self-transformation. It might be said that this is one of its key attractions. So, by following the prescriptions, internal processes, supported by positive 'paradigm shifts', it is possible to create the conditions necessary to build a momentum which is benign, irresistible and self-sustaining. What comes to mind immediately is Adam Smith's 'invisible hand' (referring to the market). So take time to reflect on the following:

- Have you found yourself in situations in which you have repeated a past mistake and felt, in doing it, powerless to stop yourself?
- How many times have you observed a group, team or even a whole workforce acting in ways, in your opinion, not only unhelpful to the organization, but to those who are part of the action themselves?

The search for such dynamics will occupy the human race for eternity. In certain situations, patterns can be observed, theories do give a high degree of validity, and no doubt we shall continue to argue with conviction about the underlying causes.

CONCLUSION

Organizational life may feel like chaos at times, but we all know that there is a measure of underlying orderliness in all situations, and how often we strive to create it, in the absence of stability. Conversely, would we like to live in a world of mind-numbing predictability? Before beginning, or perhaps re-appraising if you have begun your prescription, could it be improved by a greater involvement of those affected by it? In this book, we find examples of Total Quality Management, or quality assurance initiatives, but none yet of Business Process Re-engineering. Whatever approach is eventually adopted, it is almost certain that no-one had previously tried it in their organization. No amount of appraising the options can predict (realized and intended?) the precise final outcomes, but you can get that bit nearer.

- Is the Learning Organization an idea whose time has come?
- How susceptible are you or your people to the message?
- Are there any likely candidates for the 'organizational fool'?[16]

Senge talks of leverage, quoting Archimedes' 'give me a lever long enough and single-handed I can move the world', but we need to identify that leverage point. Stop and think for a moment about the concept of reification (treating something as an object which is not an object). This manifests itself in comments like 'society creates delinquency' or 'the company sacked me'. Can *an organization* ever *do anything*? The presupposition in these examples is that every member of the society behaves in ways which encourages delinquency, or that every member of the company agreed with and delivered an individual's dismissal.[17] People may use such terms as verbal shorthand, but they can reflect a way of looking at the world which is fatalistic, serving to sustain a very narrow outlook.[18] It is difficult to force people to learn. Without individual learning there is no Learning Organization. Individual learning is not by itself a sufficient condition to create a Learning Organization. The learning must enable the individual to excel at their own job or role, have direction (from the point of view of those leading the organization), purpose, and be efficient. Groups of learners can assist and enhance their own and each other's learning, because teams/groups are the building blocks of organizations. Ideally the learning should embrace the whole organization, its context, its phase and era.

As systems thinkers, our boundaries may extend to the outer extremities of our stakeholder universe; but can our subsequent thoughts, and consequent actions, serve the greatest good for the greatest number, or do we have another agenda?

NOTES

1 This is an excellent example of how language can influence our bias for action. By adopting simple forms, we can get closer to the customer, providing the motivation for greater productivity through our people. Look at the chapter headings in *In Search of Excellence*, Peters, T. and Waterman, R. (1982), London: Harper and Row.

2 It is interesting to observe which sources even recognize chaos theory, given its potentially profound implications. This reference was from Deepak Chopra (1991), a book which is sub-titled 'Mastering the Forces which Shape Personal Reality'.

3 It was Chris Argyris (1982) who first coined the terms 'espoused theories' and 'theories-in-use' to distinguish what managers said from what they

did. The gap between the rhetoric and reality of change is often that which creates the greatest source of conflict and frustration.

4   Personal 'states': remember a time when you did something to be proud of. How would you describe your 'state'? Confident, calm, powerful, in control, words which reflect a positive state. Now think of a time when you were less proud, or even ashamed of something you did. What is your state now? What words, images and feelings come to mind? So, when wanting to influence others, is it not best to return to that positive, resourceful state, now?

5   Before OD, the nearest was perhaps, in the UK at least, MBO (Management by Objectives). There are many tools which emerged from OD which are used widely today. There are so many excellent texts on OD it would be a major task to list them. However, a good starting point is French, W.L. and Bell, C.H. (1978), *Organization Development: Behavioural Science Interventions for Organization Improvements*, Englewood Cliffs, New Jersey: Prentice-Hall.

6   The Rover Group, as influential members of various European and international groups, such as European Lifelong Learning Initiative (ELLI) and European Consortium of Learning Organisations (ECLO), dedicated to promoting individual and company learning, began to put together ideas on benchmarking Learning Organizations in 1994.

7   In Talwar's article (Talwar, Rohit (1993), 'Business Re-engineering – A strategy-driven approach', *Long Range Planning*, **26**, (56) p.28), he describes an example of a council struggling to set nursery education budgets, then eventually reviewing outputs, rather than the traditional focus on inputs. The exercise avoided large-scale service cuts, and resulted in improvement to the budgeting process.

8   I am sure you have better examples; if so, drop me a line, at: Organisational Healing Ltd, 48 Walton Road, Stockton Heath, Warrington, WA4 6NL, England. E-mail 100436,3521@compuserve.com.

9   Is this ever likely to happen? Probably. The whole idea of comparison became widely accepted with benchmarking, and if Learning Organizations are to have any lasting impact, perhaps they may be assessed by enhancement of the Department of Employment's Investors in People criteria?

10 Sustaining achievement was put forward by Bryson (1988), as a goal for public and non-profit-making organizations, as a comparable term to competitive advantage.

11 At the time when this came out, and it is possible my views reflected my own lack of experience then, this publication was ground-breaking. To look at it now, many years later, it still contains wisdom, but perhaps the message could now (in 1997) be better communicated:

Having reflected on why a whole series of [useful] publications from such bodies as the LGTB and comparable organisations [e.g. Industry Training Boards] have not been followed or applied wholesale, the question which comes to mind is 'learning styles?', (LGTB/SAUS 1983, p.44)

12   Whether or not Pedler *et al.* have succeeded in creating a unique identity with their term 'Learning Company' (if that was their intention) will depend on many things. Equally it would be interesting to discover how many managers in the public services would or would not consider it, given the title.

13   The metaphor 'waves' was popularized by Alvin Toffler (*The Third Wave*, New York: Random House, 1980), although he acknowledged earlier uses of the concept.

14   Have you ever said to yourself: 'One part of me wants to do this, but another part of me wants to do that'? Is the idea that our personality is composed of tens, if not hundreds, of such 'parts' too fanciful to imagine? Just suppose you could communicate with those parts and secure an outcome which would satisfy them both, would you want it?

15   The idea of a learning society has been discussed by a number of authors. The reference here is Ball (Ball 1992). 1996 has been declared 'The European Year of Lifelong Learning' by the European Union. A European organization, established to promote the ideas of lifelong learning, and its translation into practice is the European Lifelong Learning Initiative (ELLI). The address is: 60 Rue de la Concorde, B1050 Brussels.

16   The Fool is the first and arguably the most important card in the Tarot pack, a set of cards used for predictions with a long and possibly obscure history. You don't have to believe in the Tarot to recognize the power of the imagery. If you have a chance to look at a deck sometime, take it. The Fool represents creativity, and the human spirit. The idea of an 'organizational fool' is seductive, though the job title may have to be changed.

17   When I first studied sociology (20 years ago), I found great difficulty in grasping the concepts. Having reflected heavily since, I realize my learning was blocked by the continuous challenges to my way of looking at the world. The power of what was termed in the 1940s 'structural functionalism' remains with us today. Functionalism assumes order, and uses the biological metaphor of society. There are forces within society which act to preserve order and stability, which if the theory is accepted, might lead us to think those forces are beyond our influence.

18   Which argues that, if those forces are beyond our control, then we might as well 'grin and bear it, after all it's only for life'. The quote is from the classic novel *The Ragged Trousered Philanthropist* (Tressell 1984).

BIBLIOGRAPHY

Argyris, C. (1982), *Reasoning, Learning and Action*, San Francisco: Jossey-Bass.

Ball, C. (1992), *Profitable Learning*, London: Royal Society of Arts.

Bryson, J.M. (1988), *Strategic Planning for Public and Non-profit Organizations*, San Francisco: Jossey Bass.

Chopra, D. (1991), *Unconditional Life*, New York: Bantam.

Deming, W.E. (1986), *Out of the Crisis*, Cambridge, Mass.: MIT Center For Advanced Engineering Studies.

Gill, J. and Whittle, S. (1992), 'Management by Panacea: Accounting for Transience', *Journal of Management Studies*, **30**, (2).

Hammer, M. and Champy, J. (1993), *Reengineering the Corporation*, London: Nicholas Brealey.

Humes, S. (1993), *Managing the Multi-National*, Englewood Cliffs, New Jersey: Prentice-Hall.

Kay, J. (1993), *Foundations of Corporate Success*, Oxford: Oxford University Press.

Kline, P. and Saunders, B. (1993), *Ten Steps to a Learning Organization*, Arlington, Virginia: Great Ocean.

Lessem, R. (1989), *Global Management Principles*, Hemel Hempstead [UK]: Prentice-Hall.

Local Government Training Board/School of Advanced Urban Studies (1983), *Departmental Development*, Luton [UK]: Local Government Training Board.

Mintzberg, H. and Waters, J.A. (1985), 'Of Strategies, Deliberate and Emergent', *Strategic Management Journal*, July/September.

Mirvis, P.H. and Berg, D.N. (1977), *Failures in Organization Development and Change*, New York: J Wiley and Sons.

Pedler, M., Burgoyne, J. and Boydell, T. (1991), *The Learning Company*, Maidenhead: McGraw-Hill.

Senge, P.M. (1993), *The Fifth Discipline: The Art and Practice of the Learning Organization*, London: Century.

Senge, P.M. (1994), *The Fifth Discipline Fieldbook*, London: Nicholas Brealey.

Stacey, R. (1993), 'Strategy as Order Emerging from Chaos', *Long Range Planning*, **26**, (1).

Stewart, J. and Clarke, M. (1987), 'Local Government and the Public Service Orientation: or does a Public Service provide for the Public?', Luton [UK]: Local Government Training Board mimeo.

Thackray, J. (1993), 'Fads, Fixes & Fictions', *Management Today*, June.

Toffler, A. (1980), *The Third Wave*, New York: Random House.

Tressell, R. (1984), *The Ragged Trousered Philanthropists*, London: Panther.

Wick, C.W. and Leon, L.S. (1993), *The Learning Edge*, New York: McGraw-Hill.

4 Is the Learning Organization transferable across sectors?

Jack Stewart, Organisational Healing Ltd

It is safe to say that the bulk of organizational prescriptions are designed with private sector/profit companies in mind. Much has been written about the differences between the private sector and, in particular, local government, and several writers[1] have highlighted the differences and similarities across several sectors, including the voluntary sector, the National Health Service, central government, newly-privatized utilities, etc.[2] This chapter explores how far those characteristics which distinguish for-profit and not-for-profit organizations are barriers or opportunities to the pursuit of the Learning Organization ideal.

To do this is not without difficulty. As we have already seen, there is no one definitive 'Learning Organization' (in theory or practice) which can be held up for scrutiny, and its characteristics mapped on to a matrix of distinguishing public/private features.[3] So, as creating Learning Organizations is in essence about system-wide, value-driven change, would the experience of the practitioners of the first such prescriptions (Organization Development) not be a useful starting point?

ORGANIZATION DEVELOPMENT IN THE PUBLIC SERVICES

Much was written about Organization Development (OD) interventions in the public services in the late 1960s, 1970s and 1980s, and there are many lessons to be learned.[4] Some of these will be covered in this section.

Thinking about starting

A very useful article, which I came across ten years ago, is 'Organization Development Readiness', by Pfeiffer and Jones (1978). The authors draw a comparison between a child who is ready to read, and can learn to read using a variety of strategies, and one who is not, when, regardless of their value, most reading strategies would fail. They then suggest this analogy can be applied to organizations. Here, 'reading readiness' can become 'Organization Development readiness' and who knows, by the end of this book, 'Learning Organization readiness' may have emerged. While this interesting approach may not guarantee the starting point, how important are the following 15 factors (highlighted by Pfeiffer and Jones) when considering change?:

1 *Size* – is it possible for Organization Development/Learning Organization efforts to succeed regardless of the size of the organization?
2 *Growth Rate* – this has had significance over the last few years for the public services, as numerous governmental and environmental changes have produced a negative-growth rate.
3 *Crisis* – is an organization in crisis more ready for change than one which is not?
4 *Macroeconomics* – how significant is the larger economic situation?
5 *Organization Development (Change) History* – however labelled, the success of previous 'interventions' will have a bearing on the receptivity for subsequent ones.
6 *Culture* – 'bureaucratic, heavily unionized, and ritualistic organizations are likely to be closed, non-trusting systems which do not invest heavily in efficiency and effectiveness'.
7 *Time Commitment* – how soon are results required? How long before transformation?
8 *Money* – are sufficient funds made available, will any unforeseen costs be met, or could the programme be abandoned mid-stream?
9 *Access to People* – are any areas (particularly at the top) off-limits? How much of a problem is it for internal change agents to have access to the top?
10 *Labour Contract Limitations* – are there limits, enshrined by employee/industrial relations agreements, which make increased employee participation difficult?
11 *Structural Flexibility* – can structures (if deemed necessary) be changed, or, as in many public service organizations, have structural changes been used too readily to solve symptoms rather than causes in the past?
12 *Interpersonal Skills* – how skilled are the members of the organization interpersonally? Are the skills of listening, conflict resolution, influencing, negotiating, establishing and maintaining rapport in evidence?
13 *Management Development* – have there been recent, comprehensive, and effective management and supervisory development programmes?
14 *Flexibility at the Top* – are those in the positions of power sufficiently flexible to be open to influence from below?
15 *Internal Change Agents* – how capable (in the medium term) are internal change agents of carrying the momentum forward in conjunction with top management?

(This list has been adapted from *The 1978 Annual Handbook for Group Facilitators* by J.W. Pfeiffer and J. Jones (eds). Copyright © 1978 by Pfeiffer & Company, San Diego, CA. Used with permission.)

All these are a matter of degree, and it is therefore possible for any one of these factors to scupper change. Equally, and more optimistically, it is possible for strengths in several of these areas (take your pick) to compensate for deficiencies in others. And what would you do with an 'instrument' which declared your organization as 'very ready', on the margin, or 'not ready' at all?[5]

Selling the unsaleable?

Twelve years ago, Harrison (1985) described some very interesting reasons why Organization Development has 'never been properly tried' in government. He cited three primary reasons. First, no-one in the UK had the credibility (as in the USA) of Argyris or Bennis to validate the ideas and practice. Second, the benefits of OD are intangible and accrue only over a long timescale. Third, the UK Civil Service (the context of his article) has never been receptive to the ideas of Organization Development. In this last instance, Harrison states that the 'psychologist class' (the obvious internal change agent constituency for OD practice) in the Civil Service has been 'locked into a conventional view of its role as a species of personnel technician'.

Who can assume the mantle of Learning Organization guru? Can Learning Organization practices be developed to yield a six-month return,[6] can public service organization change agents become torch-bearers for the new dawn?[7]

Some successes?

Sixteen years ago, Golembiewski *et al.* (1981) wrote about the successes of OD in the public sector over the previous decade (1970–80). (It should hardly be surprising that the source of these articles is predominantly American, given the origins of Organization Development, and the comments of Harrison above.) Golembiewski *et al.* note then the absence of 'satisfactory and comprehensive documentation', but go on to analyse 270 public service organization applications (which constituted 47 per cent of the total sample of all (574) Organization Development interventions from a thorough search). Of these, 84 per cent had a balance of positive effects when appraised by independent observers (41 per cent highly positive, 43 per cent definite balance of positive effects). What emerged from their study has significance.

The study classed 'interventions' into eight categories, in order of complexity and subtlety: (1) process analysis (observation, low-level working with groups); (2) skill-building activities (interpersonal skills); (3) diagnostic activities (interviews, surveys); (4) coaching/counselling; (5) team-building; (6) inter-group activities (building linkages between groups in one or across departments); (7) technostructural activities (enhancing roles, jobs and structures); and (8) system-building/system renewal (changes in climate and values, combining most of the previous seven categories and taking three to five years to implement). It was found that public service organizations tended to 'hunt the bigger game', for example racial tension, conflict between individuals, specialities and organization units, community conflict, or re-organization. There was an appreciable bias towards the more complex and subtle aspects of Organization Development.[8]

Comparable figures for private sector applications are 89 per cent positive effects (40 and 49 per cent). No data existed on the preference for, or incidence of, the eight categories of intervention (above). Golembiewski *et al.* conclude with a rather fascinating comment: '[T]he results . . . only imply that whatever constraints or conditions exist in the public sector usually can be accommodated by the kinds of Organization Development *intervenors* who document their experience.'[9]

So far, we can safely say from our research, it is not the technology of change so much as the constraints that exist in *any* organization which are most significant barriers to transformation. Exploration of the concept of 'Organization Development readiness' has already produced some of them. If we postulate that public service organizations are inherently *political* systems, then let us now go on to look at the above constraints within this context.

Resistance to change

Resistance to change may be mobilized in a variety of ways:

- *Diversion of resources* – budget changes and staff moves.
- *Exploitation of inertia* – delay action until agreement is reached by everyone, reports are circulated and commented upon, projects are fully assessed.
- *Keep goals vague and complex* – avoid pinning responsibility down, make proposals multi-dimensional.
- *Encourage and exploit lack of organizational awareness* – there are ways to kill programmes by insisting key aspects be deferred, for example union or any significant group approval.
- *'Great idea, let's do it properly'* – by involving so many people to advise and make representations, it can lead to delay and meaningless compromise.
- *Dissipate energies* – induce paralysis by analysis through surveys, data collection, reports, unnecessary visits.
- *Reduce the change agents' influence and credibility* – rumours, deliberate administrative errors, mobilizing resistance around false premises.
- *Keep a low profile* – avoid open declaration of resistance, as it enables a target to be identified.

The above, and the analysis below, have been adapted from Buchanan and Boddy (1992). Some of the counters to the above are obvious, others less so:

- *Having clear direction and objectives* – goal clarity reduces explicit resistance.

- *Establishing a simple, phased programme* – for the same reasons as goal clarity.
- *Adopting a fixer–facilitator–negotiator role* – exercising of primary change agent skills.
- *Seek and respond to resistance* – tackle it, appeal to higher values, mobilize key group support, indulge in a whole range of political behaviours.
- *Rely on face-to-face* – personal influence is more powerful than memos or reports.
- *Exploit crises* – crises can bring people together, use them to make progress in the direction of the change programme.
- *Co-opt support early* – gain support before embarking on wholesale change, turn 'poachers' into 'gamekeepers'.
- *Set up meaningful teams* – involve significant people in your membership.

Resistance may be manifest in many ways, and its resolution will trigger countermoves, which in turn may create a circle or spiral as the countermoves are countered. There may be some truth in the belief that public service organizations are implicitly more political organizations, but it is untenable to maintain that private sector organizations are less free from the kind of political manoeuvring described above.

WHAT FEATURES OF PUBLIC SERVICE ORGANIZATIONS COMPLICATE THE SITUATION?

Public service organization characteristics and implications

The following may be seen to be part of most public service organizations' make-up and, as seen in previous sections, will have varying degrees of impact:

- Multiple, sometimes conflicting service objectives.
- Multiple, sometimes artificially raised expectations.
- Many stakeholders, often with high potential power.
- Demands and expectations of funding bodies.
- Beneficiaries of service not contributing directly.
- Variable resources from funding bodies.
- Funding received in advance of services.
- Changes in ruling local parties.
- Government (and European Union) directives.
- Statutory requirements.
- Restrictions on raising revenue or capital.
- Restrictions on spending revenue or capital.
- Sensitivity to community pressure.

Is it possible to conceive of private sector organizations which have these characteristics and are subject (possibly to a lesser degree) to these influences? *43*

All organizations are public?

In an attempt to bridge public and private organizational theories, Bozeman (1987), in a book of the above title, asserts that publicness (the level of political authority emanating from and constraining the organization) is the primary concept in understanding organizational behaviour and improving management. Bozeman suggests that compliance to organizational directives has historically been seen to be born out of the influence of *economic authority* (for example, consider the role of enlightened self-interest in *laissez-faire* economics). People's actions are based on economic inducements or deprivation.

What makes citizens, organizational members and clients comply with *political authority*?

- A rational response to the quality of service received?
- Respect for the state and its laws?
- Recognition of the consequences of lawlessness?
- A sense of loyalty to shared traditions, political community and political habits?
- Influence of political symbols?

Rather than dwell on the distinctions in the last section Bozeman maintains that all organizations are public because private sector organizations are regulated by the public sector, receive funding from the government, and are subject to public scrutiny. Public sector organizations are, in turn, increasingly subject to market forces, and may actively seek profits. Bozeman goes on to discuss the implications of his hypothesis for *managing* public service organizations.

'Bottom-line' management

How often have you heard the retort that there is no 'bottom-line' (profit measure) in public service organizations? Are measures of success based on profitability the best measures?

- What is the relationship between a company's current profit and its potential profit?
- What about market share?
- How much are both of these determined by the company's effectiveness, and how much by benign (or malign) external factors?
- Can we realistically compare companies of different ages?
- Is profit the primary motive? What about growth, stability, innovation, survival, control, employee morale and health, reputation, sustainable competitive advantage?[10]

44 To Bozeman, managing publicness is about striving for multiple objectives, seeking stable growth, decision-making autonomy and control. It is not dependent on whether the organization is for- or not-for-profit.

Interdependence

Bozeman notes the increase of interdependence of all organizations, and whilst there are obvious benefits from interdependence, it can mean they are slower to respond to change; even though decisions have greater impact, actions are more difficult to reverse. The significance of this interdependence should be seen in the context of private sector organizations by reference to Kay's work on corporate success (Kay 1993). Public service organizations are implicitly and explicitly interdependent.

For organizations with high degrees of publicness (key determinants are: size; degree of government funding or percentage of turnover related to government contracts; degree of government influence over the organization's operations – all positively related), the significance of political skills in managing cannot be exaggerated.[11]

Managerial values

Bozeman poses some intriguing questions:

- What are the most basic purposes of the manager?
- What are the ends of the organization?
- How do the purposes of the manager and the organization match up with the organization's role in society?

Quoting Mintzberg (1972), if the 'prime purpose of the manager is to ensure that his organization serves its basic purpose – the efficient production of specific goods or services', Bozeman asks what happens when something goes on (for example, misuse of public funds) which contravenes the 'public interest'. In such cases (whistle-blowing is mentioned), we are reminded of the public service ethic. He asks whether this ethic is, or should be, present in for-profit organizations.

When does a manager's responsibility transcend the organization? What of the dilemma of secrecy to defend competitive advantage as opposed to the interests of the tax/rate payer? We can leave Bozeman's analysis with a final quote: 'One of the most fundamental challenges of managing "publicness" is the resolution of the tensions between the values accompanying political authority and the organization's market-based objectives.'

WHITHER LEARNING ORGANIZATIONS?

This book would not have even been conceived, let alone written, if it were not possible to create Learning Organizations in the public services. However, let us now focus on the specific aspects of Learning Organization creation which have *45* been raised in this chapter. Differing from my editorial colleagues, I lean more towards Senge's (1990) model, which I shall use to further the discussion, but will include elements from other notable authors. However, should you need reminding, a Learning Organization can demonstrate five disciplines:

1 Personal mastery (personal growth and learning; the spirit of the Learning Organization)

Are there greater barriers or opportunities to personal mastery in a public service organization? Traditionally, public service organizations have supported individual development (mainly for administrative, professional, clerical and managerial staff through further education), and many public service organizations have deserved national reputations for so doing. The contemporary barriers may be finance and time pressures through compulsory competitive tendering, local government reorganization, legislation, etc. Yet there is so much which has been done, is being done, and no doubt will continue to be done in this area. There is no obvious contender in any of the foregoing analysis which could be defined as an insurmountable barrier. Opportunities always exist, perhaps it is a question of receptivity, in the past history of learning and development efforts. Are there ceilings to be placed on personal development through service specification? Do public service organizations need innovation, creativity, and an empowered work-force?[12]

2 Mental models (how we see the world)

Senge promotes this concept to move people towards a shared understanding of interrelationships and patterns of change, that is to help identify and foster positive attitudes and presuppositions about organizations. This is perhaps the most fascinating aspect of this chapter, because in local government, while the workforce is expected to act in an apolitical way, those creating policy are there by dint of their declared ideology. Those of us who work, or have worked, in local government are well aware of the diversity of 'mental models' and the passion with which they can be described or promoted. Is it possible to be passionate in our allegiance to our constituency, and be empathetic about other groups, patients, clients or communities? Would the education of 'activists' in the ways of change be functional or dysfunctional to the organization? Closer reading of Senge's work shows that he does not wish to encourage conformity. Indeed (and this is most certainly the case with Pedler *et al.*), the opposite is true. He hints at the old OD concept of power equalization (this may be my wishful thinking!), in so far as managing, organizing and controlling (old hierarchical model) should be replaced by vision, values and mental models. This is possibly the greatest challenge for leaders of public service organizations, in particular those operating under near militaristic models of managing (for example, fire service, police).

3   Building a shared vision (the answer to the question, what do we want to create?)

Most of the above applies to this section. Is it realistic to expect a shared vision amongst such diverse and multidisciplinary organizations as public service organizations? My own previous career in, and work with, the UK National Health Service reminds me instantly of the persuasive power of the term 'patient care'.[13]

How much scope is there in public service organizations to *create*? Is publicness a barrier? Can the *public service ethic* be mobilized? Senge's preference is for visions which are intrinsic (focus on the organization, rather than the defeat or overtaking of a competitor), and which reflect the personal visions of the organization's members. (My own experience as a psychotherapist suggests we have a long way to go before people can readily identify personal visions.)[14] Senge goes on to say that building a shared vision is flawed unless done with systems thinking (as it enables us to reveal how we have created what we already have – see below). Perhaps this is one area which would merit further research.[15]

4   Team learning (a team which creates the results its members desire)

Public service organizations have as much history of teamwork as any others, despite occasional negative publicity of the committee structure of local government. Senge's team learning involves thinking insightfully about complex issues, having innovative, coordinated action, and helping achieve results, setting an example for other teams. By this reckoning public service organizations should have an advantage, not least because of the complexity issue. There has been reference earlier in this chapter to political and, some may say, manipulative behaviour. A model of political behaviour with specific reference to local government has been created by staff at the Institute of Local Government Studies (INLOGOV) at the University of Birmingham, UK.[16]

Senge borrows from Argyris (one of the originators of the concept of 'Learning Organizations') the term 'defensiveness'. For him, defensiveness is a series of habitual routines which protect us from threat or embarrassment. Defensiveness in teams can produce a glossing over of problems, or a free-for-all argument. If the top team in an organization is defensive, it spreads, and becomes part of the culture. The whole matter of power and political behaviour is too big a subject to do justice to here, but pause for a moment. Defensiveness is seen as an ever-present phenomenon which must be faced. Overcoming defensiveness can 'unlock' learning, and requires telling the 'truth' about what is going on not only outside but inside the team.

5   Systems thinking (a discipline for seeing wholes)

Despite its simple title, systems thinking embraces a range of skills and knowledge, and is itself an attitude of mind. In strategic management, many authors would maintain thinking strategically is more important to   *47* sustainable competitive advantage than is a knowledge of the tools and tech-niques.[17]

There is little to slow down knowledge and skill acquisition, but for public service organization leaders and managers the difficulty may be adopting a mind set, and an overview, which incorporates the expectations and aspirations of all their stakeholders. With reference to the creation of a shared vision, for a vision to be shared it must embrace as many constituents, stakeholders, departments, satellites, etc., as possible.

Those of you who have set in train processes to create mission or vision statements will understand the dilemma. Enrol everyone, and it is more likely to bring with it commitment and then alignment. But some groups may be ideologically, emotionally, or materially irreconcilably opposed. To attempt reconciliation and build communities[18] may save the planet, but the resources of time, and inevitably money, will intervene. We return again to the whole question of pluralism, unitarism and unstable pluralism.

BRINGING IT ALL TOGETHER – AN INTEGRATIVE MODEL OF CHANGE

We know it is possible to see barriers as opportunities and vice versa. The Organization Development research of the early 1980s suggested that those promoting change were able to overcome obstacles and report high success rates, favourable in comparison with the private sector. In an uneasy combination of 'readiness', 'era', 'phase', and 'age',[19] perhaps the trick lies in all these factors being benign and then when the time is right, the probability of creating a sustainable Learning Organization is high – or are we able to transcend this mind set?

Borrowing a concept devised by Robert Dilts (Dilts *et al.* 1991), a leading writer and researcher in the field of Neuro-Linguistic Programming,[20] that of 'neuro-logical levels', we can explore the potential for success in a more structured and optimistic way. This model has six levels, beginning with *environment* (time and place), which has already been addressed above. The environment is rarely other than a given for public service organizations. There are boundaries, legislative parameters, and these are also accompanied by a time dimension. Yet even though many public service organizations cannot secure (significant) funds by selling more services, or cutting costs without having an impact somewhere, what may be more important is a belief that it can be done.

Dilt's next level is that of *behaviour*, and in the context of this book, what would you expect people to be doing differently in a Learning Organization than they would be, had the new practices not been introduced? It is possible that employees or customers may behave in ways which could be seen as objectionable by management, but that, in another place or time, may be entirely appropriate. Have you ever looked back on serious complaints, disruptive individuals, or (dare I say it?) strikes, and thought how positive changes have since followed? Using the biological metaphor discussed in Chapter 3, imagine the organization as a body. Have you ever gone down with 'flu at the start of a period of relaxation, preceded by weeks of intense effort? It is not just teachers who are familiar with the end-of-term illnesses. Have you ever said to yourself, or been told by a concerned other, that it is your body's way of telling you to slow down or ease up? And how many of you have ignored those signs, and gone on to even more serious conditions? Is it possible to have an organization free from 'dis-ease' all of the time? You may not agree that it is possible for either, but would you rather be healthy, and work in an organization with a clear, agreed purpose, or grin and bear both because, after all, they are only for life?

Moving on, we then come to the third level, *capabilities or skills*. Skilled people can choose from a wide range of behaviours, and can more readily adapt to different environments – so maybe your disruptive individuals may lack some necessary skills, or they may not. Pause for a moment. What did most 'training interventions' consist of in the past? Remember the old formula of knowledge, skills and attitudes? If you had a similar training history to me, you knew to avoid attitudes, and concentrate on the other two. Or for those who found themselves involved in Racism Awareness Training, how useful was the old cliché, 'grab them by the balls and their hearts and minds will follow'? (This expression was OK, because during the 1980s (my time as someone involved with this training) men were the racists.)[21]

The fourth level is *beliefs*. If we believe something, we can give ourselves permission to pursue it, and it is part of what provides our motivation. If our beliefs and values support our capabilities, then we are likely to be seen as behaving in ways which are not only effective and efficient from the organizational viewpoint, but we may even feel happy in so doing. Time for the next pause. Now, think of two different scenarios at work. For the first, one when you were in disagreement with someone, possibly your boss, or a customer or supplier. Concentrate on a specific time during which the exchange was going nowhere. As you fully recall that time, ask yourself now, who are you? Do you remember getting out of bed this morning? Now, think of a time when you excelled at something, you felt good about what you had achieved, proud. As you fully recall this time, as yourself now, who are you? While there are no universally predictable responses to these questions, it is possible for the first scenario, you may have thought you were one of the following:

- only (your job title)
- the boss
- a subordinate
- the dogsbody

For the second scenario, it is probable what came up for you was 'me', or your name (what you call yourself), or your job title.

At the fifth level of *identity*, if we are fully ourselves, and actually like (can I   *49* use the word love?) ourselves, then what we believe will be consistent with our concept of self, and our performance (capabilities and behaviour), will stand a good chance of being timely and appropriate (this word is derived from the latin *appropriare*, meaning to make one's own).[22] But are we, as autonomous individuals, all that there is? If we become our congruent selves, pursuing enlightened self-interest, is there any need to do more? Sorry, but I believe (and so does Robert Dilts) there may be – remember the earlier references to mission?

The sixth level is problematic. Dilts calls it *spiritual*, but qualifies it with another term, transmission. In essence it is the answer to the question, 'who else?'. It is that quality that enables emergency services personnel to put their lives on the line, for parents to protect their children, and for countless other 'self-less' acts. Yet these instances are consistent with the self, and are real.

Imagine an organization in which every stakeholder was there to serve all the other stakeholders, because their answer to the question 'who else?' was, 'the public, the patients, the clients, the customers, the ratepayers, the tenants, the directors, the typists, the engineers'.

COMMITMENT, NOT COMPLIANCE

Having committed to these ideals, each stakeholder operates on the basis of pride in their role, and identifies themselves with it. Yet the role is only one facet of the stakeholding, because at various times, each person is a father, mother, sister, brother, or child.[23] Beliefs in this organization are supportive of diversity; diversity in every way imaginable. Beliefs are those which encourage self-development, personal growth, mutual respect and support.

Everyone is skilled beyond their current role, as their roles are multi-faceted, and enable teams to tackle projects, advise on strategy, and secure intelligence from outside. Each person behaves in ways which create and sustain high or peak performance, but never deliberately at the expense of personal, team or organizational health (they all know what this means). Occasionally, things will get out of balance, because people are human, and make mistakes. And although they learn from their mistakes, and rectify them quicker than anywhere else, it often leads to new forms, new structures, and new emphases. Indeed whereas change is always a fact of life, learning becomes synonymous with breathing, 'healing' is acknowledged, then integrated, then becomes automatic, and the new panacea is constructed with interest.

Perhaps this could be what is meant by a Learning Organization in the public services, something which is transferable across sectors, boundaries, communities and countries. Table 4.1 illustrates these concepts, combining aspects of focus (internal or external; individual, team or organization), the six levels, and a final column which suggests possible symptoms of neglect.

Wasn't it Einstein who said that imagination is more important than knowledge?

Table 4.1 Learning Organization model based on Dilts' 'neuro-logical levels'

Focus → Level ↓	Internal		Internal/External	Symptoms of Neglect
	Individual	Team/Group	Organization	
Environment (where and when)	What people, in which section or department, in what sequence?	What teams, in which section or department, in what sequence?	Which stakeholders will be affected? In what environments do/should we operate? When should specific actions be taken?	Confusion, work duplication, inefficiency, ineffectiveness loss of energy
Behaviour (what)	What specifically do we want people to do?	What does the team have to do?	What are the outputs? What outputs are demanded?	Complaints, waste, pursuit of own agendas
Capability/Skills (how)	What skills, in which people, do we need?	What skills do our teams need?	What is the capability of our organization to deliver what our stakeholders demand?	Poor service delivery, poor public image, funding issues
Beliefs (why)	Why is the person doing his/her job? What beliefs do we wish to encourage?	Why is the team pursuing its goals? How do we assimilate diversity?	What are the beliefs of our stakeholders? How do we balance competing beliefs?	Tension, conflict, division, distorted resource allocation
Identity (who)	Who is the person when they are doing their job? What is their (work) mission?	What is the team's identity or mission?	What is the organization's mission?	Alienation, stress, internal politicking
Spiritual or Transmission (who else)	Can their (beyond work) mission be served by doing this job?	What purpose (beyond the team) is being served by this task being done?	What is the organization's vision?	Instrumental behaviour, loss of service ethic, materialism

© Jack Stewart, Organisational Healing Ltd, 1996

NOTES

1   The most notable in the UK is Professor John Stewart of the Institute of Local Government Studies, Birmingham. He has written extensively on his own account, and with other colleagues. Alan Fowler has also written about the personnel function in local government.

2   Bryson (1988), and Bozeman (1987) are two American authors referred to in this book, and a search through specific sector journals will reveal the names of others.

3   Some of these distinguishing features are listed later, but if you read the whole of this chapter, the conclusion should become apparent.

4   It may now be self-evident that I have a bias towards Organization Development. The lessons (as I see them) are not all revealed herein, but will surface in numerous texts under other more recent labels.

5   Not unexpectedly, Pfeiffer and Jones have created an instrument themselves, and there are no shortages in the many fine publications about Learning Organizations. The point I wish to make is that it is why you wish to use an instrument, and how it can improve things. My preference, as a consultant, is to avoid those tools which have extremely high reliability and validity coefficients. Boxes are things we put lids on.

6   What price the quick fix? Yet it is possible for a quick return. Transformation may take time, but change can happen very quickly.

7   My own, now obsolete and therefore untenable, position regarding my peers when a trainer in local government, was their seemingly endless preoccupation with making training (their role) strategic, instead of using the tools at their disposal to secure the organizational mission. I now know this has changed.

8   The public sector *is* the big game park, isn't it? Why else bother with it?

9   This lays itself open to the charge of being a self-fulfilling prophecy. That is, excepting those who wish to star in the book about Organization Development failures, those going into change organizations will have usually conducted a distant or hands-on diagnosis.

10 It should by now be apparent that no single measure can be used to make meaningful comparisons of organizational performance, regardless of sector. The recent UK Government obsession with league tables has seduced many people who should know better.

11 How true, but not only in the public services. For political skills read communication or interpersonal skills, and for managing read influence.

12 Few would disagree with innovation and creativity. Empowerment can come with a price. Those of us who can remember the last few years of the Callaghan/Wilson Labour Government in the UK, may have forgotten the Bullock report on Industrial Democracy. The representatives of industry at the time were having none other than token worker participation: in no way would worker directors be tolerated. It would be interesting to see how these ideas would go down here in 1997. Incidentally, at the Rover Group, the largest British-based car manufacturer, workers who suggest improvements which can result in lower staffing levels are themselves free from the fear of self-inflicted redundancy. There is an employment guarantee scheme which keeps them on the payroll.

13 It may have changed now, but in the late 1970s the invocation of this term was sufficient to induce guilt for claiming (legitimate) car mileage for travelling around the authority. This was one its milder examples.

14 It was Viktor Frankl, the famous Austrian psychiatrist, whose account of his imprisonment in Auschwitz (Frankl 1964) was so inspirational, who declared that we discover our missions, rather than decide them. This is for the reader to decide. Missions and visions are often confused. A vision may be to explore space, a mission would be to land on the moon. Ask your friends how many of them have either.

15 At its most basic level, how many people do you involve in your organization to create a mission/vision statement? Top management only, the whole workforce?

16 The two staff in question were S. Baddeley and T. James.

17 Kenichi Ohmae (1982) is one who perhaps gave this idea the most credence.

18 For a fascinating account of group dynamics in its widest possible context (building communities, societies, the world) see M. Scott Peck's *The Different Drum* (1990).

19 The alternative to waiting for a total solar eclipse, is just to do it. But the pro-active/reactive dilemma is occasionally very trying. Think of the Organization Development intervenors.

20 It would be difficult to do justice to Neuro-Linguistic Programming in these notes. As a Certified Trainer of the discipline, I must declare an interest. If you wish to pursue this, contact me at: Organisational Healing Ltd, 48 Walton Road, Stockton Heath, Warrington, WA4 6NL, England. E-mail 100436,3521@compuserve.com. The two founders of Neuro-Linguistic Programming were Richard Bandler and John Grinder. Robert Dilts is one of the most prolific contemporary writers. All three are Americans.

21 Experiences of Racism Awareness Training are mixed. My own involvement was working with highly skilled trainers who induced guilt in hundreds of workshop participants about their (white) ancestors' crimes. This was not the only message of course, and the scourge of racism is one of our most pressing social ills. There are other ways of changing behaviour than through guilt. Most people on the course were men, slave traders were almost exclusively men, and the focus of anger was essentially towards men.

22 It has been suggested by many alternative/complementary medicine writers and therapists that illness is forgetting who we are.

23 The significance of our acting from different roles cannot be under-estimated. Any quality text on organizational behaviour will cover this in depth.

BIBLIOGRAPHY

Bozeman, B. (1987), *All Organizations are Public*, San Francisco: Jossey Bass.

Bryson, J.M. (1988), *Strategic Planning for Public and Non-profit Organizations*, San Francisco: Jossey Bass.

Buchanan, D. and Boddy, D. (1992), *The Expertise of the Change Agent: Public Performance and Backstage Activity*, Hemel Hempstead (UK): Prentice Hall.

Dilts, R.B., Epstein, T. and Dilts, R.W. (1991), *Tools For Dreamers*, California: MetaPublications.

Fowler, A. (1975), *Personnel Management in Local Government*, London: The Institute of Personnel Management.

Frankl, V.E. (1964), *Man's Search for Meaning*, London: Hodder and Stoughton.

Golembiewski, R.T., Proehl, C.W. and Sink, D. (1981), 'Success of OD Applications in the Public Sector: Totting up the Score for a Decade, More or Less', *Public Administration Review*, November/December.

Harrison, R.G. (1985), 'OD in Central Government: Problems and Prospects', *Leadership and Organizational Development Journal*, **6**, (2).

Kay, J. (1993), *Foundations of Corporate Success*, Oxford: Oxford University Press.

Mintzberg, H. (1972), *The Nature of Managerial Work*, New York: Harper and Row.

Ohmae, K. (1982), *The Mind of the Strategist*, London: Penguin.

Pedler, M., Burgoyne, J. and Boydell, T. (1991), *The Learning Company: A Strategy for Sustainable Development*, Maidenhead (UK): McGraw-Hill.

Pfeiffer, J.W. and Jones, J. (eds), (1978), *The 1978 Annual Handbook for Group Facilitators*, San Diego: Pfeiffer and Company.

Scott Peck, M. (1990), *The Different Drum*, London: Arrow.

Senge, P.M. (1990), *The Fifth Discipline*, London: Century.

Stewart, J. (1988), *The Management of Local Government*, Harlow: Longman.

5 The trouble with organizational learning

Anne Murphy and Chris Blantern, Re-view

This chapter, like every other, has been written from a particular point of view. It is the record of our involvement with a group of people who care about the future of their city and who want to make a difference. It is not, however, a story which stands apart from the many others which surround us, guide us and show us what our organizations and communities are and can be. Among them are the storylines many are telling about how organizations learn and can be made more learningful and how that can help us all. In this chapter we will try, then, to tell it how we see it but not how it 'is'.

THE TROUBLE WITH ORGANIZATIONAL LEARNING

A growing number of organizations are declaring that they want to be learning companies: to harness the learning of all their individuals and to learn how to continuously transform themselves. It is against this backdrop that learning has moved out of the training department and into the boardroom; that individuals have been empowered to transform themselves and their organizations; that Action Learning has become an accepted part of management development programmes; and that self-development has become a necessity and not a self-indulgent luxury. Neither is the effort directed only at individuals: people are also looking for ways to address collective learning at the level of the whole system. There has been widespread recognition among the tellers of the organizational learning story that for the system to learn more about itself there must be mechanisms for collective exchange and interpretation. We have seen The Learning Company Project's 11 characteristics of a learning company, Senge's Fieldbook for building a Learning Organization and, more recently, the emergence of large group interventions such as Real Time Strategic Change, Whole Systems Development, Open Space and Future Search. If we do enough of this (and do it well enough), one of the stories seems to go, then we will find a way to transform our organizations into something approaching reasonable places to be.

One of the most important questions we must wrestle with, however, if we are to be in some way instrumental in this transformation is, 'Reasonable places for whom?'. Our organizations are awash with visions and partial solutions: partial first because they go part of the way for part of the population; but partial also because they represent a particular world view, one which requires both change (in the way most people do their work) and stability (in the way we are able to influence the outcomes). It is our view that the current interest in organizational learning is fuelled by the desire to reconcile these seemingly contradictory positions by providing a solution which seems to do both. Its main narrative is to show how localized learning from empowered teams and individuals can indeed be made available for the organization to learn from. So, as organizations have increased their oscillation from some form of centralized control to some form of agile flexibility, the call for a way of integrating the extremes has become more audible and the development profession has tried even harder to find learning solutions to the problems posed.

However, the modernist, and largely humanistic, paradigm from which these learning stories are told has reached the very limits of its usefulness by becoming trapped in the logic of its own terms of reference. Rather than offering us a way to meet the conditions of our time, they have become so unquestionably 'true' that we have become unable to see how they also prevent us from doing what we actually want to do. The intense individualism and resultant fragmentation which has occurred since the early-1980s has brought us face to face with our need for community. In politics, management, learning and art people are looking for a way of making sense of unity within a growing amount of diversity. What is less evident, however, particularly in the way the organizational learning story is told, is the sort of critical reflexivity which enables us to see that our efforts to create unity actually deliver fragmentation. It seems to us that we face a clear choice: we can either find out which of the current or emerging stories (learning, change, systems, individuals) best fits our current needs and context and then change the people to fit our interpretation; or we can find a way of working with multiple and often conflicting needs and interpretations which enable people to do things together in spite of their differences.

Here we begin to tell another story. We do not claim that it is the latest and best way to interpret organizational learning, nor do we claim that it is the only story which can be told. All we claim is that if a pragmatic approach to doing unity *and* diversity, in preference to an ideological one, is our current task, then looking at the story differently can also offer us some means of also doing things differently. When we introduce talk about ideology we tend to associate its use with particular attitudes towards economics and politics (with a small and a big 'P') in organizations and communities. Ideology is a term often used to set apart those sets of ideas which vary from a sense of grounded reality or 'natural order of things', which enables us to assume that if we can go about our daily business steering clear of it we can somehow adopt a neutral position. However, there is no neutral orientation to the world of organizations, individuals or anything else, and the 'natural order of things' can be seen as 'what we can't help believing' – ideology which arose out of its usefulness in former times and which has become so concretized, so embedded in our processes of socialized learning, that we believe it to be true. What seems to go with the idea of a natural order is that, once discovered, it applies to all of us; it is deemed to be universal. Yet we live in times which provide us with constant examples, through increasing mobility and access to global communications media, of different interest groups seeing the world quite differently. This enables us to see too that we co-exist with different contexts, aspirations, experiences and ways of making sense in and around our organizations and communities.

Much of our energy, in organizations and more generally, is taken up in attempting to deal with difference and increasingly it is becoming a drain on our social and economic resources. Our attempts to police society and organizations in defence of unity seem unsatisfying in the face of social fragmentation and change. For example, there are more people in prison in the UK than ever before, yet the sense of a trend towards more rather than less lawlessness in society seems palpable. It also costs more to accommodate those who reside in HM Prisons than is contributed annually to the GNP (McCrae 1994) by the hotel and catering industry. However, individual free-dom and autonomy still remain powerful aspirations for democracies in the Northern Hemisphere. Organizations too suffer the same dilemma: how to promote individual autonomy and initiative whilst still retaining a sense of 'being in control'. Empowerment is acceptable as long as employees espouse the correct ideology; autonomy is desirable so long as it does not undermine the status quo; change is necessary so long as it is defined from above, and self-development is a good thing provided that people learn more or less what we think they should learn. All the while difference and diversity keep popping up!

In our era it is no longer possible to define unity from a unitary perspective. To 'get everyone on-board' or 'singing from the same hymn sheet' is highly problematic when we also require of others, and demand increasingly for ourselves, local and individual autonomy and rights of expression. Nor is absolute command and control the answer. History teaches us that the oppressed unite behind so-called strong leadership only to become the new oppressors. Rather, social and organizational methods which rely on unity as an expression (the policy) of expert leadership (power of the few) to be applied (the plan) to the rest, are increasingly less effective ways of organizing to enable us to do things together. As globalization increases we seem to be learning that ideologies are not transferable and that knowledge arises from local contexts. In this sense, the privileging of universal ideologies of how societies, organizations, and groups should be, belongs to the past. Ideology is also past-orientated when it comes to the status of knowledge. When universal ideologies are applied to local contexts sense-making is literally traditional, a historical act which inhibits the forging of collective meaning across traditional boundaries (generative learning). The growth of organizational learning can be viewed as a response to the need for both diversity and unity: $\qquad$ *57*

> A Learning Company is an organization that facilitates the learning of all its members and continuously transforms itself . . . We can design and create organizations which are capable of adapting, changing, developing and transforming themselves in response to the needs, wishes and aspirations of people inside and outside.
>
> (Pedler, Burgoyne and Boydell 1991)

Response to rapid change is a recognition of diversity across space and time and organization sustainability can be viewed as the collective need to move away from attempting to control the world through universal approaches, towards an acknowledgment of different stakeholders and interests. Even so, organizational learning itself can be viewed as a universalizing ideology locked within our traditions of managing and organizing, unless we can find more pragmatic ways of going on. In this context 'pragmatic' means ways that work for more of us – unity from a diverse perspective. In pursuit of a response to this problem our attention has turned recently to ways of working in and between organizations which shift the focus of sense-making from modernist, universal ideology to post-modern pragmatic ways of privileging relationships. Ideology, in this sense, means those deeply embedded sets of cultural ideas which, in these times, we can begin to say actively get in the way of our doing things together. Julie's story (see opposite page), though apocryphal, chimes with our sense of organizational life.

Whatever picture of the future the senior strategists paint describes, even prescribes, the context for the staff: that is, how they see themselves and the world and what action is available to them. Similarly, from the strategists' frame of reference, the staff view, if expressed openly, might look like resistance to change or a failure to move with the times. If there is compliance or a fear of speaking up, then what price 'empowerment'? How can we make sense of these different views and what is it here that we can say the 'organization' is supposed to be learning?

Julie's story may say many things. Its function here though is not as a device for helping the reader to select the right answer (which contains the assumption that someone knows the right answer) to the conundrums and riddles posed by enacting organizational learning, but rather, to consider the pragmatic consequences of simply accepting that:

- Both positions, those of staff and of senior strategists (and others, by implication), are equally true and real. These positions are strongly influenced by the significance attributed to each context. Different aspirations, values, priorities and actions arise, perhaps different worlds.
- Through relationships of power and significance each context (and those individuals who are identified through it) is instrumental in constructing the other – most likely in ways we do not know. They exist in a relationship to each other. Knowledge of ourselves and the world grows out of such relationships.

Julie's story

It was Julie's first day back in the office after attending a three-day in-house development programme on organizational learning. The message was clear. The company wants middle managers like her: to provide more learning opportunities for staff; to take their development seriously; to encourage them to take responsibility for their own learning; and to promote a climate that will encourage local innovation, creativity, flexibility and responsiveness to customers. Julie was enthusiastic, 'this could end up becoming an enjoyable place to work', she thought, though she remembered having felt similarly optimistic when Total Quality Management and, then Investors In People, had been adopted as company policy.

She sat down at her desk to catch up on her e-mails. One leapt out from the list on the screen – 'Business Process Re-engineering strategy team: Implementation of down-sizing proposals'. She knew that a specially appointed senior team had been working with consultants for the last three months.

Julie was told that in pursuit of flexibility and business focus her staff group would 'need' to contract by 30 per cent while increasing output by 15 per cent. Julie knew that most people in the organization were aware that the world was changing fast and that the organization would need to change too, but she could not help thinking that the way the BPR project had been managed (a top team defines the problem and the solution with consultation only on the means of ameliorating the effects) would become the dominant 'headline'. This would become the main story, the context from which staff would make sense of, and adjust, their behaviour – their learning! The context for the senior strategists may well be the survival of the business in its economic environment but for staff the important, most compelling, issue would most likely be surviving the down-sizing (by staying or going).

THE MAINSTAYS OF 'MODERN' ORGANIZING (MONOLOGUE)

Until recently this post-modern approach has been bypassed, both in the theory and practice of organizational learning. It is reasonable to speculate that this is largely to do with the 'problems' such an approach poses for us. Our current methodologies offer us some familiar ways of leveraging change, but more than that, they remind us that they are, in fact, 'true' by incorporating within them the 'proof' that to work in other ways will bring chaos. By allowing the following five basic tenets of modernist thought to govern our approaches to organizational learning, we have rendered any alternative invisible and not 'do-able':

1 *Control*: We are in control of ourselves and our context. Our rationality and predictive scientific abilities allow us to know that the future will continue to bring us whatever it is we need. (If we are not in control we will face certain anarchy. We will lose our ability to make things happen.)

2 *Truth*: The world is knowable and concrete. When a truth is discovered it has universal applicability. (If the world is not knowable we would never be able to agree how to get things done.)

3 *Self*: Individuals are the agents of change and the place where both learning and direction occur. (If individuals are not the agents of change then we are all powerless to change our context.)

4 *Ideology*: Action starts with ideas. We can only do what we fully understand. (If ideas do not precede action then we cannot be deliberate and purposeful in what we do.)

5 *Progress*: Tomorrow should be better than today in our progression towards an ideal future. (If tomorrow really is no better than today then we might as well give up now.)

Theories are, however, only useful in so far as they enable us to do some things and disable us from doing others. Not only do our current operating assumptions prevent 'anarchy and chaos', they also prevent 'dialogue'.

Control

We can control ourselves and our context only if we are able to influence others in the pursuit of our ends by designing ever more elaborate mechanisms for empowering them to do what it is we want them to do. What we cannot afford to do, therefore, is to accept that other people's reality is different from ours and that their own need to be in control will mean that they will do everything in their power to achieve their own ends. Attempts to address this by organizing community around a unitary vision prevent us from the need to describe our reality for ourselves and, perhaps more importantly, prevent us from hearing the perspectives of others as equally true and real.

Truth

If there is a truth, and it is universally applicable, then a different view must be wrong. Diversity is, then, no more than what can be comfortably accommodated or absorbed; anything which falls outside that is not diversity but danger. What we cannot do is to find ways of working with others who are different from us unless we either change them or make sure that they cannot change us. Furthermore, by supporting a view that the world is knowable from a unilateral perspective, we elevate such knowledge above the possibility that it is only through our relationships with others that we can actually get things done. Explanations lead us to dogma, stories to multiple views.

Self

Our preoccupation with an autonomous self leads us to the interpretation that everything must begin there. If, however, the locus of learning and change starts and ends inside the individual then we can only change our organizations if we first change the individuals in them. Quite apart from the obvious problems of 'buy in', this framework leaves us with a hole where our sense of community might be. Our only defence against the inevitable fragmentation this produces is to call for strong leadership which will unite our individual efforts behind a 'shared' vision. What this logic fails to address, however, is the extent to which a leader is only strong in so far as he or she is leading where we want to go; if not, that leader is either a tyrant or a rebel.

Ideology

If we can do only what we fully understand, we need ways of understanding the future in terms of the past and present. What matters, then, is the way we can shape our future to meet our ideas about how it should be, not what we *might be able to do* together in the present to take us towards a future we all desire. By elevating ideology (and action) over relationships (and action) we fall into the trap of having to convince others that we are right (or they are wrong) *before* we can do things together. By attempting to change the people, rather than the circumstances under which they interact, much of the organizational learning story gets channelled into action which has the function of proving that our view of the current reality is the only one which counts in the future. Organizations invest a great deal of energy in reducing multiple voices into a single 'coherent' story. What remains out of view is what we can already do together right now without the need to change anyone.

Progress

If we are to see a progression in our actions we must find ways of marking off that progress in levels or stages. Whether we draw our justifications from statistics or metaphysics, our aim must be to develop *beyond* where we currently are. In order to do this we need to put our faith into the power of models rather than into what we can currently see between us. Such models often assume a better place to be which only the privileged can see and help us achieve. By assuming someone else knows what is best, we effectively keep large groups of people out of the process of writing their own futures. Not only does this mean that much of what we all do is there to win our own privilege, it also means that the future belongs to the experts and not to us.

ORGANIZING FOR THESE TIMES (DIALOGUE)

These tenets of modernist thought effectively 'freeze meaning at a given point and thus silence voices and segment the social world' (Gergen 1994). What *61* then would it look like to begin to give attention to relationships, as post-modernism invites us to, over particular, frozen modernist ideologies. Here, of course, we are not suggesting just courtesy or care for each other (though there is little enough of that) but more particularly, what it might be like to acknowledge others' actions and sayings as valid representations of their worlds as they know them. Alongside this, we cannot pretend to know their worlds better. The shift is *from* measuring others against our (true) knowledge of the world – which, in the case of psychotherapy and even management development, includes knowing others better than they themselves do – *to* receiving others' actions and accounts as the best data available about their worlds, including what is attributed as significant and important. This is the shift from *monologue* (privileging absolutist ideology – the past) to *dialogue* (privileging relationship – what we can do together).

Much has been made of the practice of dialogue in organizational learning literature (Senge 1990; Isaacs 1993) which presents ways of going on ranging from hearing others to getting others to accept change by removing conflict. However, this practice still seems to be configured by the modernist principles mentioned above and we have drawn upon social constructionists (Gergen 1991, 1994; Shotter 1993), feminists (Calás and Smircich 1992; Rakow 1992) and anthropologists (Geertz 1993) for a more useful guide. When we turn to these cultural workers, who have long been concerned to make sense of difference in ways that enjoy humanity rather than demean it, we are presented with a different account of how knowledge comes about. For these enquirers, tales of objective truth, true selves, stages of development and even the story of emotions as pure discrete states existing within people, are largely retold as the dominant language rules of a Euro-centric, Judeo-Christian culture. This culture has been so successful in the machine era that it has largely, through its ability to exploit engineering technology for economic advantage, colonized the world. The story of 'humanistic psychology', the dominant narrative of 'management development', can be located as the cultural preferences of white, middle-class, well-off, Anglo-Saxon males. Who else does it benefit?

On the other hand, for social constructionists knowledge is not seen as a reflection of how the world out there really is, words are not representations of reality; rather words get their meaning from how they are used in particular communities.[1] Knowledge is created through social processes characterized by relationships of power. 'Conversation' is where the exchanging and fixing of power occurs and *meaning is fixed by what it is that 'conversation' enables us to do together!* What is becoming increasingly visible is that knowledge is a local and a social phenomenon (Geertz 1993). It comes out of the way people do things, work out what is the next step, how they go on together in given communities and whether those communities are separated by time, geography, function or purpose. From this frame of reference, individuals are entirely constituted by culture, the communities into which they are born and within which they move.[2] Most significantly, what this reveals is that knowledge flows from relationship not the mind of the individual (Gergen 1991, 1994; Shotter 1993; Harré and Gillet 1994).

Dialogue then, is the art of rendering visible to each other the processes by which meaning is fixed and which enable us to do things. If we are limited to the monological regimes of most organizations our range of options for action is severely limited. In the knowledge era it makes progressively less sense for organizations to minimize the voices inside which reflect the diversity outside. Dialogue enables us to see that where it is important to find ways of doing things together (the social knowledge of organizations and communities) we would be better off privileging relationships (our future together) over universalizing ideology (particular versions of the past as the way we should all live in the future).[3] Dialogue means *keeping the conversation going* by including the other, rather than freezing the meaning by excluding the other. We would be better off regarding knowledge as a story we can write with others, rather than the story which writes us. Here are some guides for acting dialogically in relationship. Each statement, of course, implies its monological counterpart:

'I try to share the conversation I'm having with myself as I talk to you.'
'I try to see others' stories as equally real and true.'
'I want to know your interpretation of the situation.'
'I listen to what I'm saying.'
'I am trying to be aware of my taken-for-granted assumptions as I think and speak.'
'I want to hear your half-baked ideas – and I'll tell you mine.'
'I don't know what's best for you.'
'I try to be honest with myself.'
'If I'm uncertain I don't try to cover it up.'
'I try to avoid fitting your stories into my ready-made categories.'
'My questions flow from my curiosity rather than my desire to steer you.'
'In what ways do I fault you in order to minimize the validity of your story/view?'

At the organization level, dialogue involves making publicly available the relationships of power and the organizational conversations which fix meaning, so that different conversations and action become available.

FUTURE SEARCH AS ORGANIZATION DIALOGUE

There has been a recent wave of interest in the UK in a number of large-group interventions which aim to involve a wider cross section of the members of an organization or community in the planning and implementation of possible futures. They all offer the possibility of doing things differently and at the same time offer the possibility of keeping things fundamentally unchanged. Our preference for Future Search is not to do with any sense of inherent superiority, rather it is the one which allows us to work with people in a way which does not at the same time demand that we collude with the way things 'ought to be'. Change, if it happens, emerges from what is common in the community and is in the hands of all the people in the room. In that sense then, it is the intervention which best fits our aspirations of how we would like to work. Furthermore, in the search for common ground, it embodies an understanding which both respects the need for differences and the need for unity and, as such, offers a tool for organizations and communities to learn in and through the relationships which make them up.

The model for this multi-stakeholder planning event is one developed by Marvin Weisbord and Sandra Janoff (1995) in the United States. The name 'Future Search' comes from both the 'futures conferences' of Eva Shindler-Rainman and Ron Lippitt (very large meetings aimed at community involvement held during the 1970s) and the 'search process' of social scientists Eric Trist and Fred Emerey which had its origins here in the UK in the beginnings of the Bristol Siddeley Aircraft Engine Company in 1960.

A future search is a task focused 16-hour planning event which involves a diverse group of stakeholders around an organizational or community issue. Its principal aim is to enable people to uncover what they are already willing and able to do without forcing or compromising. Weisbord and Janoff's view is that by bringing together many perspectives and by letting go of the need to design other people's future behaviour for them, the event is able to open up new paths and capacity for action based on common ground. In this way it provides communities with a pragmatic process for joint action in the face of a multiplicity of views and interests.

Future searching also offers a pragmatic way of using organizational learning which does not further solidify our dependence on the modernistic principles which are so much more a part of the problem than they are of the solution. Rather than reducing the future into something we can control, it allows people to take responsibility for the chaos and complexity and do something about it; rather than designing the outcome of one truth over another, it privileges what we can do together over any one view of the right answer; rather than focusing on changing individuals, it works with the skills and knowledge that they already have and focuses on changing the way it is possible for them to interact; rather than providing a platform for a unitary idea of how the future should be, it uncovers what is 'do-able' now; rather than mapping out the steps we need to take, it provides a container where we can face ourselves, each other and our intersecting futures without the need for experts to tell us how.

The event differs from typical participative meetings in four main ways:

- The *whole system* participates – a cross section of as many interested parties as practical. This means more diversity and less hierarchy than usual and a chance for each person to be heard and to see other ways of addressing the task in hand.
- *Future scenarios* are put into a *historical* and *global* perspective – thinking globally, together, before acting locally. This enhances shared understanding and greater commitment to act as well as increasing the range of possible actions.

- People *self-manage* their work and use *dialogue* (openness and commitment to listening) – not problem-solving – as the main tool. This means helping each other to do the tasks and taking responsibility for our perceptions and actions.
- *Common ground* rather than 'conflict management' is the frame of reference – honouring our differences rather than feeling the need to reconcile them. The common ground and public commitment to action emerge from the whole group so *planning* and *implementation* are in the hands of the same people.

A full account of this particular organizational learning story can be found in Chapter 11, 'Searching for Sheffield' (see page 131).

NOTES

1 Richard Rorty succinctly pointed out that all knowledge is of human invention (social construction) when he said, 'How could we know what words nature would use to describe itself?'

2 This contrasts with the traditional view that difference or culture is merely a superficial veneer overlying some essential humanness which can be known by experts. In the view presented here 'expertness' is the convention for a set of specific 'language rules' we use in a given community of practice. So, for example, using the rules of 'cognitive psychology' (a largely Western scientific community) to make sense of human behaviour in, say, Asian Islamic countries is like using the rules of hockey to make sense of cricket.

3 In this sense, knowledge points to the past, i.e. is born of a tradition.

BIBLIOGRAPHY

Calás, Marta B. and Smircich, L. (1992), 'Re-writing Gender into Organizational Theorizing', in M. Reed and M. Hughes, (eds), *Rethinking Organizations*, London: Sage.
Deetz, S. (1994), 'The New Politics of the Workplace, Ideology and Other Unobtrusive Controls', in H.W. Simmons and M. Billig (eds), *After Post-modernism*, London: Sage.
Feyerabend, P. (1981), 'How To Defend Society Against Science', in I. Hacking (ed.), *Scientific Revolutions*, Oxford: Oxford University Press.
Geertz, C. (1993), *Local Knowledge*, London: Fontana.
Gergen, K. (1991), *The Saturated Self*, New York: Basic Books.
Gergen, K. (1994), *Realities and Relationships: Soundings In Social Construction*, London: Harvard University Press.
Harré, R. and Gillet, G. (1994), *The Discursive Mind*, California: Sage.
Heckman, S.J. (1990), *Gender and Knowledge: Elements of Postmodern Feminism*, Oxford: Blackwell.

Isaacs, W.N. (1993), *Taking Flight: Dialogue, Collective Thinking and Organisational Learning*, Report from the Center for Organizational Learning, Dialogue Project, MIT, USA.

McCrae, H. (1994), *The World In 2020 – Power, Culture and Prosperity: A Vision of the Future*, London: Harper Collins.

Pedler, M., Burgoyne, J. and Boydell, T. (1991), *The Learning Company: A Strategy for Sustainable Development*, Maidenhead: McGraw-Hill.

Rakow, L.F. (ed.) (1992), *Women Making Meaning*, London: Routledge.

Rorty, R. (1992), in 'The Real Thing', *Equinox* (TV programme) for Channel 4, UK.

Senge, P. (1990), *The Fifth Discipline: The Art and Practice of the Learning Organization*, New York: Doubleday.

Shotter, J. (1993), *Conversational Realities*, London: Sage.

Waters, M. (1995), *Globalization*, London: Routledge.

Weisbord, M. and Janoff, S. (1995), *Future Search*, San Francisco: Berret-Koehler.

Part II
PRACTICE

6 Using Action Learning to enhance managerial performance

Ray Mahoney, Corporation of London

This chapter will describe Action Learning, a method of learning which I believe enhances managerial performance. It will look at two case studies, the first at Surrey County Council (Surrey being an organization of 27 000 employees, in the local government sector of the United Kingdom). The second case study is the Corporation of London, which is the local authority for the City of London. However, before I present the case studies, I will outline the method of Action Learning.

WHAT IS ACTION LEARNING?

Action Learning (AL) is a method for developing managers and their managerial actions and decisions. It was pioneered by Professor Reg Revans in the 1950s in the United Kingdom – it is no new managerial fad. It is now used as a management tool in many countries, including the United States of America, Canada, Belgium, South Africa, Australia, United Kingdom, Holland and Italy. Professor Revans was way ahead of his time as a management thinker, and his theories on learning challenged the academic and business school ideas of how people, and in particular managers, learned. Dr Ronnie Lessem of the City University Business School describes Professor Revans in a chapter of Revans' book *The Origins and Growth of Action Learning*, (Revans 1982).

Scribe and artisan: mind and body

In his early years Revans gave parallel attention to the development of body and mind. He became an Olympic long jumper and a Cambridge physicist. This particular duality was never to leave him. After his career as both athlete and physicist, he joined Essex Education Authority on the outskirts of London, soon to find himself trying to bridge the gap between the body and the mind, first within the Health Service. In 1938, while looking into 'the entry of girls into the nursing profession', he became preoccupied with the divisions between consultants and administrators on high ('scribes') and the nurses on the shop floor ('artisans'). It was this duality between matter (physical achievement) and spirit (conceptual attainment) that attracted Revans to a training and development role in the coal industry.

I have had the privilege to meet Reg Revans on three occasions and I believe he is much more than an academic tutor. His ideas that peers, when meeting, can learn from and with each other, without the so-called help of experts, are so exciting I cannot understand why it has taken the world so long to discover his genius. I can understand why some academics and business schools have found his ideas challenging, if not frightening, because he fundamentally challenged the way we learn and develop. My own introduction to this form of development was via a three-day course, run by Roger Gaunt. A management trainer for the Local Government Training Board, Roger later became a mentor and is now a dear friend. I left school with no qualifications, and during my craft apprenticeship I gained some City and Guilds certificates and spent 13 years in the telecommunications industry with General Electric Company (GEC). I then joined the London Borough of Newham as manual worker and apprentice trainer, which is where I met Roger and Action Learning. I have to be honest that as a manual worker trainer and a Millwall supporter, I found all this a bit 'touchy-feely', but I later realized that the course had had a profound effect on my trainer style. It also helped me focus on my relationships with people, both at work and privately. I have also found *my* own solutions to many and diverse problems, while I have charted through my own personal chaos.

ACTION LEARNING ATTACKS PROBLEMS NOT PUZZLES

A puzzle is something that has a solution which is known and available, you only have to find it (for instance a technical problem that can be solved by asking experts). A problem is something to which nobody knows the answer and nobody can look it up anywhere. Nobody has the appropriate experience to solve it, because nobody knows what experience is appropriate.

The style of Action Learning I introduced to Surrey County Council during my four-and-a-half years there is a consultancy/counselling model. I am at present introducing this style of operating to managers at the Corporation of London. Managers, after initial introduction to the concepts, work in groups of five to eight. These groups meet for half-a-day about every six weeks. At the start, they will have a skilled facilitator working with them. The facilitator has a guiding role, and then becomes more integrated as the skills of the group develop.

Purpose of the meetings:

- To find solutions to work issues.
- To promote understanding of group dynamics.
- To gain a wider understanding of the organization.

- To deal with the here and now issues of the workplace.
- To learn from and with each other.
- To gain the skills of a consultancy/counselling style of working.
- To develop enhanced listening skills – by listening to the meaning, the body language, not just the words.
- To develop better questioning skills.
- To explore individual development, by encouragement and challenge of personal barriers.

Some conventions for group work:

- One member of the group will offer to explore a work issue.
- They become the focus of attention for up to one-and-a-half hours.
- At the end of this time the group explores how it operated.
- The group member alone takes ownership of the issue.
- The facilitator ensures the group observe the group contract.
- Silence is permitted and often is very productive.
- Members are encouraged to suspend judgements on what is being said.

The group contract

The group contract is known as the RECIPE. The contract rules are discussed at great length before the group embarks on any Action Learning work, so that a common understanding of the conventions and contract are formed.

The RECIPE rules are:

R = Responsibility – Members of the group learn to take responsibility for their own thoughts and feelings they also learn to accept their responsibility for working as part of a group.

E = Experience-led – The group works with the current, past and possible future experiences of group members.

C = Confidentiality – To create a safe environment in which to explore personal issues and in-depth understanding of what confidentiality means.

I = 'I' Language – The use of 'I' language is encouraged where it is appropriate. This is probably the most powerful tool in the Action Learner's tool box.

P = Process – This is the means by which the group discusses, at the end of the session, how they have worked together.

E = Equal Opportunity – The group, via the facilitator, ensures that each member has a chance to contribute.

ACTION LEARNING AT SURREY COUNTY COUNCIL

I introduced AL to Surrey County Council employees in October 1990, to assist with the culture change that managers and staff were being asked to take on board, due to a policy review of the council and renewal of its working style. With the assistance of Roger Gaunt, an external consultant, I ran a workshop for 25 managers. This was a very exhausting day. Roger outlined the concepts of Action Learning and then we formed the workshop into five groups and each had three set meetings, two after the lunch period. At the end of the day, there was insufficient time to review what had gone before. This left some of the managers very confused as to what Action Learning involved. Therefore, when Roger and I, plus the three facilitators, reviewed the day, it was clear that a strategy was needed to introduce it properly.

Strategy

It was evident that 25-plus was too large a group to work with, so the following strategies were put into place:

- Awareness days: A series of awareness days was set up, with a maximum of 12 employees per workshop.
- Three-day residential courses: A series of three-day courses were set up for employees to either experience Action Learning or for group members to develop their skills. These were run in conjunction with the awareness days. They were facilitated by Roger Gaunt and other external facilitators.
- Internal facilitator group: I decided at an early stage to use internal facilitators, for economic reasons, and use Roger Gaunt to run workshops and train this group. I had no initial idea where these people would come from, but had faith in the fact I would find them as, in my capacity as Management Training Adviser, I ran various management courses and met lots of Surrey staff. I invited people from various backgrounds, but sharing an interest in Action Learning, to join this group. The group was formed in 1991 and still meets on a regular basis. Some new members have joined, but this group was central to the development of Action Learning at Surrey County Council.
- Integration with other training: This approach encourages managers to focus on their management style and was introduced to the following centrally-run programmes as well as being a programme in its own right:

  (a)   the eight-day Manager Development Course;
  (b)   the two-day Time Management Course;
  (c)   the nine-month Advanced Manager Course.

There were, at one stage, 16 working groups meeting, which had a membership of 95 managers of various levels from a cross section of departments.

I reviewed the work of all the sets in August 1993. The purpose of the review was to assess the following:

1   Was Action Learning beneficial to managers?
2   Did it have an effect on *personal* and *organizational*:

vision
values
motivation
strategic direction?

3   Did it help managers overcome weakness?
4   Were the benefits short- or long-term?
5   Did it help participants become better managers?
6   How did the learning groups work?
7   The work of set facilitators.

From the 95 questionnaires sent out I had 27 replies and below is a summary of their feedback.

The personal benefits

All 27 questionnaires reported a beneficial effect. Individuals perceived the following benefits from being in a group:

- They learned from the experience of others, by the exposure of the group member exploring an individual work issue.
- They learned how to deal with fears and uncertainties.
- There was a maximum opportunity for honesty.
- The acceptance of personal confidentiality.
- Learning how to relate feelings to thoughts.
- To practise giving immediate feedback to other people on an honest level.

The organization benefits

- A safe forum for sincere discussion.
- Openness was empowered.
- Strengthening of group dynamics, which could be transferred to work groups.
- Decisions made at the appropriate level.
- Real exploration of work issues.
- Enhanced quality of service.
- More confident managers, with a greater understanding of their own role, the organization and their personal style, with its effects on their work colleagues.

External Action Learning groups

To introduce this style of working, with its confidential nature, is a huge risk,   *73* but in my opinion one worth taking. I had become frustrated by many years of management training with course participants saying, 'Great course, but I wish I could have dealt with real work issues'. They would talk for hours in the pub about the Housing or the Chief Executive Department, but resolve nothing.

To involve senior managers in in-house sets, unless they all join, is worthless. Another option is for them all to become involved in the Action Learning process, but with internal politics the way they are this may be unlikely. So for Chief Officers and particularly the Chief Executive it is more sensible for them to work outside the organization in a stranger group.

Surrey Chief Executive comments

Derek Thomas, the Surrey County Council Chief Executive, participated in a stranger set for over 12 months. He comments as follows:

> When I became a Chief Executive I searched for a mentor with whom to share concerns and seek a reaction to alternative ways of working. Regrettably I gave up after a search. The Action Learning group can help with this role. Listening – there is a lot of listening – to a problem, an issue, as seen from the presenter's perspective and then asking questions without giving advice. This has been a rewarding experience. Recognizing that many of the issues have been confronted by others is also helpful. The whole process is based on trust and confidentiality. We know nothing of each other than within the Action Learning group. I suspect the anonymity is a strength which is vital. As Chief Executive I found it difficult to share all my concerns and challenges with colleagues. The ground rules of Action Learning appear to have at least partially filled that gap.
>
> Derek Thomas

Some Surrey managers' comments

The following are comments received from managers who have participated:

- A valuable source of personal and organization learning. Lists achievements to aim for.
- I have been able to transfer some skills to the workplace. Shown that I am not isolated with my fears and worries. Now trying to listen to others' needs and feelings. Important for self-development and has helped me enhance my skills at Surrey County Council.
- A good learning opportunity, look forward to group meetings.
- Has helped break down the barriers, communicate thoughts openly and confidently, take on board the needs of others, and gain and grow in confidence.
- Surprising depth of analysis, more than elsewhere. Any matters raised treated with respect. Capable of ever more tricky subjects as time goes by.

Surrey reflections

Surrey County Council had 27 000 employees in 1990, so the 95 managers were a significant, but small, percentage of the total population.

There were over 300 managers and other employees who attended courses and awareness days and clearly some decided to join Action Learning groups.

It has to be recognized that Action Learning does not suit all learning styles, but those whom it does not suit, who do participate, seem to gain the most.

The Action Learning groups at Surrey were voluntary, except for the Advanced Manager programme.

Fifteen of the groups were all mixed-gender groups, providing the opportunity to explore the roles of men and women working together. The other group was an all-male group.

One of the original groups is still meeting five years on and has recruited two new members. It has had two facilitators, myself and Roger Gaunt, and now group members take it in turn to facilitate at each meeting. This is one of a variety of staff development activities, but has outlasted all of the others.

It is difficult to assess what the actual contribution has been to the culture of Surrey County Council, but it has had a dramatic effect on those involved and their management performance.

WIDER ACTION LEARNING

The International Foundation for Action Learning (IFAL), set up in 1974, encourages the use of Action Learning on a world-wide basis. There are programmes documented in Holland, Australia, USA, Canada, Belgium, Sweden and many other countries. These programmes may differ somewhat, but they all follow the basic principles laid down by Professor Reg Revans in the 1950s. This learning knows no international boundary. At a recent conference in St Louis, Missouri, on 1 March 1985, the IFAL USA Chapter was launched.

They follow Revans' principle:

$$L = P + Q.$$

where: L = Learning
P = Programmed Instruction
Q = Questioning Insight

The base for IFAL in the UK is now at the Department of Management Learning, The Management School, Lancaster University, Lancaster, LA1 4YX. Telephone: 01524 594016. Their library has over 900 articles on the subject.

The Corporation of London

The Corporation is the local authority for the City of London with 4 000 staff, but has a much wider brief than simply providing services to the Square Mile. It supports the nation by financing the Barbican Centre, and open spaces such as   *75*

Epping Forest and Hampstead Heath, and supports the Lord Mayor of London who is an ambassador for the nation and the business community in the city. Action Learning is part of the Learning and Development Strategy 'Challenges, Choices and the Corporation', which was developed from a staff conference in March 1995, run for 150 staff of all grades.

There are currently three groups working as Action Learning groups, following three Effective Leadership courses. These groups (as in the Surrey experience) are voluntary and meet for five meetings following the three-day Leadership courses.

The culture of the Corporation is very different from that of Surrey County Council, but the common thing between them is that managers have the same sort of challenges, fears and insecurities.

It is far too early to assess how this will contribute to any culture change, but it is already having a profound effect on some of the leaders involved. In my position as Learning and Development Manager, I am changing the focus from Training to Learning. Action Learning underpins this by requiring participants to take responsibility for their own learning and development.

CONCLUSION

Revans is quoted as saying:

> (1) Action Learning particularly obliges subjects to become more aware of their own value systems, by demanding that the real problems tackled carry some risk of personal failure.
> (2) For doing, or Action, calls for commitment or true belief, while talking, or argument, calls only for intelligence and quickness of wit. (Revans 1982)

Mike Pedler is quoted as saying:

> Action Learning is most effective when used to confront organisational problems rather than to solve technical puzzles. As learning is at the core of its process, it is particularly valuable in developing the structures and dynamics of organisational change. (Pedler 1983)

For my own part, as I have fought to make my own concerns and fears understandable to others in my Action Learning group, I realized I was mapping my own route through my personal chaos. I have found my own experience to mean lots of hard work, much doubt and serious questioning of my own personal values. However, the experience has been very rewarding, with my enthusiasm being sustained by the generosity of others involved. I have learnt to celebrate the difference between individuals, which for me has been a great source of learning.

How Action Learning helps organization learning is, I believe, the pivotal question. First, I work from the premise that organizations do not learn, but the people within them do. I believe that Action Learning challenges the way that we operate as individuals and teams and helps us to concentrate on the here and now issues facing us. It helps to look at and change deep-seated personal habits that are barriers to changes. These habits are often the source of conflict between individuals and teams. It helps managers develop what Revans calls his questioning insight. This can be invaluable when trying to find new solutions to old problems and solutions to existing and future problems.

Organizations of the 1990s and beyond need to design the future and not re-create the past, and need employees who are prepared to operate in a more democratic and cooperative way.

For me Action Learning not only helps us discover new ways to work together but delivers the skills to put them into practice.

BIBLIOGRAPHY

Pedler, M, (ed.) (1983), *Action Learning in Practice*, Aldershot: Gower.
Revans, R. (1982), *The Origins and Growth of Action Learning*, Bromley: Chartwell Bratt.

7 Evaluating the benefits of learning

Cliff Allen, Portsmouth City Council

Possessing the skills, competence and knowledge to deliver first-class services and products is a requirement of every organization wanting to sustain itself in a competitive environment. In the public sector, the influence of market forces and competition through tendering for the delivery of services is not a transitory phase which will be reversed with time. Sustaining public sector services in the context of competition is not a matter of weathering a storm but of acknowledging a fundamental change in the pattern of our environment. The seeds of this major environmental change have given rise to a crop of learning strategies which have germinated through the necessity of surviving through competition. If the crop of learning is to flourish it must be protected from the early frosts of budget cuts. Driving down costs by reducing training budgets stems from a myopic view of the need to invest in people for the future.

To enable learning to flourish in the public sector there is a need to establish that learning is effective and leads to business benefits. Good evaluation is the key to identifying tangible benefits in business terms. Identified benefits need to be reported to investors in learning, education and training. Evaluation must go beyond the post course happy sheets if, as a process, it is going to determine that learning is effective and contributes to business success. The purpose of this chapter is to indicate how this can be done, by examining the thinking underpinning evaluation and drawing upon some practical techniques and tools in current use within the public sector.

Effective learning focuses upon four areas of concern to the management of an education, training and development function. They are policy, strategy, resources and evaluation. A task for training and development is to create a policy framework which acknowledges the autonomy of individual learners while retaining a business focus and tackling organizational needs. Training policy must identify good practice and must be sufficiently adaptive to incorporate good, innovative approaches to learning. Policy has to be framed in non-prescriptive language so that good practice can emerge. This is not an easy task and is made increasingly difficult by an increase in policies dealing with other human resource issues which might integrate with, rather than conflict with, training policy. (For example, absence management policies, family friendly policies and other conditions of service.) To ensure effective training, policy must also take account of the business planning process. Business planning will take place at different levels and will include sections, services and the organizational plan. Priorities set within the business planning process will give direction and emphasis to the learning which needs to be promoted within the organization. Policy related to effective learning will be driven by the need for:

1 *Consistency*: To ensure there is a similar approach, corporate identity, style and culture for the promotion of training opportunities.
2 *Equal Access*: To ensure fair-minded practices are used in giving opportunity to access development provision.
3 *Standards*: To ensure that development meets a minimum stated level of development opportunity.
4 *Investment*: To ensure that, in a people business, the people have development needs resourced and that resources are justified by improved performance and skill.

Policies which relate to effective learning also take account of a strategic approach to the delivery of training and development. A changing environment draws upon strategic skills. Strategy must take account of environmental context, the other competitors tendering for the business, and the skills available to deliver the service business plan. A strategy for effective learning can no longer be based upon the premise of a knowledgeable expert passing on what they know to those who do not know. Knowledge is growing at an exponential rate. Research in the 1980s concluded that the total knowledge of humankind doubled in that decade. More current research indicates that what is known now will constitute only 1 per cent of what will be known early in the twenty-first century. While strategically this may mean short, intensive development opportunities, increasing use of high-level technology using customer views as well as those of experts, and cross-professional team working, it will also mean that the nature of teaching or tutoring will change. Teachers and tutors will spend much more time facilitating and exploring issues and options for action. Learning and intelligence will be perceived as effective when the output of learning is seen to be tackling work-based problems and contributing to the performance of the organization.

Effective learning is also related to available resources. Organizations are made up of people. It is people, developed through learning, who become the assets of the organization. Investing in assets which have a mind of their own and are likely to be independently mobile requires a retention process. Offering effective learning opportunities is one way of retaining valuable assets. Investment in people has been shown to have business benefits, *79* especially when linked to a national scheme with set standards as in the Investors in People approach. Investing in people does away with poor practice, such as spending of a training budget with no analysis of the expenditure. Available resources for training, education and development can be analysed in the context of competition and used as a defence against challenges to the costs of learning. Making effective use of resources to promote learning means proactively looking at processes of price negotiation, quality standards and volume of work. Effective learning linked to effective working must give a justification and an account of the value for money that learning provides to the business.

COMPREHENSIVE EVALUATION

The need to justify, in business terms, the effective link between learning and work-based practice requires a comprehensive approach to evaluation. Comprehensive evaluation means doing more than using a post-course questionnaire, which often does no more than validate that the objectives for the course have been met. Post-course validation is an important part of evaluation; it provides evidence of good professional delivery and accesses the perceptions of delegates. Knowing that delegates are happy with the course or programme of learning is a feature of evaluation, but we must go much further if we are to provide evidence of business benefits. Comprehensive evaluation processes have been used for a number of years in local government and what follows is an explanation of how comprehensive evaluation has been used to establish the link between learning and effective performance in the workplace.

Evaluation is a process made up of a number of procedures. Procedures are made up of a number of discrete tasks. The process of evaluation is shown in Figure 7.1, which sets out an approach to evaluating learning within the framework of a management development programme.

Evaluating learning in a business context presents a number of problems common to a range of evaluation strategies. For example: where does the balance lie between knowledge and skills? Are we improving competence or awareness? Is our objective for evaluation based upon input materials or output effectiveness? Do we have access to tools and techniques for evaluating how effective learning is contributing to our business? It is common to mistake improved economy or efficiency for effectiveness.

Good evaluation needs to make clear what the terms efficiency, economy and effectiveness mean. Efficiency is a measure of the relationship between input and output. What takes place between the input and the output can be wasteful. Improvement in efficiency tends to concentrate upon reducing waste by, for example, looking at use of time and materials. Economy is a measure of the relationship between costs and value for money. Improvement in economy will tend to look at reducing costs for the same service, or expanding the service for the same cost. Effectiveness is a measure of the relationship between intention and achievement. Intention is commonly expressed in the

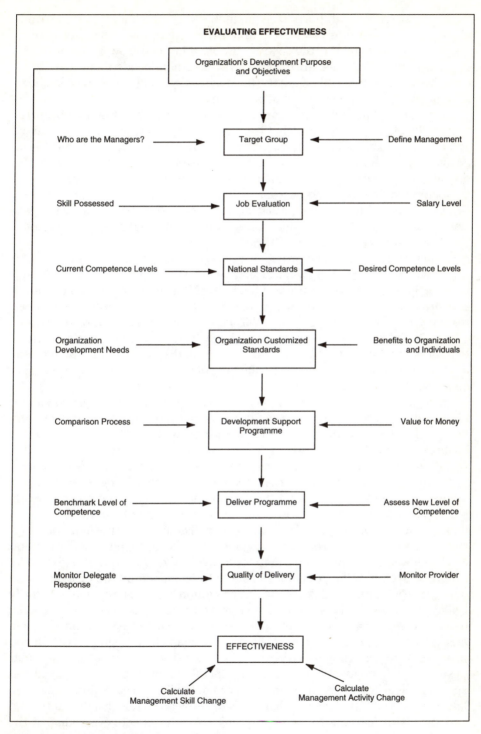

EVALUATING EFFECTIVENESS

Organization's Development Purpose and Objectives

Who are the Managers? → Target Group ← Define Management

Skill Possessed → Job Evaluation ← Salary Level

Current Competence Levels → National Standards ← Desired Competence Levels

Organization Development Needs → Organization Customized Standards ← Benefits to Organization and Individuals

Comparison Process → Development Support Programme ← Value for Money

Benchmark Level of Competence → Deliver Programme ← Assess New Level of Competence

Monitor Delegate Response → Quality of Delivery ← Monitor Provider

EFFECTIVENESS

Calculate Management Skill Change — Calculate Management Activity Change

Figure 7.1   Evaluating effectiveness

81

form of objective and purpose statements. For the most part, learning objectives are expressed as post-course behavioural objectives. Not enough attention is given to the purpose of the learning and how it fits with the organization and business plan objectives. Learning needs to be part of an organization's strategic plan and the purpose for learning needs to be linked to several levels of business planning processes.

To make the link between learning and effectiveness, it is important to express in 'big picture' terms what learning is designed to achieve. To achieve an overview may mean reviewing the organization's corporate objectives, considering the environment to identify pressures for change, reviewing the organization's policies on human resource management, identifying organizational trouble spots and assessing the organization's values and culture. Other useful techniques for gathering information about the whole organization are staff attitude surveys, cultural snapshots, and mixed professional discussion groups.

Having information which provides an overview helps to decide the purpose and objectives for learning: will learning be used to prepare staff for their next job or help them to do their present job better? Will learning be used to initiate and drive a programme of change or will learning be identified as a need resulting from a change process? Will learning primarily be used to redress poor skill performance identified through appraisal? Is the purpose of learning to address particular problems identified within the organization? Being clear about the intended purpose for learning enables a clear statement to be made about what learning should be achieving.

Once the purpose for learning has been established a target group can be identified. For example, if the target group is managers, we need to define the group and the function that the group of workers have in common. Management in the public sector is carried out in a variety of settings, at a variety of levels, by staff with a varying degree of managerial responsibility. The target group and the work they do needs to be clearly identified because not everyone with a similar job title is doing the same type and range of work. For evaluation purposes there will be a requirement to determine an improvement in the quality of management skill acquired by the individual and also to determine if more of the management function is being done. Evaluation can be viewed as a candle and a map. As a candle, evaluation sheds light on the programme of learning. It enables insights to be gained by the designers and deliverers of training and development programmes, enabling them to identify issues and recognize how and where improvements can be made. Maps can be used in several ways: as a route planner, as a means of navigation and as a means of piloting to a destination. Large-scale maps help to give direction and plan appropriate routes. Using detailed local maps enables particular destinations to be identified. Using magnified locality maps enables local and specific places to be identified and described. Similarly, evaluation as process has a number of functions which, taken collectively, enable insights, direction and details of learning to be clearly linked to the effective working of the organization.

Identifying effective learning through comprehensive evaluation processes draws upon a number of evaluation philosophies and principles, which are:

1 classical scientific principles;
2 objective-setting principles;
3 anthropological research principles.

The classical approach is to compare like with like and to make the process scientific by controlling variables. An example of this is randomizing plots of land to be sown with a crop seed. One plot is dressed with fertilizer and the other plot is not. Since weather, soil, drainage and seeds are controlled, any variation in crop yield is due to the added fertilizer. Comparisons may also be made against standards, for example weights and measures. In training and development terms, this may be applied by comparing actual competence against a standard of expected competence. It could also mean comparing a group of workers on a National Vocational Qualification programme with a similar group of workers not on the programme.

Objective-setting principles rely upon the premise that objectives can be stated and measured. In the context of learning, writing behavioural objectives and course or programme objectives is standard practice. Evaluating the extent to which objectives have been met is a way of validating learning processes but, as a single method, falls short of comprehensive evaluation.

Anthropological research principles use a process of observation, enquiry and explanation. This approach helps to discriminate between alternatives and, since the participants are actively involved, helps to make them more discriminating. Evidence generated from using these methods tends to be subjective and gives access to views and perceptions about the learning ethos and the cultural norms that cause participants to favour one form of learning to another.

Taken together, these differing principles of evaluation can be used to state valid and worthwhile outputs from learning which link the learning to effective working. The application of these principles of evaluation can be seen in the variations of meaning which can be attached to descriptions of effectiveness. For example, effectiveness may be viewed as:

1 a difference: effectiveness is showing a comparative difference; it is that which improves or betters an existing benchmark;
2 giving a better return on the investment than previously: effectiveness is doing it cheaper, lowering costs or raising profits;
3 accomplishing the objective: achieving what you set out to do;
4 making a contribution: having a positive influence which adds to or supports the desired action;
5 power: it is that which cannot be resisted and is effective because it overcomes obstacles and barriers.

Descriptions 1 and 2 link with principles of comparison, 3 links with the   *83* principle of objective-setting, and 4 and 5 link with principles of discovery embedded in anthropological approaches.

Implementing evaluation

The practice of implementing evaluation can be demonstrated by following through the process used by a local government city council to evaluate corporate management development. The organization first considered what was meant by management development. At the outset there was consensus that management was defined by the functions and task roles managers did as part of management job descriptions. This organizational definition was found to be in broad accord with that of the Management Charter Initiative (MCI). Management development was understood to be a preparation for the changing context of local government and its working. All activities which contribute to meet the growing and changing needs of the organization are subsumed into the process of management development.

Recognizing the training needs of the organization and individuals is approached by analysing the skills gap between the current organization and its skills and the future vision of the organization and its required skills. Recognizing training needs uses techniques which take account of both the organization's needs and the needs of individual staff members. Techniques which address individual needs are:

1   personal questionnaires
2   personal interviews
3   appraisals
4   personal development plans
5   job descriptions
6   competency audits
7   continuing professional development

Techniques which address organizational needs are:

1   vision, skills needed for a future organization
2   values, developing organizational beliefs
3   policies, skills to conform to organizational preferred practice
4   culture and style development for the organization
5   corporate approaches, for example Total Quality Management
6   comparing the functions in service-level agreements with the skills required to deliver the functions
7   focus groups

Recognizing training needs involves practising managers stating their development needs. It means using a process whereby managers identify, from day-to-day work issues, the needs for developmental review. Day-to-day issues inform managers what needs to be done, what skills are needed to perform better and what development opportunities are most appropriate to use to enable the organization to be more effective.

The principle of discovery – observe, enquire, explain – is used to find out what the organization has been learning. Organizations, like people, learn what they live. Culture snapshots are used to indicate what sort of learning has been taking place.

> With command, organizations learn compliance
> With consensus, organizations learn commitment
> With hierarchy, organizations learn subordination
> With responsibility, organizations learn ownership
> With leaders, organizations learn following
> With teamwork, organizations learn participation
> With criticism, organizations learn inadequacy
> With secrecy, organizations learn suspicion
> With openness, organizations learn trust

It is important to discover what the organization thinks management development is for:

> Is it to emphasize skills, or to emphasize values, attitudes, beliefs?
> Is it to drive change, or respond to the needs of change?
> Is it about a functional approach, or a characteristic approach?
> Is it about tools and techniques used by managers, or the manner and style of management?
> Is it about a brochure of training courses, or a portfolio of development activities?
> Is it about developing potential for the future, or correcting deficiencies of the past and present?

There are no right or wrong answers to selecting appropriate management development. What is important is that the selection fits what the organization thinks it is about, and also what the organization wants to achieve through the chosen process of development. By using discovery processes, a learning and development programme can be designed which links the programme with the organization's aspirations and objectives. A barrier to formulating an effective programme of development is for development specialists to produce excellent schemes of development but to do so in isolation of the organization. Many excellent schemes fail to be effective because the design stage has not included sufficient reference and relationship to business plans and objectives. Without strong links with organizational objectives and a sense of ownership of the programme throughout the organization, development can easily be seen as a bolt-on activity. Lack of organizational ownership is one problem, another is that excellent delivery can be due to a programme the specialist likes to deliver. Doing something one likes often leads to doing it really well, but if it is not what the organization really needs and wants it will *85* not be perceived as effective. When a specialist does what they like doing, they also enjoy what they are doing and want others to enjoy it as well. However, the extent to which participants enjoyed a course is more a measure of entertainment value than a measure of effectiveness. This is not to say learning should not be enjoyable; it should, but it is questionable to associate enjoyment with a measure of effectiveness. Providers are interested in the fact that participants enjoy a programme of learning because they want them to come back, they want to encourage lifelong learning and they want the programme to receive good marketing press.

Discovering the benefits from learning

Another way to achieve these aims is to focus upon the benefits of the programme to the individual and to the organization. Individuals are motivated to engage in development programmes when they can see some benefits in it for themselves. Organizations are encouraged to invest in development programmes when they see benefits to the organization in terms of better quality of service, efficiency or savings. Ideally there should be a balance where both organization and individuals perceive benefits directly relevant to their needs. If the balance is loaded in favour of the individual it may be difficult to get adequate investment. If the balance of benefits is loaded in favour of the organization it may be difficult to market the programme and sustain demand or interest against potential reluctant participants.

To analyse the benefits, a checklist can be drawn up with a rating scale as follows:

Benefits of development	Organization	Individual
Enhances career prospects	√√	√√√
Enables networking	√√	√√
Reduces stress and work pressure	√√	√√√
Improves personal skills	√√	√√
Improves quality of service	√√√	√√
Improves communication	√√√	√√
Improves teamwork	√√√	√√
Enables better resource management	√√√	√√
Provides a qualification	√	√√√

Key: √√√ Strongly applicable
√√ Applicable
√ Slightly applicable

The benefits listed are examples; an appropriate list needs to be created for each development programme. When creating the list, it is useful to canvass managers, delegates and providers for their views of the perceived benefits. It is also useful to access the views of elected members who may be fearful that training is not directly benefiting the organization or directly affecting the quality of service provided at the front-line.

An obvious benefit of development for an organization is to see that appropriate standards of competence are being used to deliver the quality of service required by the customer. Standards of competence can be formulated by the organizations in the public sector. Some organizations have used National Standards developed by Vocational Lead Bodies. The Management Charter Initiative (MCI) has produced performance competencies for managers. The MCI standards are embedded in National Vocational Qualifications which have three different levels or standards for managerial competence and they are generic, being founded upon the notion that relevant qualities and skills lead to effective job performance. The National Standards describe output performance criteria against which any manager should be able to demonstrate and provide evidence from within the job of management that they do. It is possible to use the National Standards as a basic framework and to tailor them to the organization's specific requirements and needs.

Using established output performance criteria, such as those contained in National Standards, has a number of uses and advantages:

1 They can be used to produce a specification for a development programme.
2 They can be used to evaluate a development programme against a known National Standard.
3 They can be used as a national yardstick by which to measure individual competence.
4 They can be used to benchmark current levels of competence and establish desired levels – any gaps indicate areas for development.
5 They can be used as the basis for performance appraisal from an identified 'core' of competences for managers.
6 Standards can be used to contract in output terms what development providers should achieve.
7 They can be used to measure the improved performance in the workplace of a manager and, therefore, as a measure of effectiveness.
8 They can be used to calculate financial returns by comparing costs associated with the development programme and the financial value of the development to the organization.

The public sector does make a clear connection between the job description, experience, skills, grade and salary of an employee. Many good professional and technical specialists are promoted to management roles on the assumption that experience as a technical expert has given them the necessary managerial skills. Using standards indicates that development is often required to bring performance in management up to that required by the job. When competencies are developed within existing salary structures, the organization gets the value of that proportion of the salary to the improved level of performance. To measure the improved performance in percentage terms, a benchmark of assessed performance must be established at the start of the programme and an assessment made at the end. The difference between the two assessments gives a measure of the improved performance.

Tailoring National Standards to organizational needs is accomplished through an examination of the list of units and elements contained within the Standard and noting the work-based practices required by the organization. The Standards have specific output performance criteria and are accompanied by principles, knowledge and understanding, which underpin good work-based practice. By selecting and emphasizing areas of the Standard which meet those desired by the organization, a programme of development can be specified. The specification will equip managers with the skills necessary for competent performance to a known standard. Assessment of current skills against the Standard not only identifies those who would benefit from the programme of development but it also provides a mechanism for delegates and line managers to benchmark and measure an inventory of skills. An additional advantage of this process is that the programme design targets learning to the organization's business needs; time is not wasted on irrelevant and inappropriate learning.

Once a programme has been specified and tailored to the organization's business needs, a provider needs to be commissioned. Choosing a provider is driven by a requirement to get best value for money and also to get the best variant from a wide range of management development initiatives. Researching the marketplace provides a large quantity of information. The best way to handle the information is to have a structure which enables the comparison principles to be applied – market information regarding, for example, time, finance and other benefits. When comparing time, for example, some details to look out for are:

time
number of course days
number of residential days
number of revision days
number of exam days
number of assessment days
number of support/advisory/mentor days

The focus of attention here is the total amount of time away from the workplace. A great deal of development is accomplished through the leisure, hobbies and educational activities of staff in their own time. This should be encouraged, but in terms of value for money for the investing organization, only time out of normal working hours should be recorded in the table.

Financial details can be compared by producing a table of the cost for each option. Some details to look out for are:

programme/course costs
customizing costs
venue costs

course material costs
examination/assessment costs
travel costs
residential costs
subsistence costs

There are always some accounting assumptions when measuring costs. It is important to include costs directly associated with the course programme, rather than the delegates on the programme. The kind of information most useful to this process has the following qualities:

1   information which has a quantifiable measure;
2   information which is fair and accurate;
3   information which is more objective than subjective;
4   information which is consistent and constant.

Other benefits of the programme should also be listed. These may include benefits like flexibility, specific skills, or accounts for prior learning. These are only examples; a full list should be created and used in conjunction with the tables on time and finance to compare programmes and make the best choice.

Reviewing the relationship between intention and achievement requires a measured level of development performance, a measured level of the improved value against cost of the development process, an account of the extent to which set objectives have been met and a review of the benefits of the programme. Developing the performance of employees in the workplace involves raising their awareness of current competency levels for managers. This can be done using the MCI competence model. Crediting Competence makes the point that when a manager is made aware of their own competences, they are more able to make use of them in the workplace. Questionnaires, derived from the units of competence, can be used to get the line manager's views and percentage measures of current performance levels. The same questionnaire can be used to get the delegate's views and measures of current performance levels. After the programme of development the views and measures of performance are revisited and percentage changes noted. The results of the before and after measures are entered on the matrix and used to calculate the average improvement in performance.

Example:

Competence	1	2	3	4	5	6	7	8	9	Average
Delegate Measure	10	5	5	20	15	20	10	5	10	13%
Line Manager	15	10	5	10	10	15	5	10	5	

The result in this example indicates that the delegate has improved over a range of competences by 13 per cent in work-based performance. The   *89* organization is therefore getting 13 per cent better performance value from the salary paid to the delegate to do their job.

Example continued:

Delegate's Salary		£18 000
13% of Salary	$= \dfrac{13}{100} \times$	18 000
	=	£2 340
Cost of programme was		£1 000
Financial Return	= £2 340 – £1 000	
	=	£1 340

This example also indicates that competence 6 produced the greatest average level of improvement (17.5 per cent) and competence 3 the lowest level of average improvement (5 per cent). This may indicate that the design or delivery of the programme to improve competence 3 needs to be looked at again. It could also mean that competence 3 was already highly developed and could not, therefore, be improved much by the delegate. The more delegates there are in the matrix, the clearer is the indication of effective and not so effective parts of the programme.

It is also noticeable that when managers become more competent in managerial skills, they do more management and less professional and technical work. Managers delegate more, manage people better and release more of the difficult technical aspects of their operational work. A before and after measure of the proportion of management can be used to determine the increase in the quantity of management being done. A summative report using quantitative information about choice of programme, costs and return on investment can be made to all stakeholders. Candidates are made aware of the extent to which they have improved. Chief officers are made aware of the value of their service and chief executives and councillors are made aware of the value for money and return on investment resulting from their support for the programme.

A formative report can also be given which explains the extent to which set objectives have been met. The process of evaluation eventually causes a return to the organization's stated purpose and objectives for learning and development. Comprehensive evaluation brings educators, training and development specialists, and those responsible for learning, into a strategic discussion with the organization's top managers, politicians and chief executive.

CONCLUSION

The future challenge for education, training and development will be to justify the existence of learning processes within the organization through improved performance measures and the demonstration of value for money:

- Investors want to know the identified business benefits.
- Investors want to achieve work-based effectiveness, not professional delivery of expensive programmes.
- Investors want benchmark measures against best practice and National Standards.

Processes of evaluation will be used to satisfy a number of organizational needs. They are:

1 the need to justify performance and value for money;
2 the need to explain the relationship between costs and benefits to the organization;
3 the need to explain the extent to which set objectives have been met;
4 the need to measure outputs and effectiveness;
5 the need to present both qualitative and quantitative information.

Some tools, techniques, and methods in current use within the public sector which go some way to satisfying the above list of needs are:

1 tables for comparing different training options;
2 checklists for assessing benefits to the organization and the individual;
3 competency standards written in output terms;
4 questionnaires, interviews, appraisals and observation to determine work-based performance improvements;
5 a system for comparing financial costs and return on investment;
6 a matrix which shows the levels of effectiveness of each part of a development programme;
7 post-course questionnaires to measure professional delivery and delegate satisfaction rates.

By using comprehensive evaluation, a link can be established between effective learning and effective working. Evaluation can show the benefits and quality of a development programme. Public sector organizations using the evaluation processes outlined here are able to show:

- quantifiable improvements in a range of competencies and work-based performance;
- a known level of return on the investment made in training and development;
- justifiable benefits and value for money;
- increased motivation and targeting to individual participants;
- a focus on strategic organizational objectives for the development process.

The Learning Organization will thrive and flourish when evaluation makes explicit the bottom-line benefits of learning to the purpose, mission and vision of the organization.

8 Creating learning and development processes gradually

Derek Staniforth, Leicestershire County Council

Leicestershire County Council was, for many years, regarded as a middle-of-the-road, traditional authority which carried out its duties without a great deal of fuss or publicity. As an organization, it has to deliver services to the residents of the county and these include Education, Social Services, Trading Standards, Highways, Libraries and Museums. Its Museum Service is unique in its county-wide provision at County Council, rather than District Council level. It has no responsibility for services such as refuse collection or municipal housing which are exercised by the District Council. Politically, it has been in a state of no overall party control for the last 15 years. Within this state it has also been unique in that there has been no pact between any two parties regarding direction, which has meant that every issue has been considered on its merits. It also has no elaborate rulebook or set of conventions by which it manages its political balance – only that there are no permanent chairs of committees and that there is no use of the chairs casting votes in the event of a tied decision in a committee; if this should occur the matter is referred up to the next level of the political process.

As far as the development processes of the organization are concerned, there was not a corporate approach to management development until 1988. Previously, what was carried out was on an *ad hoc*, departmental basis. It was during late 1987 that a working group of Deputy Chief Officers was set up to consider whether the Authority should take a corporate view of such developments and, if this was agreed, how it should be taken forward. This group arrived at some recommendations which, as a way forward, they took to both the Chief Officers Management Team and, subsequently, to the appropriate Member Committee.

This led to the setting up of a Management Development Unit to develop and deliver the agreed programme. This has been an evolving strategy driven by the original working group, which remained in existence to provide the necessary support and direction for the process. The programmes offered, which were originally in-house delivered, now include a partnership with the University of Leicester to deliver a tailored Graduate Diploma and a Masters of Business Administration programme. It is more than probable that these developments would not have been as successful as they are without the continuing support of the Elected Members, Chief Executive and Chief Officers. All three of these are now actively involved in the programmes. This is the context in which the development of, and belief in, the necessity for organization learning evolved.

LEARNING AND CHANGE

Some six years ago, the long serving Chief Executive moved on and his replacement, who was previously responsible for Finance and Administration in another county, arrived. He spent some time listening to a variety of people before setting out an agenda for change. This agenda was called the Corporate Action Plan and its basic task was to change the way the Authority thought, worked and acted. It was aimed at moving to a more customer-orientated, responsive organization providing an excellent standard of service to the users. The background to this plan was a realization that the organization was operating in a rapidly changing environment which was affected by:

1　increase in customer expectation and pressure about service, choice and quality;
2　economic and environmental considerations;
3　growth of Information Technology and raised expectations about its application;
4　skill shortages;
5　the proposed extension of compulsory competitive tendering and the need to change to cope with this;
6　increasing scarcity of resources in their widest sense.

The purpose of the plan was to enable the Authority to act and to be seen to act positively, concertedly and effectively in a time of growing pressure. It was to be service-led and customer-orientated which would require a culture change within the organization and it was to be continuously monitored. The plan was to address four areas of customers, resources, communications (internal and external) and the enabling authority. As far as learning in the organization, the real drive came from the enabling limb of this framework. This had two main thrusts: first, installing a 'can-do' culture, which was about empowerment and driving responsibility as far down the organization as was possible; second, succeeding in competitive tendering, which was about re-skilling and other developmental activities. Around the same time the Elected Members agreed both their priorities for the four-year life cycle of the County Council and the values for the organization.

The two values that have particular reference to organizational learning were first that the Authority is a partnership between its Elected Members and employees and depends for its effectiveness on mutual support. Second, it recognized, in the classic statement that occurs so often, that its employees are its most important asset. To this end it seeks to recruit and retain a well-motivated, well-trained workforce. This latter aspiration was enlarged in the objectives which stated how it would implement its statement of values. The key objective for learning was that it would develop and maintain a corporate training and development strategy concerning all groups and grades of employees. It is this that has been used to encourage corporate learning in the organization.

Since these values and objectives were written a further change in Chief Executive has taken place. It is worth noting that the current Chief Executive was a member of the group that moved management development on to a corporate basis and has always supported its development. As far as developing a Learning Organization is concerned he believes in an evolutionary approach with various parts of the organization moving at a pace suitable to themselves. He believes that it has to be a mixture of good management practice within a set of core values – you cannot have one without the other. There is a feeling that the development of organizational learning has taken place on a departmental basis with some corporate work. Part of the latter has been the recognition that most managers in the Authority had little contact with Elected Members or even Chief Officers. This was rectified by holding a series of one-day sessions on the Political Process led by a neutral facilitator. These involved Group Leaders, Elected Members and Chief Officers. This has now developed into a session within the programme. Members are keen, as are Chief Officers, to support this and both sides learn from the process. Elected Members of the Authority have attended various parts of the programme as participants to understand it more fully and to further the partnership principle which is one of the values of the Authority. There is still an issue as to whether more should be done to accelerate the learning process.

The Management Development Programmes that the Authority run have subsidiary benefits for organizational learning. As they are deliberately organized on a cross-departmental, cross-tier basis, that is, there are a range of grades, from Chief Officer to senior administrative assistant, on the same programme, there is a learning outcome. This may be in a better understanding of how the organization functions or a realization that people of all levels have a contribution to make to its development.

The Chief Executive has articulated his own understanding of what a Learning Organization is. He believes it is an organization which enables people within it to learn from their own experience and that of others, to develop that learning and to put it back into the organization in the form of new ideas. He believes that there has been success with 75 per cent of this but it is the last 25 per cent that is the real issue. This last quarter relates to being able to translate the outcome back into the organization. This is happening in a relatively loose way but it is not built into any coherent framework at present. It would appear that individual Elected Members would want to learn from officers to help the change process but this requires a political shift to enable it to happen.

There is undoubtedly a view that the organization has changed in the last few years to become far more responsive and even more of a listening organization. The problem that many of its staff have (and this is particularly at middle management level) is that they do not feel that the organization is moving fast enough. This may be a result of political reality, which is not fully appreciated even now by those who complain of a lack of pace.

There is a belief that things have changed and that culturally it is now quite different from what it was some years ago. This change is not, however, uniform. It has taken place at different rates across the Authority but perhaps this is only to be expected given the size and diversity of the organization as it exists. If you measure the organization against the Burgoyne model (Pedler, *et al.*, 1991)[1] you would find it is at various stages against the 11 characteristics. This is not a problem as it is a situation that one really ought to expect. Indeed the model should be used to show progress and where to concentrate effort.

EXAMPLES OF LEARNING WITHIN THE ORGANIZATION

This section will look at some of the initiatives undertaken within the Authority to involve staff at all levels in the development of organizational learning. What we were trying to do was to encourage and facilitate this process by making people feel valued and able to contribute from their unique experience and knowledge. These initiatives have varied in size and in the level within the organization at which they have taken place. The success rate has also varied. Even those that have been less successful than might have been expected when we started them have enabled lessons to be learnt by those who wish to use this experience in their own part of our organization or indeed in others.

Quality Through People

The initiative here started with one Divisional Surveyor who had been through the County Council's Management Development Programme. It arose from his analysis of complaints to either himself, other divisional staff or even to the Headquarters staff. It was his view that many of the issues raised could have been dealt with on-the-spot by the staff actually involved. The question that, therefore, arose was why this was not actually being done. The result of his questioning in this area was, as could be expected, that there was in existence a 'this is not my job' syndrome. The issue was: how could this be tackled so that the front-line staff, who were in most cases manual workers, would feel capable of dealing with these situations and feel empowered to do so? He approached the Central Training Unit to see if they could assist him with this process. The outcome of these discussions was what became known as our Quality Through People Programme.

In essence, this is a method facilitated by a trainer and requiring the commitment of senior managers to enable staff at all levels to feel comfortable when dealing with all sorts of queries. How does it work? Initially, small groups *95* of staff meet with the facilitator in a confidential setting in which they can raise any issues that they feel are preventing them from doing a good job. In this instance, in order to accommodate all the staff, several such meetings were held in groups of around eight to ten people and there was an agreement that the manual workers would not suffer financially. In these meetings a pattern of issues arose around such items as communications, how to deal with the public, and other matters of a similar nature. The outcomes of all these sessions were then analysed by the facilitator and ranked in order in relation to the number of times and importance given to them by the various groups. The manager, in this case the Divisional Manager, was then briefed on the issues raised so he was aware of the worries of his staff – these did not have any names attached to them.

Following this, a complete day was organized at a non-work venue to pursue the matter further. A non-work venue was chosen because this gave a message to participants that they and their contributions were valued and also that such 'away days' were not just the prerogative of white collar staff. The day was split into two distinct phases. In the morning there was a general intro-duction to the principles of customer care and how this affected every member of the division who came into contact, however rarely, with the public. It helped this process to remind people that their jobs existed because of the public who legitimately had an interest in the outcomes of their work. The public were certainly seen by the Senior Managers as major stakeholders in this process. The morning sessions were certainly seen as valuable by all the staff in the way that it made them think of the effect of their work on the public. In the afternoon, key issues that had arisen from the small-group work described above were then concentrated on. Participants were split into small groups containing a mixture of white collar and manual staff and each group was asked to consider one of the major issues that had been raised. They were encouraged to be as radical as they could in their solutions and not to be afraid of voicing ideas because of where they were in the organizational hierarchy. The message was very much that you are at the front-line in these issues; tell us what should be done to improve things both for yourselves, as the service provider, and the public, as the service user. It is not easy to encourage this type of process but by this stage they had started to become used to expressing views and being able to articulate their ideas. It had been agreed in advance that the Divisional Surveyor and his management group should attend in the afternoon to listen to the ideas of these small groups. What actually surprised many of the participants was that there was a rapid response to some of their proposals. Other ideas were taken on board and further working groups were organized. The outcome of this initial work was that other Divisional Surveyors went through the same process and other sections within that particular department did as well.

The outcome of this process was initially excellent and it did change attitudes and staff at all levels felt able to raise issues and make suggestions. It was not, however, realized by the Senior Managers of these sections that there needed to be continual reinforcement of these changing attitudes if they were to become embedded within the culture of that particular part of the organ-ization. It may be that we have lost temporarily some of the benefits of the learning process. It has not entirely reverted to its old ways but the lesson to be learnt is that if you want to foster organizational learning, it requires continual reinforcement if it is to succeed.

Footpath inspections

The Council's responsibilities include the maintenance of the definitive footpath map and ensuring that landowners maintain these in a condition that supports access to the public. From the public's point of view there is now an effective national lobbying organization in being – the Ramblers Association. This body is devoted to ensuring that footpaths are maintained in a useable condition and are not blocked or diverted. Although the County branch is vigorous in its pursuit of its objectives it does carry them out by seeking co-operation rather than confrontation if the latter can be avoided.

Within the Authority, there are a variety of sections who have an interest in the whole process of maintaining this network in a useable state. These are the Divisional Surveyors and their Footpath Inspectors, the Countryside Section in the Departmental Headquarters and the legal section within the County Secretary's Department. As might be expected this combination of interests could well become a recipe for delay. In addition to this it was ascertained by the Divisional Surveyors that each individual inspector had their own ways of tackling the issues that arose. Last, there was also an issue around workloads as one division, in particular, has a far greater mileage within its boundaries than do the other two. The reason for this was basically historic and was an outcome of population spread over preceding centuries.

The Countryside Section, who had a responsibility for this area of work centrally and maintained the definitive map and were also the reference point for diversions, appeals, etc., had been trying for some time to arrive at a better and more responsive way of dealing with the issues that were continually being raised. They asked a member of the Management Development Team to assist them by being a neutral facilitator at a date to be arranged to which all parties with an interest in the issue of footpaths would be invited. Prior to this date the facilitator ensured that he was briefed by all participants so that there was an understanding by him of the issues involved and what their relative importance was to each participant. From these discussions it was possible to outline a programme with an acknowledgement that this was both tentative and extremely flexible. The meeting was well attended and included all levels of the involvement but most particularly the three inspectors themselves and the solicitor responsible for the legal aspects of the work, together with his administrator from the same department, who had considerable input into the process. The initial comment by some of the participants was that this was the first time that all those concerned with footpaths had actually got together and that it was a good idea. This alone started the process in a positive frame of mind. The purpose of the day was outlined and people were asked for their ideas. Once the tentative agenda had finally been agreed, those present split into three groups ensuring representation of all interests in each group (the only problem was how to split the legal section's two people into three). Although it looked random, the groups had been pre-selected to an extent to ensure that the Footpath Inspectors were each in a different group from their divisional representative. This was done because we did not want them to feel they had to toe a party line on any issues that arose. We were after all the possible inputs and suggestions as to how working practices could be improved. Although this may sound a bit like the Quality Through People Programme outlined above, it was different in that a very specific problem area was being addressed.

The three groups were asked to detail the issues around better coordination of delivery of this service and where they thought the delivery could be improved. Again, it was made clear that no issue was too small or, indeed, too complex to be raised. They were also told that everyone present was there to learn both from the problems and then from the solutions. Plenty of time was allowed for this phase and the facilitator moved from group to group advising, assisting but most definitely not doing – each group was asked to present the outcome in some hard-copy format so that this could, in due course, be typed up and circulated.

They were also asked to be prepared to present the outcomes verbally. This was the catalyst of dialogue during the day between all the parties regarding how they could assist each other and make the necessary work easier for each other. For many of those present it was the first time they had had an opportunity to start to understand the problems that some of their colleagues had. It also enabled them to realize how some of their work practices caused problems for other people. One of the major differences in working practices highlighted very early on was the differing approach that each Inspector had to actually dealing with their landowners in order to get obstructions removed. These ranged from spending time negotiating with them, and therefore maintaining a friendly approach, to a more formal method of moving in and serving notices fairly early in the procedure. The question of differing workloads arose and many possible solutions proposed. At the end of the day an action plan was agreed and various people were self-selected to work on these points. One of the most interesting results was that three inspectors agreed to work on how to have the common approach to the various problems arising. This common approach would enable us to reduce the complaints from landowners with footpaths in more than one area that they were treated differently by each inspector. Other issues included such items as the location of inspectors, that is, should they be central and divisional, etc? Perhaps the most important single item to come out of the day was the request to meet again on an agreed date to see what had been learnt and what had been put into practice. This was actually raised by the inspectors, much to the surprise of their managers. It showed that it is possible to enthuse people and to create a climate where they want to share their knowledge, ideas, etc., for the benefit of the service user. This was agreed, a date and venue selected and the working groups left to organize themselves to produ   te proposals.

The second meeting duly took place with   tator and the same participants present. Preliminaries that had   ry to start the first meeting were not now necessary and it b   that there was a different atmosphere in place. There seeme   tor to be less need for him to be present as the groups were cc   role was to remind the group where they had reached at their la   the working group feedback and facilitate the subsequent disc   involved organizing the groups to look at each of the proposals a   they affected them and whether there were any important issue   v, or if, they would work. Again it was rewarding to see how   ogue was started, previous problems to progress were dealt w   picture should not be seen as all sweetness and light – there we   some areas where entrenched attitudes make movement slow, if not almost impossible. However any shift in these must signify success of a positive kind.

The most important outcomes of this process can be summarized as:

1   The regular half-day sessions are still continuing and are now self-facilitating.
2   The issues being addressed are moving into the major areas of cross-team sensitivities.
3   People believe they can contribute, will be listened to and the best solution will be tried.
4   There is a gradual move to harmonize work practices being worked out by those who do the job and not imposed from above.
5   Out of this came a sense of empowerment and value which made people feel better.

It is almost certain that this shift in attitudes came out of the belief that no one person or group has the right answer, if there is indeed any such thing, to any of these problems but that the group itself, provided it felt it had the authority to work, may well be able to find one. One of the parties did say after the first session that enough lip service was paid to the staff being our greatest resource but this was the first time she had felt it had actually been put into practice. This group continues to work together in small units to improve the service delivered and to learn from each other. Perhaps this initiative worked because it was felt early on that the participants were all being listened to and there was no sense of being unable to contribute.

The Foundation Programme Working Groups

The Management Foundation Programme within the Authority, in its original form, was run on cohorts of 15. These groups became very cohesive, with a strong group identity – in fact some still get together several years later on a regular basis. The Senior Officers Working Group wondered whether they could provide a means of looking at issues which the 'Authority needed to deal with'. It was eventually agreed that this should be done as part of the continual learning process. This initiative was agreed by the Chief Officers Management Team and a slot was arranged in the programme for this to be introduced by a member of the Senior Officers Group.

Initially, it was agreed that the topics to be looked at would be suggested by the Senior Officers Group and the groups would be given a choice of one or two projects from which to choose. Later on in the process the groups selected their own projects which were subject to approval by the Senior Officers Group. There is no doubt that some of these were extremely successful and a range of new ideas and ways of tackling situations were arrived at. The subjects tackled included: how to deal with women returners; green issues; advertising costs; job secondments; staff communications, etc. The aim of this approach was:

1 to get a fresh look and new ideas on some key issues;
2 to encourage the learning process of the groups;
3 to demonstrate to Senior Officers the abilities within the organization which were not at present being used;
4 to encourage a corporate approach to various major issues.

The results of these groups proved to be very good and there were some novel and interesting ways forward suggested. However, in several instances the reports moved no further than being presented to Senior Management. It was this lack of progress that reduced the enthusiasm of subsequent groups to be involved in the process. It is not that they did not have the enthusiasm or did not want to be involved that stopped the learning process but the lack of progress of ideas and suggestions made in the past. The current Chief Executive identified some of the causes of failure of this initiative as:

1 time available to participate;
2 keeping the group together – 15 was really too large but there has been an enthusiasm within each group to stay as one;
3 some resistance to topics – even latterly when self-selected;
4 concerns around lack of feedback from the Senior Management.

From what has been learnt about organizational learning since this approach was taken it would have been handled differently now. I am sure that more time would have been spent ensuring that Senior Managers were aware of the process and its advantages.

It has been accepted that there is a need to utilize all the abilities within the organization to enable it to develop. As a result of the work carried out above and its outcomes, a changed approach was tried. This involved seeking volunteers from those who had actually participated in the management development process to work on specific tasks. These groups were kept smaller as it was expected that this would make it easier to gain their commitment and to enable them to complete the work necessary. The first of these volunteer groups, which were called Corporate Action Teams, was set up to look at good housekeeping: in other words, it was asked to look at possible sources of waste and how it could be reduced. Some six people from across the Authority got together to look at this and produced a number of ways forward. Perhaps because this was a smaller, more focused group, who had an interest in the subject (or else they would not have volunteered), the outcomes were worthwhile. Some of the issues they raised have now become the subject of additional work that may not have started without being raised initially as an area with potential by this particular group. This one lasted about six months in a formal state but the most interesting outcome is that its members still look at what is going on around them with a different pair of eyes and seek to minimize or eradicate waste. The process of learning undertaken has raised the awareness of what can be achieved and, therefore, has embedded itself in a changed mind set in these particular participants.

Outcomes

What has been learned by the Authority from these examples and others that are taking place in a variety of formal and informal ways? First, that changes in the way the Authority moves towards a learning culture need to be taken at a pace that people can cope with. This will vary from group to group. It is not possible to quantify this but our experience shows it to be a longer (that is, six months plus) rather than a shorter period. Second, it has become apparent that a large organization cannot introduce a learning culture over the whole of it at the same time. It would appear to be more realistic to move into those areas which are ready for such a change. Third, it has been realized that encouraging learning requires constant reinforcement. It is no use expecting learning to happen as a matter of course, after one or two inputs. We need to spend time encouraging people to change. Similarly, it is not helpful to pronounce that we will encourage people to learn from their mistakes if the first time they make one, they are dealt with harshly. It is essential that all levels of management are seen to 'walk the talk'. This does raise some issues in certain areas of the County Council's work when mistakes could be the subject of legal or other sanctions and, therefore, this type of statement will not work. Even so there is plenty of scope for continual reinforcement of the basic message. There is evidence that a change in the Authority has occurred and is being sustained. It has been achieved by some of the ways outlined above.

However, the most important factor in this process has been the willingness of the Chief Executive both now, and in his previous role as Director of Corporate Management, to encourage this to happen and to gain support of the Elected Members for these initiatives. Without this support, progress would not have been as rapid or as rooted as it now is. This does not mean that everything is right by any means but it has changed the way we approach many issues. There is undoubtedly a great deal more we might have done and even more we could do. The gradual approach suited our particular needs but it is not the only one and other cases in this book illustrate different approaches.

BIBLIOGRAPHY

Pedler, M., Burgoyne, J. and Boydell, T. (1991), *The Learning Company: A Strategy for Sustainable Development*, Maidenhead (UK): McGraw-Hill.

9 Developing a Learning Organization through quality assurance

Janice A Cook and John Bolton, Camden Social Services

WHAT WE MEAN BY A LEARNING ORGANIZATION

As you work through this chapter you will realize that we are using a particular set of characteristics which we believe make up a Learning Organization. These are not one person's theory, but an accumulation of theories, which we believe are the best measure of our organization. This framework is:

1 Employees should feel that they are contributing something that matters; both as an individual and as a member of Camden Social Services.
2 Every member of Camden Social Services should be learning, and the organization should be using all abilities as a result.
3 Effective teamwork should be used to produce effective creativity.
4 Camden Social Services should know what knowledge exists within its organization and use it effectively.
5 Our Departmental Management Team should be setting organizational visions, and making sure that these visions are shared across the organization.
6 Employees should be able to explore assumptions and beliefs.
7 Employees should have mutual respect and trust for each other, no matter what their hierarchical position in the organization.
8 Employees should feel free to take risks and openly assess results.
9 Client and customer input to setting organizational objectives should be part of the learning process.
10 Leaders in Camden Social Services should have an enthusiasm for development, with a strong sense of self-empowerment, with the ability to empower others.
11 Structured networking should be available for all employees.
12 Changes and barriers to learning should be monitored.

WHAT CAMDEN SOCIAL SERVICES WAS LIKE IN THE PAST (PRE-QUALITY INITIATIVE)

At the end of the 1980s, Camden Social Services employed 2 000 people and provided an extensive range of services to the community. These included: care for the under-5s; residential children's homes; day centres for older people and people with disabilities; homes for older people; home care; and social work for adults and children.

This was a time of turmoil and change. The department was heading for a large overspend while central government was cutting the money available. Social workers were on strike because of a lack of recognition of their professionalism. The Senior Management Team were nearly all resigning or leaving. The Department was trying to restructure to meet the new legislative demands of the Community Care Act 1990 and the Children Act 1989. In addition, there was the threat of privatization or voluntarization for some services. Staff believed that protecting their individual service area and all related budgets and posts was the way for them and their services to survive in the organization. Training was implemented by some staff, but in an *ad hoc* way. There was also a culture where blame was prevalent, resulting in people being defensive about mistakes, and therefore finding it difficult to learn from them. In addition, the organization's ability to learn was undeveloped. There was no history of a strong training and development service and, therefore, no influence from resident learning experts. There was limited encouragement and role modelling from senior management during this period.

Quality assurance was not in the organization's vocabulary. We were still living in an old local government culture, some of which was very positive – for example, freedom to be creative with regard to tailoring services to client needs, and staff who were very committed to providing high-level social services in the community – some of which was negative – for example, a lack of systems, procedures and structured accountability.

Future plans were based solely on survival, both individually and organizationally – particularly as Camden Social Services had a poor reputation in the Council (both because of overspending budgets and some poor quality services). In this environment it was hard to think of change as a positive way forward. Change felt threatening, and was believed to result in job losses, services being diminished and a less caring and more hard-nosed atmosphere. It was a mainly negative picture that was painted, and that is probably how it felt most of the time. However, the Departmental Management Team, during this era, did allow managers the opportunity to function fairly autonomously in most parts of the organization. So, on the one hand, there was excessive control in some areas (like budgets) and, on the other, there was freedom to develop new ideas and integrate them into the service area.

LEVERS OF CHANGE WHICH LED US TOWARDS THE QUALITY INITIATIVE

Events which caused change resulted from two main areas: national government legislation and the recruitment of a new Senior Management Team. However, there were other change agents in the organization, and other events (described below), which led us to work towards a quality initiative.

We applied to national government to give us some Training Support Programme grants which enabled formal training programmes to be implemented, which had not existed previously. In order to obtain these grants, training had to be planned both monetarily and in respect of identifying needs, and this had to be formalized on paper. The grants also gave us the opportunity to fund specialist training posts in our Department. This empowered the Department because it was a way of receiving financial resources at a time of cut-backs, but within a structured approach. The other major impact of these grants was to force the compilation and implementation of a Departmental Management Development Programme. This programme was innovative for its time, using mainly external providers, and it introduced the concept of self-development into the organization. The aim was to get at least half of the managers onto this programme to develop a culture of learning from experience, rather than just attending formal training, although of course, funding for off-the-job courses was still available. This began the journey of moving away from training being used simply for punishment or reward purposes. We almost achieved the training of half of our managers on self-development programmes at one stage (before the big flow of redundancies in 1992), and this created pockets of excellence in the Department with a real shift towards the beginnings of a Learning Organization.

A new Senior Training Officer was recruited into the organization (Janice Cook, one of the authors of this chapter) and she had come from the private sector, bringing a different perspective and approach. The impact, however, was initially diminished because the training function had been devolved into each division of the Department. Therefore, she had no direct-line management authority over the Training Officers and it was difficult to achieve a departmental approach. However, this was shortly rectified at the end of 1991, with the centralization of the training function, under the Senior Training Officer's authority.

During the time of cut-backs and overspending of budgets, the Council's Chief Executive commissioned two staff from the Policy Unit to join our Departmental Management Team to assist them with controlling the budget and achieving the cut-backs. During this phase all managers in the Department felt they had to justify not only their existence but the existence of their functions. Two things happened as a result of this: (1) it embedded the competitive, fight from your own corner, culture, and (2) it made all managers realize the importance of the precise management of budgets.

At the beginning of 1992, our existing Departmental Management Team disbanded, and a new Director arrived in April of that year. His task in the first year was to stabilize the Department financially, which he achieved over the next couple of years, through strong leadership. This was a very significant lever for change because people began to believe that financial stability was possible, and our 'naughty' reputation was diminishing. This provided a more positive environment in which to work, although survival was still high on the agenda. The difficulty during this period was to stabilize without removing the space for people to be innovative and creative. The social work strike ended in 1992.

By October 1992 the rest of the Departmental Management Team was recruited, two of them were from outside of the Council, one from outside of the Department and one had already been promoted from inside in December 1991 (this is the Chief Inspector, John Bolton, one of the authors of this chapter). Not surprisingly, the newly formed Departmental Management Team found the first year difficult, but because of their new and different approaches, there was a positive impact in the organization, particularly in the area of setting standards through effective leadership. There was also a clear political priority to achieve better-quality services. (The word 'quality' crept into the Social Services language through the guidance documents that were produced by the Department of Health for the introduction of the new Children Act and the Community Care legislation.) Camden Council was trying to turn over a new leaf and establish itself as a more effective and efficient organization.

Soon after the new Senior Management Team were established in Camden Social Services, the new Director declared that he wanted to see them develop quality/good-value services. Where the Authority could not achieve this, the private or voluntary sector would be invited to run those services. This led staff in the Department to try to understand what could be done to bring about change, and develop their services as centres of excellence, thereby protecting them from voluntarization or privatization. The Chief Inspector was a significant change agent with regard to the quality initiative, working hard at the beginning to get the project going at a senior level in the Department. This has been an important strength of the initiative: that, right from the beginning, senior management have been committed and involved. In addition, the Assistant Director for Adults Division chaired the Quality Assurance Working Group in the Department from its inception. The pressure for action on quality across the board was building up. From these senior management discussions, the departmental Quality Assurance Working Group was created.

A promise of relative stability was important, and the Director indicated that large restructuring activity would not be needed for the next few years, yet the culture of blame still seemed prevalent; it takes time for people to believe that relative stability is possible, and that they will be trusted to run their own services. Staff commitment to the provision of services was still intact (although a bit bruised by the redundancies in 1992, which had affected morale), creativity was getting a bit stifled through fear of job loss and service privatization or voluntarization, but we were beginning to work hard on systems and procedures. The idea of structured accountability had not yet come into play.

All of these factors have created a new world, with a robust budget (although still within the context of national government cut-backs), and a working towards higher standards of service, with a quality initiative on the agenda. The new Departmental Management Team were enthusiastically supporting development work in the Department, to help to implement the Community Care Act and the Children Act. However, the changes required seemed so vast, with so many areas to improve and develop, that personal development seemed to be a lower priority than usual.

WHAT CAMDEN SOCIAL SERVICES IS LIKE NOW WITH THE QUALITY INITIATIVE

What Camden Social Services looks like

Camden Social Services is now 1 100 employees strong with a wide range of services provided to the community. The changes include:

- Care for the under-5s being transferred to the Education Department.
- Residential children's homes moved to the independent sector and the majority of children are accommodated in permanent placements or foster care.
- Some day centres for older people and people with disabilities being left with the Department, some are voluntarized.
- Some homes for older people left, some privatized.
- Some home care services left, some privatized.
- Social work for adults and children is still with the Department, but aligned and co-located with health.
- New multi-agency work, particularly a project in the area of learning disabilities.

How did the quality initiative begin?

Our quality initiative began in 1992, with the creation of a Quality Assurance Officer post. Initially this post was working in a vacuum, as opposed to implementing a specific quality initiative. It was not until the Chief Inspector and the Head of Personnel and Training came together to try and share their learning on quality, that the bones of an initiative began to form.

The Chief Inspector was informed by the quality language of BS 5750 of Procedures and Systems, of quality manuals and clarity of purpose. The Head of Personnel and Training was influenced by her private sector and organizational development experience, and her reading of Total Quality Management, regarding the training of staff, especially managers. Significantly, she was committed to examining the processes that could bring quality into the Department and effect change – not just the content of quality assurance. At an initial meeting both accepted that several things needed to happen to bring an understanding of quality assurance into the Department. Any initiative *107* had to be seen to be led by the Departmental Senior Management Team, and the initiative had to find a way to reach all the staff of the Department. It had to be led by those delivering and running operational services, but it had to involve all, including support services.

The birth of the Quality Assurance Working Group

These issues were discussed with the Departmental Management Team who proposed to set up a Quality Assurance Working Group. This became known as QAWG (pronounced qwag). The group was chaired by one of the operational Assistant Directors and its membership initially consisted of the other operational Assistant Director, the Head of Personnel and Training, the Head of Customer Relations, the Chief Inspector, a Principal Officer for a social work service who had good personal knowledge of quality assurance, and the Quality Officer who was part of the Strategic Planning Group (he would service the meeting). The Head of Strategic Commissioning and Development was also an early member of this group. The group set itself two tasks: to determine what it meant by quality; and to determine the process by which this concept should be introduced into the Department.

Initially, anybody who was interested could join the group, no matter their position in the organization, provided they were interested in quality. There was a great amount of learning during this period about how best to approach quality in the Department. At first, we thought it a good idea to invite managers in the Department to come and present initiatives on which they were working, which they felt were helping them improve the quality of their services. This approach was not successful because our culture is very hierarchical and it was quite daunting for managers to come forward with the ideas with so many senior managers on QAWG. However, we did have a couple of proposals to consider on consumer feedback questionnaires but it was quite difficult to deal with these in a facilitative way within the diverse group. There was also a feeling that we were trying to run before we could walk. So, we decided we had to have some measures of quality in place which would be used by managers as a benchmark for their services.

A Quality Mission Statement and 13 Quality Components

The group tried to create a Mission Statement, but the production of this statement did nothing to promote quality. It felt like empty rhetoric. The Department needed a clear model on which to shape the initiative in addition to this Mission Statement (see Figure 9.1).

One model for achieving quality of which we were aware came from the Council's Finance Department where the Housing Benefit section had received a Charter Mark. We were not keen on pushing accredited awards to targeted areas; in our culture, we were worried that resources would flood to these areas, with much attention being focused on them, when we wanted to achieve more of a holistic approach, taking the whole Department along at the same

---

MISSION STATEMENT

Camden Social Services aims to improve the quality of life for people who have social care needs in the borough of Camden. In order to achieve this we aim to arrange for the provision of social care services in accordance with the Council's Core Values which are to:

- achieve quality and equality in service delivery
- be responsive to our users
- develop our staff, and
- provide high-quality leadership and management.

Figure 9.1   Mission Statement

time. Instead, we created our own 'award', in the form of 13 Quality Components. The Chief Inspector led on the writing of these, with the help of one of the Social Work Principal Officers who had knowledge of quality assurance in her health service setting. The Head of Personnel and Training and the Quality Assurance Officer also provided wording and fine tuning. These components take on board the following accredited awards: Investors in People, Citizen's Charter, and ISO 9001, tailoring them to suit our own departmental culture and situation. These became the corner stone of the initiative.

The 13 Quality Components are broken down into four categories: Quality for Users, Quality to Improve Services, Quality for Staff and Independent Audit.

13 Quality Components

Quality for users

1   Having a clear definition of the service.
2   Having clear standards.
3   Having clear criteria for access to services.
4   Giving choice for customers and clear agreements.

Quality to improve services

5   Operating an effective complaints procedure.
6   Giving value for money.
7   Undertaking tests of customer satisfaction.
8   Having culture which encourages improvement and innovation in services.

Quality for staff

9   Having clear management systems.

10   Having written procedures which are understood by staff.
11   Offering training for staff.
12   Having a clear code of conduct for staff.

Independent audit

13   Having an independent audit for all services.

The target set by the Departmental Management Team was that all parts of the Department should be able to show how they were addressing each of these components within a two-to-three-year programme. The initiative was launched by the Director in October 1994 at a meeting for all second- and third-tier managers.

Changing the culture of Camden Social Services

In order to support this process the Departmental Management Team recognized that there would need to be a change in the culture of the organization. This change would emphasize a number of ways of working:

- A belief that everyone has a responsibility for quality.
- Delivering quality is a managed process which requires commitment and example from everyone.
- That there is an understanding of the requirements and satisfaction of people who use our services.
- That there are clear standards and procedures for delivering services.
- That equality of opportunity is a key element in promoting quality.
- That there is a pursuit of continuous improvement.
- Staff and other resources available are valued.
- That services are open to independent audit.
- That quality is part of the work, not an addition.

The criteria to assess if the Components are met are not inflexible. They are always being developed, with changes being made the more they are being used in the Department. They needed to be developed to reflect different types of services, particularly for those with internal and those with external customers.

During this time, QAWG was stabilizing in terms of membership, with roughly the same main characters, and it was decided to expand the group to include all levels of staff, with an equal mix of gender, race and disability. This decision was taken because, during the previous few months, we realized that we were having difficulty getting the message throughout the whole organization, particularly with front-line staff and management, and we needed some feedback and insight from them to help us move forward. Right from the beginning it was recognized that the only way to improve the services in our Department was to involve all staff delivering front-line services and achieve commitment to quality throughout all levels of the organization, making it part of employees' work, rather than something additional that they have to think about.

Quality can only be introduced and be seen to be effective by service users and potential users if they experience customer care from the staff with whom they have contact. There has been a strong emphasis on involving staff (and service users) to develop initiatives in different settings. This is an area that has proved to be most difficult. The challenge facing us was to try to get all staff engaged in the process. We tried various strategies to achieve this. One way of gaining staff interest and developing an understanding of the concepts involved has been the opportunity created through a seminar programme, open to different staff groups, on developing quality of service. This has led to the establishment of work groups in some settings to review how the delivery of services can be improved.

The creation of a Quality Support Force

The opportunity to both learn from one another and for individual managers to have support in the initiative was seen as vital if it was to succeed in a large, complex organization like Camden Social Services. A Quality Support Force was established under the leadership of the Head of Personnel and Training, as a sub-group of QAWG. Their role was to bring together people who had specialist knowledge of particular areas (for example, managing complaints, writing standards, developing procedures, etc.) or those who had a strong commitment to developing quality. This group both helps steer the programme (through development, support and communication work), while offering individuals advice on specific areas. The membership of this group is expanding, which could indicate an increased commitment to the initiative, but certainly means that more front-line staff and managers are involved at this practical level.

As a result of the work of this group, the Quality Officer produced a written package of information which brought together documents produced on the initiative in Camden with documents from other local authorities who were developing similar initiatives. This Quality Learning Pack is available for all staff (every person who attends a learning event gets one automatically). Eventually, every employee of Camden Social Services will have a Quality Learning Pack, which will be up-dated once or twice a year. There will also need to be an evaluation of the pack to ensure that it has appropriate information to assist staff. A quarterly newsletter is published by the Quality Officer which aims to keep staff informed on developments and progress, to share good ideas and help stimulate good practice. This is called *Quality News* and is circulated to all employees in the Department. This is our main communication tool at the moment.

More recently, money was allocated from the Departmental Training Budget to ensure that some Principal Officers could have access to specialist external consultants to help them implement the ideas. This was identified as an   *111* important area by the Quality Support Force, to help involve the more senior managers in the organization, and help to keep the momentum of the initiative going.

The Quality Support Force also requested a monthly programme of lunchtime seminars which started in 1994. This has brought together those who wish to examine particular aspects of quality. Topics have ranged from a presentation by Housing Benefits on the Charter Mark to the Lewisham Experience, and contract monitoring in Camden. Future seminars include looking at each component in turn to help everyone gain a common under-standing of all 13. A new format of half-day seminars on each of the Components is now being developed as a result of evaluating the lunchtime seminars.

Implementation targets

The Departmental Management Team decided that all service areas were to achieve components 1 and 2 by October 1995, which meant that they would all have service definitions and service standards in draft form by this date. Also, the Department of Health (SSI) have set a range of standards for Social Services during recent years and many parts of the Department are taking their stan-dards and either adopting or adapting them for their setting. A growing resource library of information is being built in the Department to assist managers with this.

The Leader of the Council speaks

Alongside these developments in Social Services, and strongly influenced by both this initiative and the award of a Charter Mark to Housing Benefit services, the Leader of the Council expressed his commitment to quality by requiring that every Department in the Council had to have an initiative – like Social Services. He also asked all Departments to put forward specific service areas for external accreditation, for example Charter Marks, ISO 9000, Investors in People, etc. This announcement assisted in promoting the Social Services work but caused some concern, because we were still anxious that all service areas were brought along simultaneously, rather than a few targeted service areas being in the limelight attracting resources.

Staff involved in the Social Services Initiative were asked to go and share their experience with other Departments, which gave an early opportunity for those involved to reflect upon what they had achieved and what the task ahead required. The problem of 'centres of excellence' was also discussed. Social Services did not want to promote a few well-run places – they wanted some-thing that would permeate the whole Department.

LEVERS OF CHANGE WHICH WILL HELP US FULLY IMPLEMENT THE QUALITY INITIATIVE

Equality and communication

The Quality Assurance Working Group is currently working on two important areas to help implementation: equality components and a Quality Communication Strategy. The development of equality components will ensure that this very important area is interwoven into the process of implementing the 13 Quality Components. A major development since June 1995 has been a recognition in the Department that equality is an intrinsic part of quality. In line with the Council's policy on valuing diversity and with the support of an external consultant, the quality initiative has been developed to ensure that for each component of quality the components of equality are clearly incorporated. A separate document was produced to guide managers and staff in this area. This did not prove to be successful. Staff found addressing equality issues hard in this context. More work is certainly required to simplify what is required in a quality system to promote equality.

A Quality Communication Strategy will help send a message out to the front-line, even more so than currently is being sent, and will ensure that quality is part of every member of staff's everyday working life. Some ideas were recommended by the Quality Support Force for 1996, including a re-launch of the quality initiative with all managers from across the whole Department attending a communication seminar run by the Departmental Management Team. We are also looking at Employee and Team Awards and upward appraisal.

QAWG and Quality Support Force

The involvement of all levels of staff, at both the Quality Assurance Working Group and the Quality Support Force, is helping to develop a quality organization, and the commitment of managers, at all levels, is equally crucial to the initiative. We allocate plenty of time at meetings for all people to contribute by giving feedback, and so therefore feel part of the initiative as their involvement influences their behaviour and decisions back in the workplace.

The Quality Support Force is currently exploring formal evaluation of its support, development and communication work. Results from this were received in the autumn of 1996.

Top management commitment

The continuation of the top management commitment is a great strength during the implementation phase and will continue to help to reinforce the line management role and responsibilities. From December 1995, the Director of Camden Social Services has chaired QAWG, which means the whole of the Departmental Management Team is a member of this policy group. This will not only be visible leadership, but will also help speed up decision-making and, hopefully, agreed action.

Quality and Internal Communications functions

The transfer of these functions into a newly named Human Resource Group (previously called Personnel and Training) will emphasize the importance of quality through people in the organization and link those functions' work into the development of the organization as a whole, thereby helping to enhance the impact of the levers of change described above. The Quality Officer is now a Quality Consultant, and there is a new post of Internal Communications Consultant.

Cultural Analysis

Another important project which is currently being developed is a Cultural Analysis Project. This project is the first of its kind in Camden Social Services, based on researching the organization to evaluate the existing culture in the Department, to help the Departmental Management Team develop the culture and assist them with implementing strategic objectives over the next few years (including quality). This is a long-term project which will eventually use comparative information to assess cultural changes over the next few years.

Implementation Action Plans

Action Plans have been received from every Principal Officer to implement the 13 Quality Components identified for all services run by the Department. These were reviewed in January 1996, and extra resources for training and consultancy support have been made available (endorsed by Social Services Committee) to support managers with implementing these plans.

Quality Audits

One of the Quality Components is independent audits and it has already been agreed (and they have already started) that our own Inspection Unit will conduct these Quality Service Inspections. Initially, they inspected against Components 1 and 2 (plus others as agreed with the Service Manager) until after October 1996, by which date all service areas in our Department had done some work on all the Components.

The Department instituted a 'Quality Service Inspection' programme which looked at how each section was developing the Components. This proved to be both a threat and an opportunity. There were common anxieties in the anticipation of being inspected. Most managers know their weaknesses, but having them spelt out on paper in a report on their section feels different. However, this provides an excellent feedback mechanism in order to see how

progress is being made and it provides an opportunity for managers to discuss their difficulties with experienced Inspectors in order for them to get help and advice.

In the spirit of continuous improvement, a model of self-auditing is an essential part of the way forward. Some managers and staff in our Department have passed their Lead Assessors course for ISO 9000. On this course, auditing techniques are learnt and this should help with this work. In the personnel and training function, a self-auditing process is being designed, with the help of the Chief Inspector.

Consumer views

In order to meet the Quality Components all service areas have to use staff and user surveys to help them improve the quality of their services. The results of these surveys are a good measure of success.

Change management

It has proved hard to effect change in this large and diverse Department as quickly as was hoped for. There are pockets of excellence where the initiative has supported the development of quality services. There are parts of the Department which have either not been affected by the initiative or have resisted participation. Ways of addressing this are being explored by both the Departmental Management Team and QAWG. The role of the Quality Support Force is also crucial to help promote the change of culture in the Department. The Director set a target for every Principal Officer to produce their definitions of service and their service standards (with performance indicators) by October 1995. Following this exercise there is an intention to publish all the service definitions with their standards and performance indicators, in a publicly available document. This will include the Community Care Charter. All remaining Components had to be realized by October 1996.

QAWG is aware of the limitations of the initiative and is now examining more and different ways to ensure that managers are supported in implementing their Action Plans with the full participation of all staff. The essence of quality assurance is that it is an enabling rather than a punitive process. It concentrates on reviewing failures to get things right, rather than punishing the perpetrators. The emphasis must be on ensuring that staff are trained and equipped to do the job effectively, if this is at all possible. At the same time it must be user (customer) focused. The bureaucratic, hierarchical and legislative frameworks set up for the Local Authority can militate against this. The challenge for managers in Camden is to create the quality of service within the constraints that are placed upon them. For this to happen the whole culture of Camden will be affected.

Areas that need particular attention in the Department include responding appropriately to complaints (this has improved remarkably in some services). It also includes: being clearer with users of the options available to them; giving more written information to users; being able to be clear about the   *115* criteria that have been used to determine a particular service; and developing effective and efficient ways of monitoring performance.

It may be appropriate to call the initiative 'working to improve quality'. We know that we still have a long way to go in some areas, but the initiative has helped to act as a focus for developments that are taking place. This must be sustained as the programme develops.

WHAT CAMDEN SOCIAL SERVICES WILL BE LIKE IN THE FUTURE, WITH THE QUALITY INITIATIVE

At the moment Camden Social Services does not specifically talk in terms of being a Learning Organization, but the characteristics of a Learning Organization, outlined in this chapter, are certainly on the agenda and talked about. The area of real challenge is learning from mistakes rather than blaming mistakes, which seems difficult when working with democratically elected Councillors, accountable to their constituents. However, if we wish to sustain ourselves in this newly challenging and competitive environment, these difficulties will have to be overcome with time. Our image and profile will improve significantly as we accumulate accredited awards and all service areas meet the 13 Quality Components.

It is hard to get everyone in a diverse Department to support any initiative for change. We will need to have a number of strategies that rely on both hierarchic and matrix models of communication. We will need to constantly review the strategy – get honest feedback – look at where there are identified weaknesses and attempt new strategies or re-enforce old strategies. We need to learn from experience both at the strategic and the practical level. Not all managers can appreciate the objectives of the programme. They cannot relate it to their service area. It seems to work well for those delivering direct services and harder for those providing indirect/planning services or assessment services. We need to find ways of engaging these managers and find things with which they can identify to meet their needs. Many have seen the initiative as an additional extra rather than a vital way of ensuring the quality of their services. People could not see the benefits, and this is still a challenge.

Senior managers can divorce their work on a working party from their normal line-management duties, but it is important that the initiative is built into everyone's work programme, into their targets and accountabilities. Two-way communication throughout the organization has proved to be the most critical factor for the successes and failures of any initiative. In addition, we have found that once staff are clear on the service they are providing, and have standards by which to judge those services, the other objectives become much clearer and easier to address.

SUMMARY POINTS

- An organization needs to have a framework for a Learning Organization to work towards.

- Camden Social Services has a difficult history with major cut-backs and resources continuing to be threatened.
- National government legislation was a strong lever of change.
- Top management commitment is a crucial factor for success in implementing quality assurance.
- Quality initiatives created in-house (with external expertise) have more chance of being sustained.
- Effective in-house working groups involving front-line staff and management can help a quality assurance initiative to succeed.
- Top management must set clear implementation targets to keep the momentum going, especially when the quality initiative is large.
- Accredited quality awards should be part of a quality initiative, with a holistic approach taking precedence.

10 Creating the conditions to become a Learning Organization

Jo Somerset, Manchester City Council

To be or not to be?; that is the key question facing the local authority of the 1990s. Gone are the heady days of the early-1980s, when District and County Councils could embrace new initiatives, welling up like newly discovered North Sea oil. Undoubtedly, gains were made in the areas of community consultation, awareness of service users' needs, and equal opportunities. Employment policies were updated, official gobbledegook revised (not eliminated!) and people were transformed from 'cases' into clients. Town Halls made great efforts to slough off their impenetrable exteriors and become 'of the people' rather than 'for the people'.

When I entered this world in 1985, Manchester City Council's 38 000 employees provided housing, education, roads, parks, leisure facilities and a wide range of social services to the local populace. Ten years later, there were 28 000 people working for the Council. Further Education colleges, much management of schools, elderly people's homes, funding for house-building and the associated support and maintenance functions had been hived off to independent status or withdrawn. Now the organization was grappling with issues which would ensure the Council's survival against economic and political pressures. The challenge was to transform the organization into one which could cope with, if not thrive on, a process of continual change: defined as a Learning Organization.

In 1995 Manchester City Council served a population of 432 000, made up of a range of diverse communities. Manchester is the regional capital of the North West, providing the greatest concentration of job opportunities in the county. Its inner-city areas experience high levels of deprivation and unemployment is twice the national average. The City Council is working to attract jobs, investment and prosperity and secure the city's position as a centre of national, European and international significance.

In 1984, when the Labour Left took control of Manchester City Council, many of the foundations of today's Council were laid. The determination to address the unemployment and poverty of the city, and get results, has paved the way for large capital partnership projects: the Nynex Arena, the new Halle concert hall, the Velodrome, and the re-development of the 1960s planning disaster called Hulme. A bid to host the 2002 Commonwealth Games finally succeeded. Internal policies aimed at ensuring that Manchester residents are well represented in the Council's workforce have begun to take effect, and continue to be implemented. Ramps, lifts and dropped kerbs continue to appear, slowly but surely.

Not all the initiatives survived the new realism of the 1990s, however. The dream of a multifunction council office in every neighbourhood had to give way to hard financial realities, with only six neighbourhood offices in existence, rather than the 20, 30 or even 40 that had been envisaged. The Manchester Information Centre became a dodo – it seemed that Mancunians had not received the message that the Town Hall was now approachable, and did not call in for their information needs. A complex structure of equal opportunities sub-committees which sought to give disabled people, black people, women, lesbians and gay men a direct influence on the Council's decision-making process was found to be unwieldy. The Council would have to take other steps to involve these communities more effectively. Peace education became a thing of the past, and the Nuclear Free Zone unit soon followed suit.

However, the Council did change irrevocably from the old dinosaur to something more in line with the needs and aspirations of a large city forging new pride in itself and warding off the threat of a spiral of decline signified by a dwindling population and steel-shuttered shops. There is no doubt that the pace of change in introducing the new initiatives was fast. There is no doubt that it resulted in widespread uproar and confusion. Change was effected at a price. Partly, the changes were temporary measures, aimed at filling the gap until a Labour Government came to power, when local Councils would have their central government support reviewed, and would be able to spend the receipts on council house sales. There *was* a review, a whole series of them, but none of them favoured Manchester or any other City Council, because the Government that carried them out was still unremittingly Conservative. In the 1987 and 1992 general elections the Conservative Party became more, not less, entrenched. Not only did they continue the squeeze on local government in financial terms, but they launched an all-out attack on their pet bugbears, forcing local councils into a programme of unwilling privatization. Manchester was no different from any other Labour local authority in having to switch the focus from a future Labour Government to the realities of now.

EARLY MOVES TOWARDS THE LEARNING ORGANIZATION

The name of the game had changed. The key word now was survival. For me, working in a central support department (Personnel, later absorbed into the Chief Executive's Department) with a corporate overview, my objectives also changed. Training and Development staff could not simply enhance skills and provide new information; the new imperative was towards efficiency, *119* improvement in performance, business-like operations, and above all, the implementation of change, change, change. Suddenly, my cosy ideas about the Council becoming a Learning Organization took centre stage in my work programme, and I saw how crucial this was to the creation of a streamlined, fast-moving organization that needed to be able to rapidly change its shape to adapt to new conditions: becoming more of an amoeba than the traditional pyramid structure of the hierarchical organization. It became imperative to focus on creating 'an organization which facilitates the learning of all its members and thus continually transforms itself' (Pedler *et al.* 1991).

There were some parts of the new style required already in place. I had been conducting one-to-one supervision with my staff for some time, and our management skills training courses advocated this approach. Throughout the Authority there were pockets of a style of management which emphasized teamwork and involvement of staff. Some managers were committed to communicating with their staff, although this was an area which was pinpointed as being sadly lacking in a MORI survey of all employees conducted in 1990. The Chief Executive, newly arrived in 1992, threw his weight behind a vastly improved management information system, and resolved to improve what he called the 'bread and butter issues' of the Council: the accounts, effective documentation, and tools for management education. Although the promised new financial management system was slow in materializing, internal trading between departments had been partially implemented, and financial responsibility had been devolved to unit managers via a system of cost-centre management in some departments.

However, the Council was riddled with departmentalism and operating in many ways as 15 separate organizations, loosely held together at Chief Officer Management Team level. Traditional structures and forms of management were entrenched: technical experts with little up-to-date knowledge of management practice were likely to be heads of service and charged with the successful management of their department.

The Training and Development Service was attempting to contribute to changing this, to some effect, but the emphasis was still on short courses, with, later, follow-up consultancy with individual managers. Yes, the courses were (and still are) good; yes, they were relevant to the Council's needs, delivered by excellent in-house trainers, providing a balance of theory and appropriate practice – but these were only touching those who attended, and it was never clear how much of the learning was transferred back to the workplace, let alone whether the beneficial effects were experienced by anyone else in the department.

I was keen to move beyond this, and on to a model of individual learning where the effects spread beyond the learners – not quite a ripple effect, more the way oil spreads in the sea: gradually growing in size and taking larger and larger areas under its influence.

ENHANCING INDIVIDUAL LEARNING

It had become increasingly clear that, whilst the need for training had not diminished, the ability of managers to release employees for training had been severely restricted, particularly in services affected by Compulsory Competitive Tendering. I realized that if I wanted a reasonable number of people to participate in a learning programme that was more substantial than a short course, I had to devise a formula which did not involve releasing people from the workplace for days at a time. A corporate Positive Action Training Programme for black and women employees was the programme that enabled me to do this. This had been identified by Councillors (always useful) as part of their strategy for meeting equality targets. One focus of the Council's commitment to redress inequality is to ensure the workforce proportionally reflects the diversity of the population of the city. This is measured by a system of yearly equality targets, culminating in final targets for the year 2000. In 1990 the Council noted that representation of black people in higher grades was poor and the targets for women at higher levels had not been achieved. It was therefore resolved to establish a Positive Action Training Programme. (Equality targets also existed for disabled people, but other initiatives were afoot to increase the number of disabled employees in the workforce.) Because of the size of the undertaking, it was split into three phases from 1991–4, covering five Council departments in each phase. The first phase acted as a pilot, and served to create a vastly improved model for the two subsequent phases. It is this model which I shall describe and refer to throughout.

The content of the training was not particularly innovative; the style certainly was (for Manchester City Council anyway). Two parallel programmes took place, each with three strands (see Table 10.1). The National Examining Board for Supervisory Management (NEBSM) Introductory Award was followed by the NEBSM Certificate (with some 'graduates' from the Introductory group, but mostly direct entrants to the course). The Management Charter Initiative (MCI) Management Standards Level I (NVQ in Management Level 4) formed the third strand. Around 80 people participated in each phase, of whom 75 per cent completed Phase 3 (50 per cent in Phase 2).

What was different was the way in which the training was delivered, and the context in which it took place. Remembering the goal of affecting the whole organization, not just the participants, the programme was designed to have maximum effect with decidedly limited resources (one Training Officer supervised by myself and a maximum of £30 000 per year). The innovations that formed part and parcel of the Positive Action Training Programme became fully integrated into the regular practice of the Corporate Training and Development Team and took Manchester City Council several steps closer to permeating the concept of learning throughout the Authority and becoming a Learning Organization. It was an additional bonus that women and black employees were at the forefront of this pioneering approach, rather than being left behind in new, exciting management initiatives.

A number of practical innovations were implemented, with the objectives of *121*

Table 10.1   Positive Action Training Programme

Course	Introduction to Supervisory Management (4 Months)	Being a Manager (10 Months)	Professional Qualification in Management (Accreditation of Prior Learning) (10 + Months)
Targeted employees	Supervisors and potential Supervisors	Potential Managers	Managers
Qualifications	NEBSM* Introductory Award	NEBSM Certificate	MCI** Management I/NEBSM Diploma

Key: *   NEBSM – National Examining Board for Supervisory Management
       **   MCI – Management Charter Initiative

maximizing the learning gained by individuals, the transfer of this learning to the organization through projects completed during the programme, and collaboration with line managers and mentors, as well as improved individual performance. These initiatives had varying levels of success. None were a failure, and some, particularly the use of accreditation of prior learning and the introduction of Management Standards, were significant in paving the way for further policy developments in the Council.

The most basic innovation was to use open learning. In order to significantly reduce the amount of time spent off-the-job, and to create a more flexible course structure, the Positive Action Training Programme adopted a model of open learning supported by tutored workshops on Council premises, delivered by a local college. The Introduction to Supervisory Management course required 40 hours of study, of which only 12 hours involved attendance at workshops. Sixty hours out of the 300 hours of study time for the Being A Manager (NEBSM Certificate) course was workshop time. In-depth courses were therefore provided with a maximum of two half-days per month away from work. Managers were asked to be flexible about allowing study time of at least one hour per week, supplemented by participants studying in their own time. This model proved to be a popular way of making training accessible and a general Supervisor Training Programme was developed, incorporating the same courses, and using an almost identical model. Importing the college to the Council's location enabled the training provided to be more specifically work-related and relevant to the trainees.

All the initiatives moved training practice more and more into the workplace to become less reliant on learning which is divorced from people's jobs. Work-based projects, set by participants in consultation with their line managers, were an integral part of the Being A Manager course. This form of learning was later adopted for wider use by the Corporate Training and Development Team.

Providing qualification-based courses from the corporate centre was a new departure. The change was partly in response to employees' wishes, but clearly it was also necessary to adapt to the changing climate of the working world, where competencies and qualifications (including National Vocational Qualifications (NVQs)) have an increasing role in ensuring quality staff, and in developing a competitive workforce which can meet specified standards. Although it would be inappropriate to link all training and development activities to qualifications, this side of the operation has increasing significance.

Several groups of managers pursued accreditation at level M1 of the Management Charter Initiative's (MCI) national Management Standards through the Positive Action Training Programme. This was the first time that the Standards had been used in the Council, and the value of the approach was recognized, although the language and assumptions contained in the MCI Standards did not fit well with the Manchester context. So, led by Chief Officers, a project was initiated to draw up a set of Manchester Management Competency Statements. These have provided the foundation for a comprehensive appraisal scheme for all managers.

For the first time the Council has an Authority-wide way of measuring the performance of its managers, and systematically planning for their development where there are gaps in skills, abilities, knowledge or experience. The chasm between performance and development has been bridged by the definition of competencies. Using this powerful tool, conscious learning should become part of the culture of the Council, and is within the grasp of all managers. Management development is now progressed following the Management Competency framework which defines our concept of the management function. Training for managers now enables participants to develop the skills needed to produce work for which they may prove competence.

Through the work on the MCI Management Standards, the use of Accreditation of Prior Learning was developed. Again, the skills required in advising people in developing a portfolio, plugging knowledge gaps, and using a variety of means to demonstrate competence extend beyond the Positive Action groups. The Council now has a solid NVQ strategy, putting competence-based development to the forefront and currently providing accreditation in 18 occupational areas. Portfolio building is one of the commonest development activities taking place across the Council, supported by a strong Assessors' Network resourced from the corporate centre.

Involvement of line managers was, and continues to be, the most important aspect of the whole matrix. For Manchester City Council to become a Learning Organization, development of employees has to be part and parcel of daily practice. The Positive Action Training Programme briefed line managers on how to be involved with their employees' training. A 1995 evaluation survey found that 57 per cent of participants' line managers or mentors had been involved, in some way, in supporting the employee's learning. While this figure is not nearly high enough, it provided a useful base-line, and showed how much could be achieved with a small amount of input and impetus from the centre. As the area is now defined as a Manchester management competency in both the areas of delegation and training/coaching, the figure could be expected to increase significantly in the next few years.

So that individuals could gain as much benefit from the Positive Action Training Programme as possible, a mentor system was established for each participant. With only a minimum of resources available, support for mentors was limited to the provision of a pack containing the wider policy framework and articles on the learning process, as well as details about the programme. The vast potential of this approach is being explored, and mentoring will be a key ingredient for development at many levels, from graduate trainees to senior managers.

A certificate presentation ceremony, presided over by a Councillor (and attended by line managers, representatives from departments and the college, and Elected Members from the Personnel Policy Sub-Committee), turned out to be as rewarding to the visitors as it did to the participants. As well as being a public relations exercise, with a mention in the local press, they provided concrete evidence for Councillors that the workforce is being trained to a particular standard, giving more meaning to statistics in a report.

Clearly, all was not plain sailing and the achievements of the Positive Action Training Programme resulted from a considerable amount of sweat and determination by all involved. Phase 2 had several faults, leading to a lower rate of achievement by participants than expected, and some friction between the corporate centre and participating departments. The key initiatives identified that were needed to resolve these problems seemed to be: consultation, commitment, communication and control.

Departmental management were, on the whole, committed to the principle of Positive Action Training, but detailed consultation with Personnel Officers, senior managers, line managers and potential participants was necessary to ensure that the new style of development (open learning, line manager involvement, work-based projects, portfolio building) was understood by departments. The consultation was a two-way process, with information about the specific situation and needs of each particular department being incorporated into the training brief. Consultation with the Council's employee-led women's and black groups had taken place since the beginning, and had informed the design of Phases 2 and 3.

Communication is one of the problems of all large organizations. There never seems to be enough of it, and even the most conscientious attempts seem to fall short of the ideal. By the time several pieces of Phase 2 had been picked up and stuck back together again, it was clear that attention had to be paid both to clarifying the relationships of all the parties involved, and setting

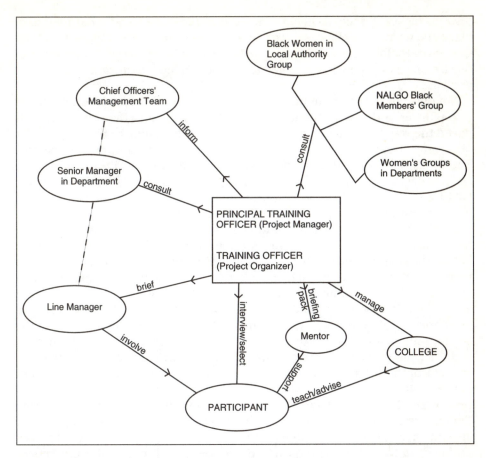

Figure 10.1   Key relationships in the programme

up communication systems with and between each of them. (See Figure 10.1.) Once this was established, and channels had been created for dealing with day-to-day issues, many of the major problems dissolved. Tight control of the project was needed throughout its life, since it did not run itself, and there was a danger of it being effectively run by the training providers rather than the Council. With a simple project management system in place, I set targets, measured performance and planned the details of the project with confidence.

The ability to get the most out of consultants (internal or external) is crucial in these days of internal trading, increased accountability and the duty to provide value for money, brought to bear in part by the Audit Commission's annual performance indicator exercise for local government.

FROM INDIVIDUAL TO ORGANIZATIONAL LEARNING

The effects of the Positive Action Training Programme went far beyond the original objective of aiding the progression of women and black employees   *125* towards higher (Principal Officer) grades. It is true that a substantial number of black and women employees were trained to an appropriate standard, and the Council did achieve its interim equality targets at higher grades. The number of black managers had nearly doubled to 83, and 100 more women were in higher grades.

Not only did the programme contribute to achieving these objectives, but it also pioneered the use of management NVQs throughout the organization. It paved the way in competence-based development, leading to the Manchester Management Competency Statements and the Performance Appraisal Scheme. The ideas developed during the Positive Action Training Programme were absorbed into the wider corporate climate, leading to a transition from specific Positive Action objectives to corporate objectives like performance management and progress towards the Learning Organization.

At this stage, it is important to outline some other initiatives which had been taking place, and influencing the progress towards the Learning Organization. In 1991 the shape of the Corporate Training and Development Service had been re-defined to create an internal consultancy role, which was to take primacy over the direct training and advice/information roles. Progress towards achieving this model was initially slow, due to the size of the organization, inexperience of training and development practitioners in this area, the insufficiently high profile of the corporate training and development function, and the heavy weight of tradition throughout the organization. However, the concept of the internal consultant now permeates the Council, applying not only to training and development professionals, but also to other providers of central services. Chief Officers, who called for the help of the Corporate Training and Development Team to provide a specific training course, learnt instead to work with a Training and Development Officer to examine key problems in the functioning of their department, and to identify solutions to these, some of which had a training/development aspect to them. This form of process consultancy enables departmental management to own and lead the change programme, with the support of a skilled professional who has both the clarity and the time to devote to the department's goals. A move from *training* and development to *organizational* development was quietly taking place.

The approach to organizational development which was materializing was firmly embedded in our understanding of, and commitment to, quality of service issues. Following the advice of management experts like Handy (1985) and Peters (Peters and Waterman 1982) towards flatter organizational structures, training and development activities were to be primarily focused on the 'invisible organization' (90 per cent of the whole) to enable the visible 10 per cent on the front-line to meet the needs of the service users/customers. (See Figure 10.2.) The concept of the Learning Organization was later embraced within the context of the quality banner.

On a national level, the introduction of NVQs and competence-based development dovetailed with the expansion of the training and development role. Making the organization's goals the central feature of any development activity, and using a wide variety of methods to achieve individual

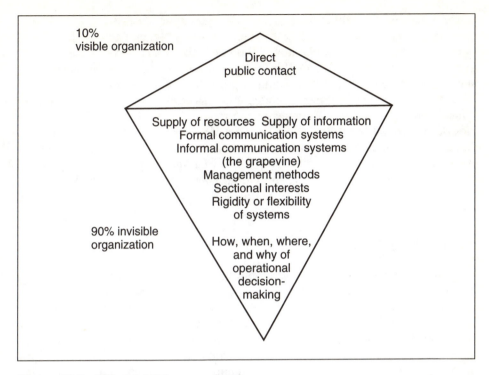

10%
visible organization

Direct
public contact

Supply of resources Supply of information
Formal communication systems
Informal communication systems
(the grapevine)
Management methods
Sectional interests
Rigidity or flexibility
of systems

90% invisible
organization

How, when, where,
and why of
operational
decision-
making

Figure 10.2   The invisible organization

development which would contribute towards those goals, meant a shift in emphasis for the whole organization. Individual development was likely to be taking place over a longer period of time than previous short courses, and within the workplace, rather than on day-release college courses. The Council has had to gear itself up to job rotation, managers setting developmental tasks, experts (in accountancy or health and safety for example) offering workshops to NVQ candidates, line managers developing skills in assessment and being primary figures in their employees' development (or otherwise). Add to this the concept of lifetime learning inherent in the government's National Education and Training Targets, and clearly the issue of individual learning has to be on the agenda at all levels.

Moves towards becoming a Learning Organization have been accelerated by the Council's major change project of the mid-1990s: the creation of a new style of management through the installation of an up-to-date, state-of-the-art Human Resource Management Information System (the HURMIS project). Driven by the Chief Executive, involving all departments, and supported by a massive amount of customized new technology systems, this project touches every manager within the Council. It was an early decision that HURMIS should not be limited to the installation of an integrated Personnel and Payroll system. Rather, the technology should be used to spearhead changes in the funda-mental ways in which the Council was run at the operational level. An organic system of departmental and issue-based project sponsors, review boards and project managers complemented the central project team. Each Review Board was encouraged to 'think big' about the effect that its role could have on the organization as a whole: hence the Training Sub-Project saw that it could set as a goal the achievement of 'a learning organization that can effectively manage change whilst improving performance' once HURMIS had been implemented. The thorough Project Management System ensured that the systems developed are suited to the users as much as possible, and that, having been involved in their design, managers will *use* the information and systems available to manage more effectively. The HURMIS project enabled the leap from accepting and supporting individual learning to committing the organization itself to learning, and putting the benefit of that learning at the disposal of all involved in the Council's operations.

THE WAY AHEAD

A snapshot of the Council in 1993 would have revealed an organization which had partly adopted a contract culture, and in which no contracts had been lost in the compulsory competitive tendering arena. An emphasis on value for money and greater financial accountability was apparent. The organization had been streamlined in many areas, with its central support services honed down correspondingly. The area of performance management was beginning to be addressed. But enormous problems endured. The uncertainty and increased pressures following reorganizations, restructures, reductions in staff and re-deployment had taken a heavy toll of staff morale. Although senior management was tighter and more results-focused, departmentalism was still rife, and there was a wide difference in skills between Council employees: from excellent technical abilities, customer focus and/or overview of the organization, to a very limited range of skills that provided a minimum of achievement, rather than the maximum required. This disparity existed at all levels, and there was no uniform system in existence which set standards and against which performance could be measured.

Over the next two years, initiatives were developed which took the corporate whole from a situation which was both chaotic and static to a more integrated and organic entity. The seeds for this were sown in the preceding years' initiatives, some of which are described earlier in this chapter. The single most important measure has to be the development of an appraisal system based on a set of Manchester-specific management competencies, supplemented by departmentally defined performance indicators. With this tool, performance is measured, job targets identified, and development goals established – in a collaborative format between line manager and employee. Eventually, the system will be extended to cover all employees.

To many organizations, this is probably old hat. However, to Manchester City Council, it is a key factor in pulling the organization together to produce common standards towards a set of common goals. This is an essential building block for an organization committed to continuous development and learning. Now that managers know what is expected of them, and have had detailed feedback on their performance against those expectations, they are much better placed to both carry out the organization's functions and to support their part of it to grow towards the future.

Interestingly, the management competencies' development was embedded in the goals for the HURMIS project, thus linking several of the new initiatives and trends. In fact, the management competencies themselves grew out of a Black Managers' Development project. Right at the start it became clear that it was ludicrous to attempt to develop a target group in a vacuum, without knowing what standards they were being developed against. The project was put on ice while the appropriate standards were drawn up, consulted on and finalized. So the seeds of management standards within Manchester City Council were born out of equality initiatives: the Positive Action Training Programme and the Black Managers' Development project. Rather than being tacked on, equality considerations were therefore at the heart of the standards.

From the viewpoint of the corporate centre, having a meaningful set of standards, and an effective appraisal system, underpinned by a strong consultancy and training and development framework, with an up-to-date Information Technology infrastructure, the conditions have been created for Manchester City Council to take on the status of a Learning Organization.

Will the Council actually take it on? I would say that actually it has, and the challenge now is for the culture of planned change and welcoming challenges to become a strong motivating factor in all departments. There is a corporate commitment to achieving the Investors In People kitemark department by department – with several departments well on the way to accreditation. Those departments subject to Compulsory Competitive Tendering are facing the challenge of creating successful trading organizations, and all contracts are still retained in-house. To sustain this momentum against increasingly fierce competition, the Direct Service Organizations will have to achieve the symbiotic relationship of commercial success combined with a proactive work-force.

The Council is clearly going to survive. It has developed the strengths necessary to ensure it can withstand onslaughts, adapt to almost any change, and continue to sharpen its focus as required. The ride will continue to be bumpy, there is ample room for improvement, and major tensions exist between conflicting priorities and consequent resource allocation. However, it is fair to say that Manchester City Council is on the way to adopting a Learning Organization approach, remembering that the Learning Organization is not an end result, but a process. As with the concept of continuous improvement, the destination is never reached, but the essential elements need to be in place to ensure that learning is part and parcel of the Council's everyday processes, from front-line contact to strategic planning. It would be wrong to be complacent – in order to retain the flexibility inherent in Learning Organizations the Council needs to be undertaking a process of continual change.

BIBLIOGRAPHY

Handy, C. (1985), *Understanding Organisations,* Harmondsworth: Penguin.

Handy, C. (1990), *Inside Organisations,* London: BBC Books.

Lawton, A. and Rose, A. (1994), *Organisation and Management in the Public Sector,* 2nd edn, London: Pitman.

Leach, S., Stewart, J. and Walsh, K. (1994), *The Changing Organisation and Management of Local Government,* London: Macmillan.

Pearn, M., Roderick, C. and Mulrooney, C. (1995), *Learning Organisations in Practice,* London: McGraw-Hill.

Pedler, M., Burgoyne, J. and Boydell, T. (1991), *The Learning Company,* Maidenhead: McGraw-Hill.

Peters, T. and Waterman, R.H. (1982), *In Search of Excellence,* New York: Harper and Row.

Ranson, S. and Stewart, J. (1994), *Management for the Public Domain: Enabling the Learning Society,* London: Macmillan.

11 Searching for Sheffield

Chris Blantern and Anne Murphy, Re-view

LOOKING BACK

The city of Sheffield has been a Labour stronghold for 70 years and has been dominant/hierarchical (unchallenged) in style (for example, housing policy – officially *everybody* can look to the local authority for housing, but in practice only a small proportion are housed because of huge waiting lists created by the policy itself, a legacy of 1950s modernist, socialist thought). In the mid- to late-1980s this style (one right way) was manifest as extreme ideological recalcitrance faced with the impact of Thatcherism (rate-capping, etc.). It seemed more important to be ideologically defiant than to productively manage the new and current social and economic realities. Sheffield (the People's Republic), like Liverpool and a few London boroughs, adopted a strategy of commercial borrowing, high-profile, but risky, projects (the World Student Games) and dependency on the hope of rescue by an incoming Labour Government. The context was ideologically adversarial (privileging one right answer) rather than collectively pragmatic (community building). The industrial and commercial sectors were alienated and some local groups were effectively privileged over others.

After John Major's election victory in 1992 the Leadership of the Local Group changed. This coincided with the growing voice of people across economic sectors (commerce, industry, education, recreation, health, media) that Sheffield's future as a community (with all the attendant benefits) had been neglected in favour of ideological posturing.

LOOKING FORWARD

The City Council began to look more and more to cross-sector partnerships and embraced more pragmatic politics. The Sheffield City Liaison Group is one important manifestation – the City Council in partnership with public and private sector organizations – forging a more collaborative future. So far, this future building has been undertaken with the traditional managerial tools of 'mission, vision and empowerment'. There is, though, some concern that this is not working as well as might be expected: 'we have lots of visions and plans but implementing them is the problem'.

Two main issues existed without the practical means of doing anything differently in pursuit of this more collaborative future. First, the Liaison Group could only reach the current leaders in the city and had no way of providing the context within which the next generation of leaders across sectors could begin to see their interdependencies. Second, the lack of unilateral leverage over these complex problems without boundaries left too many of the ideas locked into perpetual planning. A future research conference was planned to address both of these issues. The planning was carried out by a group whose individual stakes in the future reflected a community of practice and influence in the city. These people worked on the task of the conference and on defining the cross section of people who needed to be invited if the event were to impact the future network and its ability to implement its plans. After some interesting exchange around the nature of the current reality in Sheffield a task, which invited personal commitment, was framed as 'Sheffield – our city, our responsibility, our future, our contribution', and a list of 64 participants was drawn up. The planning group aimed to reflect a broad cross section of Sheffield society in order to get 'the system in the room', and divided those interested into eight, loose, stakeholder groups of: politicians; public sector; education; health; corporate sector; voluntary and community; culture and media; and entrepreneurs. The compelling nature of bringing together a potential new network of the next generation of Sheffield leaders tempered the planning group's desire to search for a cross section of the people who also are affected by what those in positions of influence decide. Consequently, after some deliberation the idea of having a stakeholder group of citizens – people who were there simply because they lived in Sheffield – was abandoned. In retrospect, we are sorry that we did not push a little harder on this point as there is a difference between having diversity and fragmentation in the room. Nevertheless, this view was not, and is still not, shared by the 'search community' which, of course, begs the question of why we think we know better.

THE TASKS

The event itself followed a tightly managed time schedule of five basic tasks:

Task 1: The past; society, self and Sheffield.
Task 2: The present; trends affecting Sheffield.
Task 3: 'Prouds' and 'Sorries'; us and Sheffield.
Task 4: The future; desired scenarios.
Task 5: Common ground and action planning.

The tasks honoured diversity, the exploration of common ground, complexity and confusion, and our ability to learn from experience. The work was mostly undertaken in groups of eight people, either working in their stakeholder groups or in mixed groups where a variety of views were present at any one time. In between the small-group tasks the group convened as a whole conference so that everyone got to find out how the pieces make up the whole. There was no pressure to shift positions (views) and everyone heard all the perspectives.

Our shared past

The conference began with an activity which invited everyone to write down what they remembered of local, global and personal events over a specific time span. The three long sheets of paper where the time lines were completed were then hung under each other to provide a rich picture of the world we all share. What the group saw is that there are differences and similarities but that we live in the same world. The whole group got the chance to hear and see that our past shows both despair and potential, and that our own actions, both responsible and irresponsible, have brought that past about. For the group in Sheffield, what this brought into view was the recognition that, temporarily, in the same room, were enough of the city's fragmented interest groups to reach across the structural boundaries of our daily lives in order to consider that the future, just like the past, is of our own making.

Our current reality

The conference then gathered to make a Mind Map® of the current trends that affected our joint future. The different and often contradictory views which all make up our current *reality* were drawn on a very large piece of paper – it was a mind-boggling task, and one which caused some anxiety: our usual preference is not to really look at the trends affecting all of us but to offer our solutions which we think will help us get the future we want (over the future someone else can see). There was more complexity and more confusion than with our more reductionist methods and one thing came over very clearly to everyone: if we do not do something about this *together* then we do not stand any chance of success.

After working in small groups on our stakeholder view of present trends the conference moved on to expressing what it is they are both proud of ('Prouds') and sorry about ('Sorries') in relation to the present situation in Sheffield. This was a time to talk about how people felt about whatever it was they either were or were not doing, and to do so in public. These declarations were extremely powerful: the challenge to own our own actions, rather than bemoan those of others, gave the whole community a fuller picture of the nature of the current task than ever before. That the corporate sector was 'under-represented', that the media and arts described their present as autonomous, that the education

133

group was angry at their current powerlessness and that the public sector recognized their tendency to follow the rules were treated not as problems to be solved, but as current reality – part of what needed to be accepted if collaboration were to make any sense at all.

Our joint futures

In small mixed groups, where the different stakeholder views are reflected, the conference moved on to look at desired futures where a staggering amount of overlap among all the participants was visible. By presenting the ideal futures in a dramatic and creative form, the common ground was experienced as a real possibility. What the futures represented at this point of the conference was the turning point from our preoccupation with what is wrong (with everyone else) at the moment, towards what it is we might do together to bring about a different world. The futures painted a picture where diverse groups worked in partnership, where communities ran their own affairs, where transport was clean and efficient, where politicians were locally accountable, where electronic communications supported everyone's work and leisure and, above all, where the fragmentation of our current experience was replaced by a strong sense of pride and belonging.

Our common ground

The final task was to capture what was common in the ideas and projects expressed in the scenarios, and as a whole group to engage in dialogue about what was 'do-able' now. It was here where the face-to-face confrontation with our own assumptions about how things should be done was most palpable. The group was asked to decide which of the projects, taking us all towards the future we all want, were to be confirmed as common ground upon which the whole conference was ready, willing and able to do right now.

The initial dynamic was to express a preference for possible futures, that is, those which people wanted to pursue individually but which were not agreed by the whole conference. People were, at first, far more motivated to continue working towards their own ends than to do something differently for the benefit of the whole community. It was indeed a struggle, and one in which the anxiety levels soared. Everyone had to make their own personal choice about doing more of the same and risking getting what we already have, or doing some things across the current physical, structural and mental boundaries. It was here where we, as conference managers, also faced our most anxious moments. Quite apart from our struggle not to wade in and 'save' everyone by designing the discomfort out of the activity, we also found ourselves confirming to ourselves that our analysis about having gathered fragmentation rather than diversity would indeed mean that the conference was doomed. While we still believe that it is only with the feedback, ideas and dreams of the groups we do not usually meet that the potential for breakthrough occurs, we also have now learned that our preoccupation with our own 'view' was more to do with reducing our own anxiety than with any disembodied notions of 'success'. Doing things differently is not easy.

ACTION

The group decided upon the goals that they were prepared to work towards together and made a public graffiti wall of ideas and plans of how they all wanted to begin. From this, voluntary groups formed to do detailed, short-term action planning and produced the following projects:

- Creating and communicating a more inclusive vision for the future of Sheffield.
- Raising multi-cultural leadership and personal awareness.
- Leadership and personal development skills in the voluntary and community sectors.
- Health promotion in the Asian community.
- City-wide lifelong learning.
- Sheffield's environment.
- Making things happen.
- An electronic networking infrastructure to support the interaction of initiatives, now and in the future.

The conference took place in March 1996 and the first follow-up meeting occurred in May. At the time of writing the following activities had taken place:

- The action groups had met and made sense of the masses of data they produced. A picture of the whole conference was subsequently circulated.
- The first newsletter had been circulated outlining the main action points and reminding everyone how to stay connected.
- A 'getting connected' electronic networking workshop had been offered free of charge so that the community could remain connected.
- Thoughts and feelings about the event had been solicited so that an article could be written.
- Free Mail and Internet connections had been offered to everyone.
- A newsgroup conference had been established on the Internet.
- An Asian meal and get-together had been organized and invitations sent out.

SO IS THIS ONLY ONE STORY?

From our earlier discussion of the compelling task for organization learning what is perhaps the most interesting aspect of all this activity is that the Sheffield City Liaison Group (as sponsor and potential 'leader') has neither had to suggest action nor follow up on delivery; people are simply getting on together in pursuit of their futures with a renewed sense of common purpose.

Given the space to uncover this purpose, the strong unitary leadership so called for during the most anxious moments of the conference, and in the debates around organizational learning, seems no longer to be an issue.

The event, like any other, uncovered many views of what our past, present and future have been, are and might become. Perhaps the lack of diversity across the system uncovered a deep fragmentation in Sheffield society which prefers to work in pockets rather than together; or perhaps a few small ripples of collaboration of a different kind have done enough to start the journey of what it is we can do together; or perhaps, and this is much more likely, it is both at the same time.

12 Learning at the whole organization level

Liz Wallace, North Warwickshire NHS Trust

The 'Learning Organization' or 'learning company', as defined by various academic writers, does not simply refer to an organization where employees learn, but to a specific sort of learning which takes place within those organizations. This is not learning in order to perform a task, but the kind of learning which questions the assumptions behind the need to perform the task, or indeed whether that is the most appropriate task to perform. This is the sort of learning of which revolutions are made; it is about constantly re-inventing, constantly questioning, constantly challenging. It requires people who do not recognize boundaries, people who think in terms of 'how' and 'why', rather than just getting on with the task in hand or striving to meet objectives. It describes not only a way of working, but a way of *being* for an organization. It presupposes self-responsibility for employees and an equality of importance for people within it. In short, to me, it would seem an ideal environment in which to work.

In my enthusiastic response to the concept I began thinking about what I could do to make it work in my place of employment, which at the time was a medium-sized Metropolitan Borough Council, where I was working as a Training and Development Officer. As I looked further into the concept, I experienced blocks around every corner which set me on a train of other blocks, along the lines of 'this can't happen because that can't happen', and so on. In fact, my feeling is that the changes required for public service employers to become Learning Organizations would actually be so fundamental as to require changes to current legislation. For example, how can a Learning Organization function as a committee-run organization?

In coming across these blocks I felt (and indeed feel) uncomfortable. This was helpful in that it led me to explore the discomfort, and this I share here as a background to my perspective, which may also have some links with yours. My thoughts now are that it is viable to take elements of the idea and apply them where possible, but that to take the whole concept and attempt to apply it to the whole organization cannot, in my view, work. If this is attempted, I think that little but frustration and disillusionment will arise. Instead, there may well be pockets of a Learning Organization within any organization, or parts of its constituents, which are appropriate for you.

On first contact, I felt enthused by the concept, wanted to believe that it could work in my own organization and wanted to believe that as a Training and Development person, I could help it on its way. After all, if I couldn't be enthusiastic about learning, who could be? However, I believe that being enthusiastic about learning does not preclude critical analysis of a concept defining learning. I emphasize again that the concept does very definitely not just refer to an organization where people learn, but

> can only happen as a result of *learning at the whole organization level.*

What I attempt to set out here are some fundamental questions underlying the appropriateness of applying the Learning Organization concept to public service. This I do from a background of some twenty-one years working within local government and the National Health Service (NHS). From my own experience within local government and the NHS, a number of issues immediately spring to mind:

- Is the Learning Organization concept a good one *per se*?
- Is it a helpful concept to apply to public service?
- How might it work in public service?

My immediate reaction is that yes, of course it must be good *per se*, to be part of an organization where everyone is constantly learning, but further study reveals that this is not exactly what the Learning Organization is about.

THE PUBLIC SERVICE CONTEXT

Taking Pedler, Burgoyne and Boydell's[1] definition of the 'learning company', as being one which 'facilitates the learning of all its members *and* continuously transforms itself', it is not easy to imagine how this relates to public organizations (in this case, local government and the NHS), when these are, by any definition, large and complex bodies. A local authority usually employs hundreds and frequently thousands of people, as do NHS Trusts.

This is not to imply that the people working within these organizations are not learning or changing what they do. Far from it. But look hard at that definition, '**facilitates** the learning of **all** its members *and* continuously **transforms** itself'. How would anybody possibly know if this were happening? How would it look, feel, seem? A public service will not go out of business and cease to operate, for example, if the capacity of its employees for learning fails to exceed the rate of change within its operations, neither will it make more profit if it does. This definition is not just about the people who work in an organization learning, but about a very particular sort of learning, which affects 'all its members' and from which continuous transformation stems. It has profound implications for public service organizations in terms of structure, and for its employees in terms of status and role.

My suggestion is, therefore, that the notion of the Learning Organization (as it is currently understood) is not a useful one to apply to these organizations as a whole, primarily for the following reasons:

- Structural inflexibility for example, local authorities are bound by statute to operate through a committee structure.
- Government-imposed rules and restrictions; for example, NHS Trusts are not permitted to make a profit.
- It would be politically unacceptable for a local authority or an NHS Trust to go out of business.
- The majority of these organizations' customer bases are relatively secure.
- Subjectivity to political 'whim'.
- Bureaucracy.

This list is not exhaustive, but is formed of the dogmas behind the whole complex business of public service 'culture', driven by expectations, roles, constraints and demands. Context cannot be ignored within the concept of the Learning Organization and to my mind, culture is a large part of context. The context of public service is particularly complex and is affected internally and externally by a multitude of factors, some unique to public service, others not.

This is not to say that people employed in public service organizations do not learn, or do not need to learn. On the contrary, the pace of change for such people is enormous. However, the sort of learning required for a Learning Organization, as I understand it, is not so much related to its capacity to cope with rapid change, but rather to achieve 'transformation'. Bob Garratt, in *The Learning Organization*,[2] writes of 'second-order' change as the sort of change required to achieve this transformation. This is brought about by people who see the need for change in a wider context and perspective and so are able to 'reframe' their problem – people within a Learning Organization need to be able to do this.

Change is stimulated by a variety of sources, of which national government is one. External trends and changes also have their effect, like membership of the EU, the Charter movement and Investors In People. These combine to produce consumers of services who expect value for money and a customer-friendly approach, from service providers who are able to respond flexibly and quickly. Speedy decisions affecting service provision are also expected by the customer of today. These demands presuppose an organization where operational decisions are made by those closest to the customer, and one which strategic planning develops and informs. Also, people working in public service are frequently their own customers and as such, subject to the same external influences as everyone else. So the 'aware customer' becomes the 'aware employee', who not only wants, but expects, involvement in decisions affecting service provision. If the culture of the organization, that is, 'the way we do things around here', actively promotes this way of working through its style, structures and its 'feel' then all is well. If, however, the employee experiences a tension, a contradiction perhaps, in how s/he is an adult in society, as compared to how s/he is able to be in working life, then I would suggest that stresses and difficulties arise.

These difficulties are pointers towards the need for public service to become a Learning Organization and become a cause of tension and stress if the individual finds that his/her employer either does not expect this, or cannot deal with it. The consequences of this, in times of high unemployment, when the employee needs a job, but is unable to find a new one (or a new one that offers what s/he wants), can be alarming. Who wants to be cared for by a nurse who finds working life in today's NHS unrewarding, insecure and de-motivating, for example, or a Social Services' employee with the same outlook? By no means everyone in public service feels unhappy in their work, but few people would suggest, I think, that high employee morale is a common feature of working in public service today.

One of the questions put by Pedler, Burgoyne and Boydell in their book *The Learning Company: A Strategy For Sustainable Development* is, 'What is the reaction to failure in your company?' They go on to identify a learning company 'litmus test' for this: 'just look at the way the last three errors, break-downs or failures were dealt with'.

- Did people talk openly about them or did they hide away and avoid the subject?
- What was learned from the mistakes?
- Did people get blamed or did they feel empowered as a result of the post-mortem?

If local government workers ultimately have a politician to answer to for their mistakes, and NHS workers a lawsuit, I think the results of the 'litmus test' are easy to anticipate.

It may be that some mistakes or failures in this context are indeed acceptable, if they are not life threatening, politically unacceptable or expensive to the public purse. It may also be a reasonable consequence of true teamwork and non-hierarchical management for mistakes and failures to have an 'empowering' effect.

Public service organizations are, however, by their nature hierarchical. Within the NHS, different professions and staff groups are frequently described as 'tribes' divided, rather than united, by their roles, responsibilities, expertise and loyalties. These divisions have been underpinned for decades by pay and reward structures, career paths, professional training and everyday culture. Local pay bargaining, CCT and self-governing Trusts may outwardly force change on public service, but a hierarchical management structure remains, as does tribal professionalism. This for me, is the single, strongest factor militating against a public service organization becoming a 'learning company'.

It feels almost as if people are frightened to behave in any other way, it seems so ingrained. Yet it is not difficult to see the reasons for the insecurities which mitigate against anything but defensive behaviour.

Pedler, Burgoyne and Boydell define the characteristics of a learning company in the following terms:

- *The learning approach to strategy*: strategy formation as a conscious learning process and not as a 'gung-ho' approach. Managerial acts are seen as conscious experiments, rather than set solutions.
- *Participative policy making*: all members of the company have a chance to take part, to discuss and contribute to major policy decisions. Commitment must be made to airing differences and working through conflicts as a way to reaching business decisions that all members are likely to support.
- *Informating*: Information Technology is used to inform and empower people.
- *Formative accounting and control*: systems of accounting, budgeting and reporting are structured to assist learning and, hence, delight their internal customers.
- *Internal exchange*: all internal units and departments see themselves as customers and suppliers. The purpose of a department is thus to 'delight' its internal customer.
- *Reward flexibility*: recognition that money need not be the sole reward; a whole range of things might be considered 'rewarding'. Underlying assumptions are brought out into the open, shared, examined and alternatives discussed and tried out.
- *Enabling structures*: roles loosely structured. Departmental and other boundaries are seen as temporary structures that can flex in response to changes.
- *Boundary workers as environmental scanners*: data collected from outside the company by all members who collect and carry back information that is collated and disseminated.
- *Inter-company learning*: engaging in mutually advantageous learning activities with its customers. Getting together with competitors for mutual learning.
- *Learning climate*: managers see their prime task as facilitating members' experimentation and learning experience. Senior managers lead by questioning their own ideas, attitudes and actions. Continuous improvement is seen as important.
- *Self-development opportunities for all*: resources and facilities for this made available to all members of the company. People are encouraged to take responsibility for their own learning and development.

The above is a summary of the characteristics as Pedler *et al.* define them, but my proposition is that there are too many seemingly immovable structures, cultures and externally imposed rules and regulations within the public *141* service environment to make the 'learning company' a constructive target to aim for. In fact, I believe that it could even be unproductive to take elements of the above characteristics and seek to apply them indiscriminately. Surely, the characteristic of 'self-development opportunities for all' is dependent upon a particular sort of 'learning climate'? Have any of us in public service ever felt that we are there to do, rather than to learn, or that this is what our customers expect, or our patients, or the elected officers?

Instead, I suggest that we look more closely into what affects adult learning and specifically to this in the context of public service organizations. There are reasons why it is as it is and these may benefit from being explored – some of them I have suggested above. For example, take the characteristic of 'participative policy making'. This may initially seem easy to achieve. Perhaps policies in their formative stage are sent out to managers for comment? Perhaps there is a specified consultation process via Trades Unions and other internal organizations before the policy is finally adopted? This is participative, surely? If such a policy lands on your desk do you read it, or comment on it, by phone, e-mail or memo? Do you find time to talk through, explain, discuss it with your staff? Do you ensure that your staff know about it? Do they want to know? Do you check their understanding? Do you check yours? Have you had a similar discussion with other colleagues about it? Is it an important and live issue for you? For them? For everyone? Do you understand it? Do you and your staff understand it and its implications? Are they interested? Do they care? Do you? What will happen if you or they want to change something in it? Will you know if comments have been listened to? How? Have your customers/patients also been consulted? How? Do you know their views?

Public service employers are so large, so unwieldy, and seem to have to exist on so many assumptions, that true participation would appear to be an impossible dream; yet how can this be? For local government and NHS workers, there exist hidden and overt parameters in which the culture particular to public service operates, and we can benefit from clarifying these.

There exists a wealth of academic writings on the subject of adult learning, but applying this practically, to the context of adults working within organizations, is another issue. Before we enthusiastically rush ahead (as we Training and Development or OD practitioners are wont to do) I suggest that an exploratory pause may be advisable.

IMPLICATIONS FOR TRAINING AND DEVELOPMENT

The Training and Development function in any public service organization exists as a product of itself. It may be a product of its own success, or perhaps one of managers' neglect. This is because a training function may have come about as the organization grew and busy managers did not have time to organize the training that was needed. The Training and Development specialist took this onerous responsibility from managers' shoulders. In doing so, the specialist also developed an expertise in identifying what the need for *142* training was, in order best to design or commission a targeted programme.

Thus, a key skill was inadvertently removed from the managers' practice. The irony is that with the currently fashionable de-centralization of the Personnel function, in which trainers often find themselves housed, many are now working with managers to re-instil Training and Development into their role. Trainers themselves having taken up residence in the more strategic (in name anyhow) Human Resources function. No wonder that many practitioners believe that we are striving to do ourselves out of a job – we know how unrealistic it is for managers preoccupied with service delivery, often having to work shifts themselves for absentees, or maintain a caseload of clients, for example, to spend time on training and development issues.

Working in the NHS and local government, for years I genuinely believed that once a manager could appreciate the value, indeed necessity, of training and developing his/her people, then all would be easy thereafter. Perhaps I was particularly unskilled at helping managers do just that, but I recall few managers 'out there' meeting the pressures of directly delivering a service to customers, clients or patients, who were able to take time to assess training needs, brief and de-brief if a course were involved, and give regard to an individual's personal development needs. There is, I'm sure, an argument that applies to some, if not all at some times, that if they remain operational rather than managing operations, they are poor managers. Some, however, are operational as well as managerial of necessity; in a time of low staffing levels or high absenteeism perhaps. What hope then for 'self-responsibility'? Many I come across feel so demoralized and stressed anyway, that they are as unable to devote time and skill to their own development needs as they are to their team members'.

However, as this separation of training into a specialist field was happening, the considerable body of academic work applicable to Training and Development and adult learning was impacting sporadically on public service. Delivering courses continued to be the main function of the Training and Development specialist. Linking this to the business plan emerged as an issue, but only for the training and development manager and possibly his/her director. Other directors were concerned with their own areas of the business plan (which training and development of course was not, having become a specialism in its own right). Furthermore, it appeared inappropriate for other directors' targets to include anything related to training and development issues when this was the remit of the manager for that function. This in itself seemed to demonstrate the level of importance of training and development held by the top managers to everyone else in the organization.

In some public service organizations the capacity to address wider change issues was/is tackled via the appointment of specialists in Organizational Development (OD). This can serve to hive off the responsibility which rightly belongs to a chief executive and his/her managers. The testing time for the OD specialist comes when they begin to have an impact on how things are done and are thus seen to be doing more than tinkering around the edges. It is at this point that they become perceived as dangerous by other directors. Infrequently directors or chief officers themselves, they are vulnerable and   *143* expendable. Those who survive either find themselves unable to make a difference by doing the job they are paid to do, become immersed/indoctrinated in the existing *modus operandi*, or are consultants external to the organization anyway and used perhaps by the Chief Executive in the role of personal guru.

For me, the Training and Development, (and indeed OD) specialist, is likely to feel caught between a rock and a hard place, or at least, to be in the throes of an identify crisis. In short, in much the same position as anyone in public service today. The major difficulty, though, lies in seeking to affect the behaviour of others for whom they bear no line management responsibility. Moreover, those whom they are trying to affect are not fooled; they know that they can choose 'not to play' and that it is they who have to survive at 'the sharp end'. The training and development specialist faces a similar conflict. Managers seeking a 'quick fix' expect training courses to be on the menu. What else is a trainer for? This is the trap of a training course. Expectations are such that people on training courses generally expect to be taught – rather than to learn. The managers who require/allow them to attend have similar expectations. On the other hand, the trainer who believes that, in itself, a training course can change practice, may well be viewing the world through rose-coloured spectacles. The course may be a masterpiece of design, varied in process and content, the group may have 'gelled' phenomenally well, but what happens once back in the workplace? Who cares, who notices, who is able to do anything about it (unless that is, the course has involved a whole work team, and even that does not guarantee success)?

In fact, in my experience, it will be a mark of success if a course results in one or two individuals making just one or two changes to their working practices. Somehow though, this seems insufficient – for the time spent away from the workplace perhaps, or at least insufficient for the trainer to admit. Who would come on courses if it were outwardly acknowledged that such low success rates might result? Yet if asked a common response from individuals is that they feel pleased if they can take away and use just one or two ideas. Neither should a trainer feel disappointed if this is the case. However, it may be that there are different and more rewarding ways to achieve the same results.

The sort of learning that courses often achieve, though, frequently stems from the idea of 'single-loop' learning, a concept referring to learning within existing organizational norms when, in learning organization terms, 'double-loop' learning is needed, so that norms are questioned and challenged. A course may indeed serve to challenge the status quo, but what will be the result? In the Learning Organization, practices and procedures must be flexible and adaptable to change through learning.

THE 'VIRTUAL REALITY' OF A LEARNING ORGANIZATION

There are some intriguing conundrums for public sector workers which directly affect our capacity to form a Learning Organization. One way of exploring these can be through language; by analysing the transactions between employer and employee. This 'transactional analysis' is defined by Thomas A. Harris in his book, *I'm OK – You're OK*.[3] It involves analysing the language in terms of a stimulus by one person and a response from another, which then becomes a new stimulus for generating the other's response. Each stimulus and response is originated from the perspective of Parent, Adult or Child. The origin of the stimulus and response can be discovered through the analysis. The Adult-to-Adult transaction is demonstrated by the book's title.

Within the culture of working life, expectations are held by employer and employee of the other's behaviour: that is to say, the way we do things around here. It may be affected by where the individual sits within the hierarchy of the organization, or perhaps by a manager's personal style in one team or department, or by the nature of the work, for example. I suggest that where transactions are experienced as Adult-to-Adult, a Learning Organization may grow or exist. Where they are not, I believe that a Learning Organization is precluded.

The 'I'm OK – You're OK' position is one which allows for uncertainty; that I'm OK and you're OK essentially – whatever your experience, whatever your beliefs and philosophies may be, and that that applies to me too. For the 'learning company' to become a reality, this then is how we must experience ourselves and others within it:

As a customer of my organization, it is agreed that my views should be sought, listened to and responded to.

As an employee, it is agreed that I will get on with the job, expect to be involved if my manager requires me to be and share my views if my manager asks me to.

Difficulties arise if, at work, I am expected to be a passive vehicle for my employer's expectations when, at home, I behave as an individual with rights and expectations of my own; or if, as a worker, I am expected to adapt to my manager's personality and style of management. If I think s/he is wrong and I question, then I may expect to feel myself in a position of a child questioning a parent.

As a customer, I expect to be listened to and have my views discussed on an Adult-to-Adult basis.

This is to analyse an organization in terms of how I experience its culture as operating in practice. If you are finding some puzzling contradictions, or paradoxes, between what people say and what they do, analyse the transaction which is going on. The words used may represent one adult to another, but the practice may feel very different. In local government or NHS terms, a Chief Executive or his or her representatives, line managers, will usually be seen by an employee in the 'parent' role, for most practice purposes. No wonder managers often feel they have a thankless task; it feels quite schizophrenic to be a parent to some and a child to others! For someone to experience themselves as working in a Learning Organization, in transactional analysis terms, their daily interactions will be experienced as Adult-to-Adult. *145*

One adult may hold more power than another, as in the line-manager relationship, but in order for a real Adult-to-Adult interaction to be possible in this circumstance, the non-manager would have to have, expect to have and be expected to have, a genuine influence on the line manager's decision making. In a Learning Organization, we may also expect to influence, Adult-to-Adult, those above, below, or in the same lateral organizational slice as ourselves, and to do so directly; not through organizational hoops like committees and management groups, etc.

CONCLUSION

My experience has revealed that there are a number of tasks to be completed when considering the Learning Organization concept and its applicability to public service. They are:

- Find out what it's about. Delve into the literature. Don't assume.
- Analyse it critically (and don't feel bad about doing so, after all, a considerable industry has been built up around the whole idea).
- Consider what will make it work and what may act as blockages (and find others to do this with you if you can).
- Take the model and mess around with it – use what you can, but if you cannot apply the key constituents remember that you will be working on something else, not on the Learning Organization.
- What would it *feel* like to work in a Learning Organization? Can you imagine having that feeling where you work? What makes it happen? What prevents it?

I have never worked in a Learning Organization. I have and do work in an organization where people learn, but it is very seldom the sort of learning required for 'second-order change' – the capacity is certainly there, but the blockages get in the way: bureaucracy, legislation, hierarchical management, 'tribalism', fear and many more. I am used to the idea that in public service it is the people at the top (themselves constrained by public accountability) who hold the responsibility for decision making, and for the rest of us it's a case of 'what the Chief Executive says, goes'.

The Learning Organization concept is a vision for learning and a way of being for an organization. Although I remain cynical that such a vision might become a reality throughout public service, I am far from cynical about the power of learning for an individual. My own experience of learning and that of others I see, like Care Assistants, or managers on a National Vocational Qualification (NVQ) programme, for example, or indeed anyone who captures some learning for themselves, is that it is a force to be reckoned with. It is self-responsibility in action and self-responsibility is a key component of any Learning Organization. It is this that leads people to question, to challenge, to seek solutions of their own.

A way forward for the Training and Development/OD specialist may be to encourage and support learning wherever and however that can be done, not on a grand scale necessarily, but at a team and individual level. Define for yourself which part/levels/individuals in the organization can be influenced and determine this (try the transactional analysis test – if Adult-to-Adult transactions are not a possibility find somewhere where they might be!). Use the 'litmus test', but apply it to individuals or teams. Equally powerful, I believe, is for oneself to model Learning Organization practice – more difficult than it appears.

REFERENCES

1   Pedler, M., Burgoyne, J. and Boydell, T. (1991), *The Learning Company: A Strategy for Sustainable Development*, Maidenhead: McGraw-Hill.

2   Garratt, Bob (1988), *The Learning Organization*, London: Fontana.

3   Harris, Thomas A. (1993), *I'm OK – You're OK*, London: Pan Books Ltd.

13 Investors in People and the Learning Organization

Kenneth Franklin, Department of Employment

PEOPLE COUNT

In *Nice Work*, David Lodge's funny and perceptive novel about the interaction between a West Midlands foundry and the local university, Vic Wilcox, the factory manager, speaks with feeling about the challenge facing all organizations as we approach the millennium: 'You can have the greatest ideas in the world for improving competitive edge but you have to rely on other people to carry them out, from senior managers down to labourers'. What he says applies not only to manufacturing firms but to service industries and to the private and public sectors alike. In place of 'competitive edge' we could equally well substitute 'greater efficiency', 'improved effectiveness' or 'increased customer satisfaction'. At the end of the 20th Century, what Vic Wilcox is uttering is close to a universal truth. In the car plant, the tyre factory, the hospital, the benefits office, the bank or the council planning department, the message is the same: 'people are the key to improving performance'.

THE LOCATION

This chapter is a case study of a project designed to bring together Investors in People and organizational learning. It took place in a policy branch of a central government department, the former Department of Employment, between 1993 and 1994. The Department of Employment, in 1993–4, employed some 7000 staff in three head office locations and ten regional offices. Its functions included employment policy, vocational education and training, policy for the payment of benefits to unemployed people, job-finding services (administered through the Employment Services Agency) and industrial relations. The Department was organized into three directorates each headed by a Deputy Secretary (Grade 2) and subdivided into divisions reporting to an Under Secretary (Grade 3). Each division would typically comprise between four and

148

six branches managed by an Assistant Secretary (Grade 5).

The project investigated the possible link between Investors in People and the Learning Organization in the sense of the former promoting 'single-loop' learning and the latter providing a platform which could lead to 'double-loop' learning (Argyris and Schön 1978).

The Department of Employment's Further and Higher Education Branch was formed in July 1992 by the merger of two branches which, until then, had dealt separately with the Department's policy, operations and development work for further education and higher education. This organizational change was not novel. It had been preceded less than two years earlier by another structural realignment. Prior to October 1990, the Further Education Branch also had responsibility for education–business partnerships and Compacts (in both cases, involving schools and business). In October 1990, responsibility for partnerships and Compacts was transferred elsewhere. The Strategy and Further Education Branch was established in October 1990 as part of a more general response to the emergence of Training and Enterprise Councils (TECs) and their assumption of education programme responsibilities. That Branch's purpose was twofold: first to complete the transfer of responsibility for the Department's work-related further education programme to TECs, and second, to develop a broader, overarching education strategy and provide a focal point for integrating and coordinating policy on all TEC strategy, plans and operations concerning vocational education.

In July 1992 the new Further and Higher Education Branch was a 40-strong unit, one of five Branches constituting the Youth and Education Policy Division. Its purpose, as set out in the operational plan, was 'to develop and maintain effective national policies that promote further and higher education which are accessible, flexible and relevant to the present and future needs of employers, individuals and the labour market'. The Branch was unusual in having hybrid responsibilities: for policy, development work, contract management and programme delivery. In addition to the 40 career civil servants in the Branch, there were also five professional advisers, working virtually full-time under service contracts, advising the Branch on policy and operational issues affecting both further and higher education. In 1992 this was an example of new and more flexible working arrangements in which the advisers, who were not employees, provided access to a wide range of external networks.

HRD strategy

Since 1980, the Department of Employment has experienced important changes in its approach to Human Resource Development (HRD). Potter's report (1987) for the Manpower Services Commission recommended a HRD strategy for the organization designed to encourage all staff to develop the competence to deal with unpredictable change in the future. The strategy was focused on competence, commitment and increased capacity to handle change. It signalled a change of direction, from an emphasis on specific job training to more broadly based personal and professional development. It was taken up by the Department of Employment which, in November 1988, published its HRD strategy document, *Developing People in the Employment Department Group: An Agenda for Action*. The Department's success was said to depend on 'the effectiveness of the people who work for it ... If we are to increase our ability to carry out our tasks and to cope with change, we must develop the skills of each individual. ... HRD is about creating a climate in which people can seek to fulfil their potential, both in their own interest and in that of their organization' (Potter 1987; p.2).

To signal the strong commitment of the whole of the Department to HRD it added an additional objective to its existing corporate objectives. This stressed the importance of making the most of the existing talent and future potential of each employee with the aim of increasing overall effectiveness. A further change in the direction of HRD in the Department began in October 1991 when it made a public commitment to become an Investor in People. Three phases can therefore be identified in the Department's approach to HRD during this period:

1   pre-1985: traditional job training;
2   1985–91: an increased emphasis on personal and professional development;
3   1991 onwards: strategic HRD closely linked to the delivery of business objectives.

Investors in People

The Department of Employment's unpublished briefing guide to Investors in People notes that HRD is increasingly recognized as one of the keys to improved organizational performance and is the Department's main initiative to encourage employers to invest in the skills needed for business creation and growth. As such, it is designed to improve any organization's business performance by linking the training and development of its employees to business objectives. It is based on a rigorous Standard which employers must meet to be recognized as an Investor in People. The Standard is national but is delivered locally through Training and Enterprise Councils.

The Standard is built upon four key principles:

1   top-level commitment to develop all employees to achieve business objectives;
2   regular review of the training and development needs of all employees;
3   action to train and develop individuals on recruitment and throughout their employment;
4   evaluating the outcomes of training and development as a basis for continuous improvement.

The commitment to become an Investor in People was taken at the top level within the Department. Following its announcement there was uncertainty among some staff about the future role of HRD in the Department's activities as it made the transition from its 1988 HRD strategy to becoming an Investor in People. There was a perception on the part of some staff that the Department was moving to a more instrumental approach to HRD. This carried the risk of lessening their individual support for the Investors initiative unless they believed there would still be opportunities for personal development, consistent with longer-term organizational objectives, but not necessarily directly linked to short-term business goals.

Once the commitment was announced, all parts of the Department were actively encouraged to produce action plans for Investors in People including a comprehensive portfolio of evidence to demonstrate how the four elements of the Standard were satisfied. The Branch appointed an Investors in People coordinator who also had responsibility for HRD. The established tradition of job training and personal development in the Department formed the basis for more systematic arrangements, for example by identifying key areas of skill and competence and by developing action plans to meet any shortfall. The three elements of the Standard concerned with management commitment, planning and review, and action planning posed no serious problem for the Branch. Evaluation, however, was more difficult. The evidence from a number of studies is that this particular element of the Standard has been the most challenging one for organizations to meet. In the Branch a need was early established for more systematic record-keeping of development activity and particularly follow-up to identify whether, and to what extent, activities had contributed to improved performance, both at a personal and organizational level.

About a year after the commitment to Investors in People, in the spring of 1993, the Branch began to explore the possibility of making a link with the Learning Organization.

The Learning Company project

My initial interest in the Learning Organization had been stimulated by the realization that the *Learning Company Project Report* (Pedler *et al.* 1988) had been commissioned by my own organization (then the Manpower Services Commission) in October 1987. This report referred to a speech, in February 1986, by Geoffrey Holland (now Sir Geoffrey), then director of the Manpower Services Commission: 'Excellence in Industry: Developing Managers – A New Approach'. He called for a new management development initiative, the precursor of the Management Charter Initiative, but also advocated creating a new tradition in Britain in which 'every company must be a learning company' (Pedler *et al.* 1988; 3, p.5). The call to create a tradition of 'learning companies' was to be picked up by the National Training Task Force, formed in December 1988, which culminated in the launch of Investors in People. Thus, in Britain, the 'learning company' and Investors in People sprang from the same seed. Investors, however, does not specifically or overtly make a connection   *151* between individual learning (or HRD) and organizational change and development.

The Learning Organization is still garnering interest on both sides of the Atlantic. Pedler *et al.* (1988) expressed a preference for the term 'learning company' rather than 'Learning Organization'. However, Hendry *et al.* (1994) argue that the 'Learning Organization' is preferable since it enables non-profit, public sector organizations to be more readily embraced than is possible when using the term 'learning company' with its connotations of the private sector and profit making. Theirs is one of the most interesting reviews of the Learning Organization.

It draws a valuable distinction between the Learning Organization and organizational learning. They also discuss 'organizational capability', a term used by Pettigrew and Whipp (1991), which they suggest deals with the 'intricate and often unnoticed or hidden learning that takes place and which informs and influences what occurs in any organization'. They regard 'organizational capability' as 'not just the sum total of the organization working in unison in changing values and mental models. Capability also means expanding and building on that which remains undeveloped and this is the focus of the learning organization concept'. Garvin (1993) expresses his frustration and dissatisfaction that there is no single definition of organizational learning which commands widespread support. He believes there is 'a large measure of agreement that organizational learning is a process which unfolds over time and ... [links] with knowledge acquisition and improved performance'.

There are important differences, some believing that behavioural change is required for learning, others insisting that new ways of thinking are enough. The cyberneticists argue that information processing is the mechanism through which learning takes place while others propose shared insights, organizational routine, even memory. In an attempt at greater clarity Garvin has offered his own definition: 'A learning organization is an organization skilled at creating, acquiring and transferring knowledge, and at modifying its behaviour to reflect new knowledge and insights'. This definition has considerable attractions and was used to inform our thinking about the project in the Branch.

Utilizing action research

The project adopted an action research framework predicated on a belief that the best way of learning about an organization is by attempting to change it. It involved an exploration of the impact of management behaviour on staff's disposition to learn and to alter the norms and values of the organization in which they worked (or using Garvin's definition 'modifying [Branch] behaviour to reflect new knowledge and insights'). However, I needed to take care not to delude myself and others that unwitting manipulation of staff or the use of more coercive, or covert, methods could be presented as 'empowerment'.

Those involved in the project quickly became aware that virtually all the writing and theories about the Learning Organization and organizational learning derive from a Human Relations perspective. The industrial relations discipline from which springs most of the theoretical work on industrial democracy and employee participation appears unconnected with developments in organizational learning. This may account for the concern of Ross (1992) that the political and industrial relations' dimensions of the Learning Organization seem to have been overlooked. This is a fruitful area for further research which could lead to developing a more integrated model of organizational learning taking into account unitary and pluralist theories of organizational behaviour.

As an exercise in action research I believe the two features normally associated with it were both achieved, namely that the action researcher is best able to learn about an organization by trying to change it and that the people involved in the change process should be involved in the study. It gave me an invaluable opportunity to surface and question some of the deep-seated and unconsciously accepted – indeed, hidden – assumptions about the way the organization works. It also offered opportunities for staff in the Branch to explore different ways of working, including examining their expectations of themselves and their managers.

As a result of this project I believe the concept of the Learning Organization, as put forward by Pedler *et al.*, may be too narrowly drawn; its focus on the nexus between individual learning and organizational norms and standards may serve to deflect attention from the need to address the learning of individuals holistically. In so doing this it should, for example, embrace issues of individual motivation, the extent to which the organizational environment is favourable to learning, management style, the identification and communication of primary purpose and what Senge (1990) calls 'shared vision'.

At the time the project began the Civil Service was at a point where the relationship between policy making and management roles was not altogether comfortable. In theory (and, perhaps, largely in practice) the Civil Service executive agencies, freed from policy making, may be able to concentrate their attention more fully on the management role in ways which are more difficult for Civil Service departments which continue to have traditional and more direct relationships with Ministers. For Civil Service managers working in policy branches the double challenge has been to respond to the new role of 'manager' while coming to grips with changes in the responsibilities of the role itself, particularly the balance between 'management' and 'administration/policy making'.

Reasons for the growth of interest in the Learning Organization include:

- innovation;
- competitiveness;
- cost reduction;
- learning and its encouragement;
- skill formation;
- participative management;
- organizational change.

In this project we attempted to develop understanding within the Branch as a precursor to engaging in action. This is not, perhaps, the usual way of proceeding in many organizations. The understanding in question was not about the nature of the learning concepts, still less about the concepts of single- and double-loop learning. These are theoretical constructs which, while of interest to some members of the Branch, were likely to be off-putting to others. Lewin's dictum that there is nothing as practical as a good theory is appealing but managers are well advised to tread softly in presenting theories to unprepared staff. Interestingly, this approach is paralleled by that of Hendry *et al.* (1994) in their work in developing a Learning Organization approach with Courtalds Advanced Materials.

Critchley (1993) has written about the illusion of managing organizational culture in the sense of top management producing a statement of values which the organization is expected to adopt. He writes: 'It takes managers courage to explicitly undertake to work with the dynamics of their culture and allow changes to emerge from what they find, rather than impose apparently desired changes on what they do not fully and deeply understand'.

In retrospect, this is very similar to the approach we adopted in seeking to work with the 'dynamics of the culture' rather than imposing my own views and perceptions on the Branch. It resulted in a number of developments such as the 'culture group' – an informal working party which any member of the Branch could attend, to share ideas, identify issues of concern and suggest ways of bringing these to wider attention. However, this approach gave rise to some uncertainty on the part of some members of the Branch, particularly, perhaps, in not meeting their need for a stronger sense of direction. This, I believe, was a necessary and, for some, disorientating phase, particularly for those inclined to adopt Bion's basic assumption of dependency in relation to management (de Board 1978). It was a learning experience for me and members of the Branch to ride with the flow. It helped encourage a belief among staff that they too would play an active part in helping shape the itinerary for the journey and be fully involved in the regular reviews of progress as we proceeded.

It needs to be made clear that the research did not take place on an organizational 'greenfield site'. On the contrary, a number of the changes and processes covered by the project were already in train when it commenced. They included:

- Management of change: activities arising from the reorganization of the Department's Training, Enterprise and Education Directorate (TEED) in 1992;
- Communications: a major focus of organizational activity which led to the introduction of team briefing in 1992, and the inception of a regular monthly Branch meeting in February 1993;
- National Vocational Qualifications: the introduction and take-up of NVQs in the Branch as part of the developing HRD strategy and in response to the findings of a Branch skills audit published in October 1993.

The project revealed that many staff had difficulty in recognizing or accepting that a Learning Organization could be realized in a Civil Service setting, embodying systems and structures which emphasize grades and roles, and the authority associated with them.

THE STORY OF THE PROJECT

In preparation for Investors in People we held an initial one-day workshop involving all staff in the Branch. Six months later, in May 1993, we held a second Branch workshop. This concentrated on our preparations for the 'dry run' assessment for Investors in People to be held in September 1993. We also used this workshop to explore the idea of the Learning Organization. The 'dry run' involved a mixed team of assessors from within the Department led by a national, accredited assessor from Henley Management College. In all respects this simulated the actual assessment process including the preparation and submission of documentary evidence and interviews with a sample of staff chosen by the assessment team.

The dynamics of the day's event in May were very positive. People worked actively together. There was evidence of mutual support and a good deal of interchange. Three working groups were set up involving staff from different sections in the Branch to develop ideas and produce solutions on (1) induction arrangements for staff joining the Branch, (2) the evaluation of training and development activities, and (3) a Branch system for recording training and development undertaken by staff. The working groups met regularly between May and early September. Leaders were selected from within the groups without regard either to seniority or grade. There was clarity about the required outcomes but with each of the groups having considerable freedom about how they would produce results. The group working on the induction pack was led by a clerical officer who had joined the Branch only three months earlier. She therefore had direct personal experience of the strengths and weaknesses of existing induction arrangements in the Branch and was able to use this to help define the group's approach to its task. In September, following consultation within the Branch and research on induction in other parts of TEED, the group produced a comprehensive and well received induction pack for use within the Branch. Similar high-quality work was produced by the two other groups.

A third one-day workshop was held in October. The tasks for this were (1) to consider the outcomes of the Investors' assessment report, (2) to agree actions at section level to meet the Investors in People standard by April 1994, and (3) to plan to meet its evaluation requirements. Compared with the initial event a year earlier this was altogether a more lively and participative meeting characterized by:

active discussion and debate on whether the Department's commitment to become an Investor in People was primarily motivated by top management's desire to secure the award or to treat HRD as a serious issue with proper *155* regard for individuals' aspirations as well as improved 'business' performance;

a strong feeling this was just another initiative being pursued by top management;

a belief that, like other management fads, it was 'flavour of the month' and would quickly be forgotten on the other hand, as the sponsor Department for Investors in People, we could hardly be seen to be unsuccessful in securing the Award;

a worry that the commitment to Investors in People – with its direct connection between staff development and business objectives – would limit the range of development opportunities previously available. I explained that the business performance connection was now clear and explicit but that we would define business objectives in a Departmental context, which broadened the scope for development, rather than the narrower focus derived from a Branch or Division perspective.

In addition to the one-day workshop and the working groups, we set up a Branch culture group, held regular meetings for all staff, drew on the results of the annual Departmental staff attitude survey and used the results of a specifically commissioned skills need analysis.

In September 1993 the Branch was invited to take part in an inter-departmental consortium project organized by the Development Branch of the Cabinet Office to explore management and leadership styles in consumer-led organizations. This had strong connections with the Citizen's Charter and the government's emphasis on creating a more responsive public service. The project, involving some 16 government departments and executive agencies, was supported by a team of external management consultants which had previously worked with the Cabinet Office on a similar consortium project in 1992, addressing issues of quality. The Branch decided to take part in the project to explore organizational learning and its implications for management style in the Branch. We used the Cabinet Office project to develop a question-naire, based on the 'learning company' profile in Pedler et al. (1991, pp. 26–27), to gauge the Branch's position as a Learning Organization. Of the 40 question-naires issued, 25 were returned, a 63 per cent response rate. From this we identified those issues on which 'high scores' (60 per cent or above) were recorded and compared them with those questions with 'low scores' (34 per cent or below). The survey suggested that the Branch was strong on operations and action but much weaker on policy matters – in the sense of staff lacking a well developed, collective understanding of the wider policy framework in which operations were conducted. Similarly the Branch's organizational framework (its structure and systems) was underdeveloped in so far as it did not fully facilitate the interplay between ideas and policy or provide channels for transforming ideas into action.

In a workshop, for all members of the Branch, to discuss the survey's results, some interesting points surfaced:

The idea of Branches as 'customers and suppliers' was a difficult concept to handle.

It was not helpful to use words like 'customers' and 'suppliers'; some staff felt the only 'real' customer for the work of the Branch was the Branch head. Staff did not like the idea of 'Branches speaking openly to challenge each other'; this was not the way the organization worked.

There was a need for more coordination of work in and between the sections in the Branch to help people understand what was happening around them.

There was a perception of a lack of structures in the Branch to help staff contribute to improvement of policy. There was also difficulty with the concept of staff contributing to improving policy 'outside their normal work boundaries'. On the other hand, the current definition of work areas was beginning to become flexible and open up.

In connection with issues of recognition, the Department now had limited scope to increase pay and offer promotion.

The new Departmental performance management system seemed to be designed to prevent people getting pay rewards other than at the very lowest level of the grade.

However, there were ways of recognizing good performance other than by pay and promotion.

Nevertheless, there were strong feelings that the new performance pay system would increase the level of staff dissatisfaction (45 per cent in 1993) in the 1994 staff attitude survey.

Key issues

Some of the key issues which emerged from the study were:

There was concern about the lack of promotion opportunities and restricted pay (the Chancellor's limits on public sector pay increases).

There was a perception that performance-related pay (PRP) is a system of getting more out of people but without adequate reward.

There was a continuing suspicion about the Department's motives for seeking Investors in People status:

- to gain the recognition of the Award
- to limit the development/training/education opportunities formerly available under the Department of Employment's 1988 HRD policy.

However, there was recognition that work in preparation for the Investors in People assessment had focused attention on systems and procedures to formalize the Branch's arrangements for staff development, its evaluation and linking with operational planning.

It was the staff's wish to have a clearer sense of a mid-term strategy.

The staff's primary focus was on the immediate task in hand but there was a growing wish to know more about related work in other parts of the Department.

There was an increased understanding of the benefits which could flow from teamworking in the Branch, but an awareness that systems and structures did not always encourage this, for example:

- performance-related pay is based on individual performance
- staff reporting arrangements reinforce the pattern of single-line vertical accountability
- the pervading power of grades and hierarchy in the traditional Civil Service organization
- the 'hidden assumptions' which underpin organizational life had partly, if not completely, surfaced
- the processes of socialization in the Department were deep-seated in their effects on individuals
- within the Branch some staff appeared to have adopted, in Bion's terms, a basic assumption of dependency
- the dynamics of the relationship between managers and those being managed in shaping expectations of behaviour; staff expect managers to behave in certain ways which can constrain the development of new patterns of behaviour.

For some staff in the Branch, management-inspired initiatives, which may seem coherent at senior management level, can appear incoherent and sometimes in conflict. It would be worthwhile developing a strategy for further work on Investors in People, based on an analysis of all activities which contribute to, or impinge on, HRD policies. Such an analysis might seek to identify the extent to which other initiatives are consistent, or in conflict, with the HRD strategy itself.

The Department was responsible for, and actively pursuing, a range of national policies, such as, Investors in People, individual commitment to training, employee development and employee participation initiatives. The connection between these initiatives, particularly the first three and the last, could be more clearly articulated, particularly as they have similar purposes though originating from different traditions. It would also be worth exploring the extent to which these initiatives, including the first three, might be presented in a more coherent way to the wider community including the Training and Enterprise Councils which have a key role in explaining these initiatives to local partners.

QUESTIONS RAISED BY THE PROJECT

This project raised a number of interesting questions:

Was Investors in People a help or a hindrance?
Is it possible to develop a Learning Organization within a unit of a wider organization?
What are some of the key requirements to secure a Learning Organization?

What are the consequences for management?
How do staff react to the idea of organizational learning?
What are the implications for the distribution of power within organizations?

SOME CONCLUSIONS

The key conclusions from this study are:

1   Our experience of working towards Investors in People in the Branch was that it is a powerful lever with which to raise awareness of HRD and to put in place systems and processes to secure a stronger link between training and development, and business objectives.
2   As such, Investors in People could help to promote single-loop learning ('learning which enables an organization to examine the extent to which it is meeting existing norms and standards', Megginson *et al.* 1993).
3   However, Investors in People, because of its exclusive focus on HRD and business objectives, does not necessarily lead to double-loop learning ('learning to change norms and standards, and to do so in a way which takes into account the views of those affected by the change', Megginson *et al.* 1993).
4   The approach to learning (and also to HRD) in the former Department of Employment was characterized by a fragmentary view of the organization at all levels. This made it difficult to develop an appreciation among managers and staff of the interaction between the various elements of the organization's systems. More seriously, it encouraged the introduction of internal initiatives which were not wholly consistent one with the other.
5   Staff at all levels in the Branch had a strong wish to know more about the work of their colleagues, both within the Branch and in other parts of TEED, to help them contribute more fully to improving performance and shaping policy.
6   Staff also wished to engage in more teamworking within the Branch.
7   The skill of leading teams and individuals, which was recognized as an essential competence among senior staff, was not seen in this way among junior and middle managers. At all levels in the Branch there appeared to be a significant degree of self-misperception of managers' existing competence (expressed as a lack of need for further development) in this and other key areas to do with management of people.
8   The Learning Organization, in the sense of an organization 'skilled at creating, acquiring and transferring knowledge and modifying its behaviour to reflect new knowledge and insights' (Garvin 1993) challenges many of the accepted orthodoxies of organizational behaviour. It encourages a searching review of management style, particularly on how to provide leadership and direction while, at the same time, devolving responsibility to staff and encouraging their increased participation.

9   A more participative management style challenges managers to develop new skills and competences based on a broader and deeper understanding of organizational life. It also provides opportunities and creates uncertainty for those being managed as they are faced with new demands and enhanced responsibilities.

10 Empowerment and a more participative management style should not be seen as reducing or eliminating the need for management to give a clear sense of direction and to provide a framework in which staff are encouraged to review and measure their performance.

For those studying the Learning Organization from within the academic community, the following suggestions may be useful:

●   The distribution of power within organizations which are seeking to become Learning Organizations might usefully be analysed using the concepts of unitary and pluralist organizations, taking account of Lukes's radical view of power (1974).

●   Research might be pursued seeking to integrate the theoretical perspectives derived from the industrial relations and the human relations traditions regarding employee participation and the Learning Organization.

●   An interesting area of research would be the dynamics of the relationship between managers and those being managed in organizations which purport to engage in organizational learning, having regard to issues of staff dependency, staff expectations of management and the implications for the role of managers in managing 'empowered individuals'.

BIBLIOGRAPHY

Argyris, C. and Schön, D. (1978), *Organisational Learning: A Theory of Action Perspective*, Harlow: Addison-Wesley.

Critchley, B. (1993), 'Organizational Culture – Is it just an illusion?', *Leadership and Organizational Development Journal*, **13**, (1), p.8.

De Board, R. (1978), *The Psychoanalysis of Organisations*, London: Tavistock-Routledge.

Employment, Department of (1991), *Investing in People: The Benefits of Being an Investor in People*, Sheffield: Employment Department.

Employment Department Group (1988), *Developing People in the Employment Department Group: An Agenda for Action*, London: Employment Department.

Garvin, D.A. (1993), 'Building a Learning Organisation', *Harvard Business Review*, July/August.

Hendry, C. and Jones, A. with Cooper, N. (1994), *Creating a Learning Organisation: Strategies for Change*, Sutton Coldfield: Man-made Fibres Industry Training Organisation.

Jones, A.M. and Hendry, C. (1994), *The Learning Organisation: A Review of Literature and Practice*, Coventry: Warwick University.

Lodge, D. (1988), *Nice Work*, Harmondsworth: Penguin.

Lukes, S. (1974), *Power: A Radical View*, London: Macmillan.

Megginson, D., Joy-Matthews, J. and Banfield, P. (1993), *Human Resource Development*, London: Kogan Page.

Pedler, M., Burgoyne, J. and Boydell, T. (1988), *The Learning Company Project Report*, Sheffield: Manpower Services Commission.

Pedler, M., Boydell, T. and Burgoyne, J. (1991), *The Learning Company*, Maidenhead: McGraw-Hill.

Pettigrew, A.M. and Whipp, R. (1991), *Managing Change for Competitive Success*, Oxford: Blackwell.

Potter, A. (1987), *Developing People in the MSC: A Human Resource Development Strategy*, Sheffield: Manpower Services Commission.

Ross, K. (1992), 'The Learning Company', *Training and Development*, July.

Senge, P. (1990), *The Fifth Discipline: The Art and Practice of the Learning Organisation*, London: Century Business.

14 The Learning Organization and the voluntary sector

Mike Aiken and Bruce Britton, Save the Children Fund

Does the concept of the Learning Organization have an application to the voluntary sector? Do voluntary organizations possess any characteristics that make it easier for them to become Learning Organizations? Are there examples of voluntary organizations using the ideas of the Learning Organization? What potential blocks to becoming a Learning Organization have been identified and how might they be overcome? This chapter arises from an analysis of our own organization and others we have been involved with, as well as from recent discussions with medium-to-large UK-based voluntary organizations on the theme of the Learning Organization.

We begin with an examination of the term the Learning Organization. This is followed by some of the features of voluntary organizations that make them different to the private or public sectors and we consider here the needs and benefits of organizational learning in the not-for-profit arena. Third, we look at the main functions of the Learning Organization and map them to examples of voluntary sector endeavour. Finally, we illustrate some of the blocks to organizational learning and describe some potential solutions to these.

THE LEARNING ORGANIZATION

A Learning Organization is described by David Garvin of the Harvard Business School as one which is 'skilled at creating, acquiring, and transferring knowledge, and at modifying its behaviour to reflect new knowledge and insights'.[1] This is a helpful definition since it provides some insights into what a Learning Organization must do, but does not address why organizational learning is important. Pearn *et al.* in their book *Learning Organisations in Practice*,[2] caution against concentrating on *the* Learning Organization since, in their view, this tends to prompt the wrong kinds of questions, such as: what is a Learning Organization? How can you tell if you belong to one? How does an organization become one? What does it do after it has become one? According to Pearn *et al.*

these questions assume that being a Learning Organization is a steady state which one achieves as a result of following certain prescribed action. In their book, Pearn *et al.* emphasize the *process* of organizational learning rather than the state of being a Learning Organization. This focus is a useful one to bear in mind. However, most people do ask the kind of questions listed above and therefore a vision describing what we are aiming for can be useful to help voluntary organizations effectively direct their energies to learning.

Gareth Morgan[3] points out that organizations cannot, themselves, learn. However, they can be organized in such a way that learning can be a prominent feature at a number of different levels. According to Morgan, the key aspect of a Learning Organization is that it exists only as a set of complex systems and relationships which link the organization's vision, mission, values and behaviour to desired outcomes and results. An effective Learning Organization will constantly question its assumptions and review its objectives in the light of both its own experience and changes in the external environment. A Learning Organization will be arranged in such a way that it encourages:

- individual learning;
- team or work group learning;
- cross-functional learning (for example, between departments or sections);
- operational organizational learning (which focuses on how the organization can improve its day-to-day operations);
- strategic organizational learning (which concentrates on how the organization can use its experience to decide what its overall priorities should be).

Our own preferred definition of a Learning Organization is one which actively incorporates the experience and knowledge of its members and partners through the development of practices, policies, procedures and systems in ways which continuously improve its ability to set and achieve goals, satisfy stakeholders, develop its practice, value and develop its people, and achieve its mission.

Why should voluntary organizations seek to become Learning Organizations? Much of the literature on Learning Organizations describes benefits in private sector terms, such as gaining competitive advantage over rival companies. At first glance, this does not seem to be a suitable approach for organizational learning in the voluntary sector. However, a closer examination of the competitive advantage model shows that even this does have a place in the not-for-profit world. In the competitive world of fundraising, for example, voluntary organizations vie with each other to attract the interest and the donations of the public and large corporations. Innovative fundraising practices may not retain their competitive edge for long, but learning quickly what works and what does not can avoid wasteful use of fundraisers' time and energy. Similarly, a voluntary organization which is seen to be 'first' to a new social issue will gain a reputation as being far-sighted and ahead of others. This can give it a higher profile and an increased possibility to raise funds.

In the voluntary sector, other benefits apply to organizations which learn. A group of voluntary sector managers we worked with identified the following advantages for a voluntary organization of becoming a Learning Organization:

- improved cohesion – unity of purpose across different parts of the organization is encouraged;
- increased adaptability – the organization is better placed to take advantage of opportunities and deal with challenges and unpredictable events;
- increased impact of the organization;
- increased effectiveness and efficiency – the organization makes better use of its resources;
- increased staff motivation – staff feel more valued and influential;
- ability to retain staff and their knowledge – better systems for rewarding the contribution staff make to the development of the organization;
- legitimizes grass-roots knowledge and experience – learning is valued no matter where it takes place;
- greater opportunities to be creative – learning encourages creativity and teamwork;
- increased ability to initiate change – learning provides the organization with the confidence and information necessary to take initiatives and risks.

If voluntary organizations do not learn to adopt organizational learning they are likely to cease to exist because they are unable to adapt sufficiently well to the changing circumstances in which they find themselves. This is the classic $L \geq C$ equation of the 'Action Learning guru', Reg Revans, who stated that, to ensure survival, the rate of learning of an organization must be greater or equal to the rate of change of its environment. A more proactive answer is that it is only by learning lessons, and applying the learning, that voluntary organizations will stand any chance of fulfilling their missions. Sometimes learning is an implicit part of the mission statement of voluntary organizations. For example, the Save the Children Fund (SCF) mission is:

> Save the Children works to achieve lasting benefits for children within the communities in which they live by influencing policy and practice based on its experience in different parts of the world. In all of its work Save the Children endeavours to make a reality of children's rights.

Although learning is not mentioned explicitly in the Save the Children mission statement, it forms the implicit bridge between 'experience' and 'influence'. Without learning, and the wider application of the lessons gained from experience, there is no possibility for an organization the size of SCF to have a significant impact on the lives of any but a very limited number of children in *164* the 50 countries worldwide where the organization works.

A failure to learn from experience can be a fatal weakness when it comes to planning at any level in an organization, but this is particularly true at a strategic level where it is necessary to make sensible long-term choices about goal-setting and resource allocation. In recognition of this strategic role, learning has been identified in SCF's Programmes Department as one of its main strategic priorities.

The stewardship of resources is a particularly important reason for voluntary organizations to be proficient at organizational learning. All voluntary organizations manage their resources on behalf of their constituency – service users, members of the organization, the general public, grant-awarding bodies and other donors. They are therefore accountable to these bodies for the efficient use of resources and have a responsibility to ensure that these resources are used wisely in the pursuit of their constitutionally agreed purpose.

Learning from their own and others' experience to avoid repeating avoidable mistakes is an important way of ensuring that the maximum impact is gained from limited resources. Indeed, given that learning is going on all the time throughout any organization, it could be argued that it is a misuse of resources *not* to create a framework which both encourages learning and makes lessons freely accessible. This does not necessarily mean formalizing the process of learning since informal learning can be just as powerful as that which is more planned. Rather, it means creating a working environment which enables the organization to make the best use of its experience and, hence, its resources. Later in this chapter we provide some examples of voluntary organizations which are doing this.

CHARACTERISTICS OF THE VOLUNTARY SECTOR

Let us examine some of the distinctive features of voluntary organizations that will underpin their approach to organizational learning. Voluntary organizations have a goal or purpose for which they were originally set up. A statutory organization (like a social services or education department) has a legal duty to provide certain services and perform specified operations. Charities have a much wider scope which can at times be empowering, at other times overwhelming. For example, should a children's charity provide more direct services for children and their families, or should it involve itself more in lobbying for their rights and needs? Should it become more research-led, develop as an advocacy organization, or seek attitudinal change amongst the public? A charity has the possibility to make far-reaching choices about its strategic direction; about what kind of organization it wants to be to fulfil its purpose.

The equivalents of mission statements existed in not-for-profit organizations for over a century before they became widely fashionable in the early 1980s in the commercial and, more recently, public sector. SCF, for example, was based by its founder, in the early 1920s, on a set of principles entitled 'The Rights of the Child', which appear, virtually unchanged, on its annual reports and publicity to this day.

The notion of values is integral to the very concept of a voluntary organization and some might say it is their key distinguishing feature. They are often written into the constitution and are regularly appealed to in the day-to-day operations of the work; they are seen as establishing the culture of the whole organization not just its end product. Supporters (and critics) of an environmental organization would expect and demand concern for the environment to be demonstrated in its day-to-day work, by attention to using sustainable resources in its own operations at the very least. Depicting people in developing countries as miserable and helpless as part of a fundraising campaign used to be common among aid agencies. International charities today usually seek images which are more positive and confer dignity on their subjects to be consistent with organizational values of respect and mutuality. Learning in such a context, then, must take account of these all pervasive and unmeasurable values. This will involve judgment and debate and cannot be appealed to on the basis purely of 'inputs and outputs'.

Many public sector organizations, in health, housing or social services for example will, of course, have ethical standards. They will, however, need to combine an ethos of say, care, accountability or providing a service to the public, with a statutory mission. These two elements may at times conflict, for example due to a lack of resources, and present different challenges to organizational learning for statutory organizations. 'Values' have also become more important in the commercial world over the last decade. Environmental awareness and multicultural workforces are just two obvious areas where companies have recognized the need to be responsive to the wider community of which they are part. Cynics may see this as a strategy to present a company in a favourable public light in order to maximize their profits, but the fact that there is a need *to appear*, at the very least, to be a commercial organization that upholds values illustrates the shift that has taken place. Ford Motors developed a multi-ethnic advertising poster in the early 1990s in the UK but the subsequent 'deletion' of some of the black engineers depicted in an advertising campaign in Poland a few years later led to complaints, compensation and a public relations disaster for the company. Shell, the oil company, eventually backed down in its attempt to bury an oil rig at sea in 1995 following enormous public protest. The public's perception of a company's ethical considerations is one of the factors large corporate concerns must now take into account. Whether organizational learning in such cases took account of substantive issues of values in the company or remained at the level of avoiding public relations disasters we do not know.

Voluntary organizations are, by their nature, very people-intensive. The main resource, of small voluntary organizations in particular, is the volunteer's time. Every year over 23 million adults volunteer and it is estimated that in the UK they contribute nearly 62 million hours of voluntary work each week.[4] Staff, essential to carry out the mission of the larger organizations, are frequently the biggest cost and therefore a vital resource. In 1990 more than 438 000 people were employed in the voluntary sector.[5]

Passing on learning is vital in such labour-intensive environments where the expertise of volunteers or staff in key development roles can disappear quite rapidly. Funding considerations can mean staff are on short-term contracts and a volunteer's circumstances may change swiftly, leading to their abrupt departure. We return to examine this particular challenge in more detail towards the end of the chapter. The problem is similar for larger charities seeking to develop innovative approaches to work at national or international levels, or attempting widespread attitudinal change. Demonstrating a new way of using aid with poor communities; modifying the general public's attitude to disability; lobbying a local authority on the needs of Gypsies and Travellers; campaigning for black and Asian people's rights in the criminal justice system, all require a considerable range of skills and abilities, not to mention ingenuity, tenacity and determination. The tools and systems to record and transfer learning in these situations are not easy to develop. This is particularly so when a success, for example, in lobbying Parliament for a legislative change, may be perceived to be attributable to a particular, charismatic, leader. A failure in this situation may, conversely, be seen as a one-off setback, beyond the control of the organization. These kinds of activities differ in form and substance to some public sector operations, a library service for example, where the goal may be delivering a regular and repeated service to the public and the learning issues are more about assessment of need, diversifying the service and improving quality rather than using innovative problem-solving processes.

The Management Committee members, resembling the non-executive board members of some public and commercial organizations, play a central policy and accountability role in most voluntary organizations. While they may have a deep awareness of the issue of the voluntary organization, either through personal or professional knowledge, they receive no pay for their long hours of service and, often, no training. As trustees they can be ultimately financially liable for any debts of the charity. Voluntary management committees were, in total, accountable for between £4.5–£4.9 billion, according to a 1990 estimate of the voluntary sector's total income.[6] Their own learning and understanding of what is a sophisticated and delicate management task may not be recognized or recorded. They can often be a vital continuity link, both on goals and values, in an organization, particularly if key staff leave. Any Learning Organization needs to take account of their contribution to the charity's achievements.

Equal opportunities are high on the agenda of most voluntary organizations of all sizes, and this is not surprising. Notions of justice or rights are embedded in many voluntary organizations' constitutions and are frequently quoted in their publicity material. The work which has been done in the voluntary sector to apply such thinking to practice has been a serious and preoccupying pursuit since the early-1980s at least. Empowering and supporting those involved in their organizations to learn and contribute by being able to speak out for themselves, is a fundamental, related concept for many voluntary organizations, particularly those working directly with user groups. There is frequently an expectation among voluntary organizations that users should be enabled to participate and share in setting the direction of the organization. Keeping close to the user's needs, fashionable in the private sector through the notion of customer satisfaction and quality service, is an issue many voluntary sector organizations would state as having always been their highest concern. Evaluating how far practice matches what is preached on both equal opportunities and participation remains a concern in many parts of the sector.

These are some of the features we think are distinctive about the voluntary sector. That is not to say that the issues of values, participation and empowerment, to take just three, are not important to other sectors. Nor is it to say that the voluntary sector necessarily outperforms other sectors in these areas. It is to say, however, that these are central preoccupations of those involved in not-for-profit organizations which have an important bearing on the voluntary sector outlook on the Learning Organization.

How do voluntary organizations perform in practice? Does performance measure up to stated ideals? Are shortfalls in sound organization (resource management, human resource development, strategic planning) disguised by appealing to the very worthy intentions? Are voluntary organizations able to adapt, grow and remain relevant and creative in the light of the changing environment around them – socially, politically, technologically?

The environment in which voluntary organizations are working is undergoing fundamental changes and rapid adaption is necessary. The degree to which voluntary organizations can adapt to these changes may decide their fate. This is the $L \geq C$ equation referred to earlier. It is worth touching on some of these changes and challenges to underline the current importance for the Learning Organization in the voluntary sector. The recession has had a mixed effect. While many small charities were forced to close, some very big charities were still expanding as recently as the early 1990s. Many very local neighbourhood groups and self-help groups, highly responsive to their communities, relied heavily on small grants from the local authority – these have become harder to obtain with the fiscal squeeze on local government and in some places have disappeared altogether. The National Lottery's effects are beginning to become apparent. Large sums granted to some small organizations with no guarantee of continued funding, while temporarily welcome, could have a distorting, divisive and ultimately destructive effect on local communities. Meanwhile, research is indicating the effect on overall charitable giving has been negative. The growth of the contract culture whereby organizations, commercial or voluntary, can tender for services previously delivered by a local authority – or grant conditions that amount to a contract – in some cases threatens the very identity of the voluntary sector as an independent force. The purchaser–provider split opens up similar opportunities and threats to the character of the sector. Access to European money and UK regeneration budgets is invariably via partnerships with local authorities or private industry. This is forcing new kinds of collaboration, in some cases positive and in other cases ultimately undermining of the voluntary sector's unique contribution to society.

A commission ('Meeting the Challenges of Change, Voluntary Action in the 21st Century', NCVO) on the future of the voluntary sector reported late in

1996. A few years earlier there were controversial suggestions that the voluntary sector reform itself by defining two different kinds of action. The first kind would be, 'authentic voluntary action, prophetic, vision led, reformist, independent of government, pursuing independent energy for moral purposes'. The second kind would be 'part of the wider social economy. It acts philanthropically on sub-contract from the state'.[7] Such a proposed split ignores what many in the sector consider a vital special relationship between work 'in the field' and advocating/campaigning independently from the experience this generates. However, it is illustrative of the way the voluntary sector is being scrutinized and is scrutinizing itself as never before.

This is the challenging background against which the voluntary organization must operate. How the sector will respond and adapt to these changes and challenges, both current and imminent, is not yet clear. Arguably, these represent fundamental questions similar to those any business faces when large changes to its customers or suppliers or product are taking place, or a public sector department with compulsory competitive tendering about to be implemented.

We have concentrated here on some of the differences in characteristics between the public, private and voluntary sectors. However, organizational theories apply equally to the people, structures and processes of organizations in the not-for-profit sector as to others. We should not be surprised, therefore, to find similarities between the organizational behaviour of voluntary organizations and that of other sectors. A small women's training charity in Belfast, struggling with limited grants, uncertain cash flow and emergent organizational structures, may have much more in common with a small business in Peckham than either has with IBM. On the other hand, a large international charity may superficially resemble more a local authority or a quango or even a multinational corporation than a black self-help organization in Birmingham. It follows that, despite the key characteristics of the three sectors (voluntary, public and private) outlined earlier, some of the organizational learning of voluntary organizations is likely to be applicable to other sectors and vice versa.

THE FUNCTIONS OF A LEARNING VOLUNTARY ORGANIZATION

In our work on developing mechanisms for organizational learning in the voluntary sector we are often asked what organizations can do practically to improve their capacity to learn. We always suggest that organizations take stock of their current abilities by using a model which focuses on the key functions, which all organizations must do if they are to learn effectively.

We will now look at eight key functions of Learning Organizations and illustrate these with some current voluntary sector experience. We believe the model in Figure 14.1, which illustrates the eight key functions of a Learning Organization, is a useful one not only for the voluntary sector but for any organization which is serious about learning.

If organizational learning is to be a genuinely organization-wide endeavour it   *169*

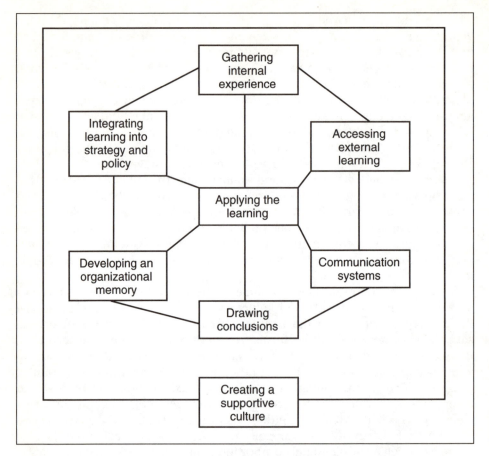

Figure 14.1   The key functions of a Learning Organization (based on Slim, 1993)[8]

must become part of the organization's culture – the way the organization does things. This requires both a positive attitude to learning and a commitment by everyone to contribute to the process. It also requires the organization itself to be seen to support the learning of all its members.

Many voluntary organizations are very 'action-oriented' and this implicitly tends to downgrade the value of the other stages in the experiential learning cycle – reviewing experience, concluding from the experience, and planning implementation (which are all necessary, of course, for effective learning). In such a culture, learning tends not to be rewarded either overtly or implicitly and it therefore becomes viewed as an activity which individuals are expected to do in their own time or at quiet periods when their 'legitimate' work permits. This has to change if voluntary organizations are to take learning seriously. Because culture sets the scene for the other functions, it is depicted in Figure 14.1 as being 'all embracing'.

170   An initiative which aims to build learning into the organization as part of its culture is the use of the Personal Development Plan (PDP). This scheme formed part of Voluntary Service Overseas' Management Development Strategy and was designed to enable VSO managers to take more responsibility and give time to their own individual development. PDPs give a strong message to staff that it is legitimate to use resources to meet individual learning and development needs which are linked to the goals of the organization.

We will now look at the other functions in turn and illustrate examples of good practice from organizations with which we have worked.

Gathering internal experience

The process of gathering internal experience needs to be one based on sharing and exchange. This requires an awareness inside the organization of what it does and the impact of what it does. There are particular 'paper' mechanisms which can be used for this which may include evaluation studies, annual reports, documentary information systems, policy documents, strategic plans and research reports. Many voluntary organizations admit that they are not rigorous enough in evaluating and documenting their work. If administrative and decision-making processes are included as legitimate subjects for evaluation, there are likely to be even fewer examples of good practice.

Water Aid has sought to address this problem by producing a 'Working Methods Directory' which describes the technologies and planning approaches used in each of the organization's overseas programmes. The Directory enables staff to see what experience exists in other programmes and provides opportunities for them to seek advice directly on a specific area from those with the most experience rather than having to go through head office. This example usefully illustrates how the production of a written document can change communication routes in an organization, reducing dependency on a head office and encouraging internal networking.

Discovery – accessing external learning

Organizational learning in voluntary organizations has two major sources: what the organization itself does; and what others do. It is not enough to be clear about what the voluntary organization itself is doing, it must actively seek out learning from elsewhere. In general, the voluntary sector scores high in this area. Voluntary organizations tend to be good networkers and often co-operate in sharing information and taking joint action, particularly in the field of advocacy and campaigning. This requires a genuine openness and willingness to share their own learning with others (which means being willing to share the learning from failure as well as success).

The concept of 'benchmarking' is useful here with its recognition that organizations may learn a lot from looking at 'best practice' in a wide range of other organizations. The voluntary sector has only recently woken up to the idea of benchmarking in the corporate, public, and even the multilateral and bilateral agency sectors (for example UNICEF and the Overseas Development

Administration of the British Government respectively) as well as other voluntary organizations. Some voluntary organizations second staff to agencies which have developed 'best practice' as a way of accessing their experience in a direct and practical way. Others seek outplacement staff from the corporate sector to carry out particular pieces of work, for example in the field of Human Resource Management.

Another source of practical lessons from experience can come from working in partnership with other agencies on joint projects. Partnership with other agencies is a common feature of work in the voluntary sector in the UK. Development organizations such as Oxfam and Action Aid often go one stage further by channelling their funds directly to Southern Hemisphere Non-Government Organizations (NGOs) rather than setting up their own projects in less-developed countries. This creates opportunities for increased exposure to new ideas in a setting where learning can be immediate and influential for both partners.

In an interesting piece of research, INTRAC (a UK-based international training and consultancy organization working in the development field) has been examining the way in which NGOs in the Northern Hemisphere go about strengthening the organizational capacity of their Southern partners. This is a rare example of a voluntary organization setting out explicitly to benchmark good practice and make this information widely available throughout the voluntary sector by producing publications and offering training and consultancy services.

Communication systems

If learning is the lifeblood of the organization, then it requires a circulatory system to enable it to constantly stimulate and refresh all its component parts. Communication systems – both formal and informal – are the circulatory system for learning. Circulatory systems must be designed and maintained in such a way that information and lessons learned reach the other parts of the organization which could use them, and the supply should not be so anaemic that the information offers little or no stimulation to the organization.

The communication style in voluntary organizations we have worked with, for example, has sometimes tended to reflect circulatory systems which are both sclerotic and anaemic. At the sclerotic end many voluntary organizations produce lengthy evaluation reports which are so focused that they often do not encourage a lateral transfer of knowledge – you have to be a dedicated seeker of specific lessons to read them – and which rarely lead to changes in practice. At the opposite end there are informal conversations which identify important lessons which disappear into the ether if they are not shared more widely or documented in some way.

An example of a communication system which has the potential for circulating lessons has been established by the Save the Children Fund (SCF). SCF has developed a 'Global Information System' (which is a database which brings together all significant internal documents which may be of interest to any staff in the organization), and produces a range of internal newsletters and briefing sheets which keep staff and supporters informed about what is going on in the organization. However, like many organizations in the voluntary sector, SCF does not yet provide its staff with universal access to e-mail (which might encourage greater sharing of information between colleagues and would reduce communication costs) and computer networking (which would allow on-line searching of computer databases developed inside and outside the organization).

The voluntary sector has been rather slow to exploit the benefits of the Internet and, particularly, the Worldwide Web. Some notable exceptions to this have been campaigning organizations in the voluntary sector, such as Greenpeace and Amnesty International, which have developed Web sites as a tool in their advocacy work. Newer organizations like The Development Trusts Association are pursuing, with others, computer networking as a way of keeping in touch and sharing learning between members in their federation, which is spread throughout the UK.

Drawing conclusions

The process of drawing conclusions and identifying lessons learned is the main characteristic which differentiates organizational learning from simple information exchange. Drawing conclusions is a process which needs to be seen as the responsibility of the whole organization and should, ideally, happen as near to the source of experience as possible. In many voluntary organizations at present, it tends to be concentrated in those specialist parts of the organization which are associated with research and information. This reflects a division of labour which is commonly (but unhelpfully) associated with organizational learning and which is analysed by Swieringa and Wierdsma in their book *Becoming a Learning Organization*.[9]

One simple mechanism for sharing out the responsibility for drawing conclusions is to insist that all documented experience must have a section considering its learning points and its implications for policy, strategy and practice. From our discussions with voluntary sector managers, most voluntary organizations have a long way to go before this becomes an organizational norm. All agreed that drawing transferable conclusions is a skill which needs to be developed through training, teamwork and good management practices.

The British Red Cross provides a good example of a voluntary organization which attempted to evaluate and draw conclusions from a major campaign. The organization undertook an evaluation of its response to the crisis in Rwanda which focused on management and decision-making processes. A number of recommendations, based on a rigorous analysis of the information, were made and these have subsequently been acted upon. The Red Cross also identified areas of 'best practice' which have been written up for wider distribution. This kind of evaluation requires ready access to the necessary information and an openness about discussing the strengths and weaknesses of the organization's practice.

Developing an organizational memory

Remembering is a crucial element of organizational learning. Although it is true to say that organizations cannot learn, it is reasonable to say that organizations can forget. If learning is locked inside the heads of individuals, the organization becomes very vulnerable if those individuals leave or themselves forget what they learned! The old African proverb that 'when an old person dies, a library is lost' should no longer have to apply within organizations in these days of Information Technology. A Learning Organization needs mechanisms which effectively enable an individual's memory to be 'down-loaded' into an information system so that everyone can continue to access that person's experience and their analysis of that experience long after the individual has left the organization.

Through the use of documentation, databases, resource centres, policy papers, guidelines, training, staff supervision and appraisal, and discussion of experience, an organization can enhance its members' collective memory in ways which unlock each individual's implicit knowledge and place it in the public domain. An excellent example of an organization setting out to improve its memory is the development of a 'Field Office Handbook' by Christian Outreach. The handbook draws on both internal and external experience and covers all the major elements of setting up an overseas office. It was written with the express purpose of preventing the organization 'constantly re-inventing the wheel'. The process of producing the handbook had a useful spin-off for Christian Outreach by helping all those involved in the production of the handbook feel more valued by the organization.

Informal sharing related to problem-solving is also an effective way of ensuring that the corporate memory is expanded and refreshed. In addition, many voluntary organizations have recognized the importance of unlocking each individual's memory but few have, as yet, developed systematic ways of ensuring that their members' knowledge and understanding are made widely accessible to colleagues. This requires an investment of time and other resources in individuals to ensure that they are willing and able to analyse their own experience and make it available to others. One of the key skills here is being prepared to listen to what others have to say. Organizations themselves, though, may have to rethink what they expect from their staff. Learning itself takes time and it must be seen as a legitimate endeavour if staff are to feel safe about devoting time to it.

Integrating learning into strategy and policy

One way of building lessons learned into the fabric of an organization is to develop policy, procedures and practice expectations which reflect organizational learning. This can provide the voluntary organization with a framework for decision making and resource allocation which is grounded in the organization's own experience and that of other agencies. We have come across good examples of integrating learning in our own organization and in others. For example, the Save the Children Fund (SCF) produces a series of 'practice guidelines' on subjects as diverse as 'Evaluation' and 'Communicating with Children' which are based on what it has learned through hard-won experience. SCF also promotes good practice in the field of development by sponsoring international workshops. In conjunction with the Institute of Development Policy and Management at the University of Manchester, SCF organized two internationally acknowledged workshops on the role of non-government organizations in development. The workshops drew heavily on the work of the sponsoring organizations and their partners and the books which were published as a record of these conferences have become very influential in the thinking of development practitioners and policy-makers worldwide.

If policy development is seen as a participative learning process in itself, this strengthens the process of integration and builds the staff commitment necessary for effective implementation. SCF's policies on equal opportunities, for example, were developed in a highly participatory way by involving practitioners as well as managers and policy analysts and are widely recognized as a benchmark standard by many other voluntary organizations.

Integrating learning into organizational strategy is more complex but, potentially, more powerful. Strategy development in voluntary organizations is often a more flexible process than the strategic planning approaches used by many large-scale private and public sector organizations which concentrate on anticipating changes in the external environment and developing contingencies for these. Henry Mintzberg[10] provides a useful model for strategy development which acknowledges the importance of what he calls 'strategic learning'. He suggests that, in the real world, the strategy which is actually implemented and realized by an organization is rarely what was originally intended. Some strategic priorities emerge from opportunities and constraints which the organization faces in its operational work, many of which could not have been anticipated in advance. Some of the organization's strategic intentions may never be realized for whatever reason – perhaps because the window of opportunity passes before the organization can respond; perhaps because the organization prioritizes other strategic goals over those which no longer seem relevant and are allowed to 'fade away'. Ultimately, the importance of a learning approach to strategy is that it enables the organization to respond flexibly and thoughtfully to significant changes in the external environment without simply reacting to events.

Applying the learning

The ultimate test of learning is the ability to apply what has been learned. Only when learning is applied in the work setting can we say that a continuous learning cycle has been created. For many voluntary organizations, the application of learning is not limited only to their own organization but also to the practice and policy of others through the processes of scaling-up and advocacy.

175

Scaling-up is the term used in the voluntary sector to describe the process of increasing the overall impact of the organization. In common with many other voluntary organizations, SCF uses the learning gained from its international work to influence the policy and practice of governments and development organizations worldwide. SCF's impact is based on the reputation and credibility it has developed as an organization involved at grass-roots level with communities worldwide. Reputation and credibility come from an acknowledgement of the quality of its work at local, national and international levels.

Where its work has achieved a high level of recognition, the voluntary organization can build on its experience and then generalize from and use the lessons it has learned to influence the policy and practice of others. A major challenge for voluntary organizations is, therefore, to maximize the impact that they can make by mobilizing the knowledge and skills they have already gained in their work. Many voluntary sector managers have told us that their scaling-up and advocacy work are based on what is probably a relatively small portion of the total knowledge and skill that they have at their disposal. Overcoming this problem requires them to identify the blocks which prevent or constrain learning in their organization, then to develop a strategy for dealing with these blocks.

OVERCOMING BLOCKS TO ORGANIZATIONAL LEARNING

We have suggested that there are considerable benefits to be gained by voluntary organizations which commit themselves to developing their capacity to learn. Many voluntary organizations readily admit that their practice does not always match up to these aspirations even when the importance of organizational learning has been recognized. In discussions with the staff of many voluntary organizations they have acknowledged (with varying degrees of frustration) that their organization has characteristics which make the process of organizational learning difficult. We have found that these blocks – which prevent effective organizational learning – can be usefully categorized under the following:

strategy
structure
systems
human resources
culture
resourcing
values

Strategy here refers to the way in which a voluntary organization uses its resources to achieve its mission; *structure* means the way in which the different functions of the voluntary organization are grouped and allocated to enable the organization to implement its strategy; *systems* are those mechanisms which enable the functions to be carried out effectively and with an efficient use of resources; *human resources* are the volunteers, staff and managers of the organization; *culture* means the basic ideologies and assumptions that guide and shape both individual and organizational behaviour; *resourcing* refers to all the 'non-human' resources such as finances, equipment, buildings and time; and finally *values* are the enduring beliefs about what are desirable and accept-able views and behaviour within the voluntary organization. Each has an effect on the others as can be seen in Figure 14.2.

In our work researching organizational learning in SCF, two main blocks were identified by managers as being related to structure and resourcing in Figure 14.2. The problem of 'departmentalism' was identified most frequently by those interviewed. At the time of the research, SCF was an organization comprised of five departments, each of which had developed its own organiza-tional culture which was determined, in part, by its functions and the profes-sional backgrounds of its staff. This 'departmentalism' sometimes expressed itself in an unhelpful diversity of goals and behaviour which led to departments 'hoarding' information or failing to communicate lessons learned throughout the organization. This rather compartmentalized approach to organizational learning is very common and can lead to the interests of a department being prioritized over the interests of the organization as a whole. As one manager put it: 'We have this tremendous wealth of experience in this organization but

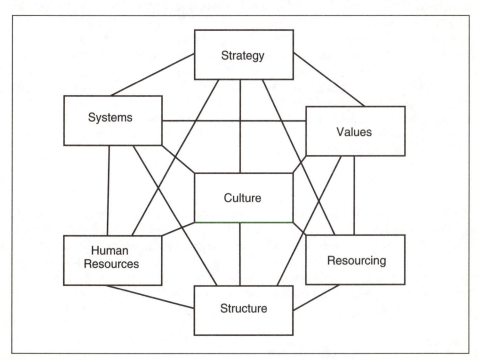

Figure 14.2   Organizational Development framework, based on 'McKinsey 7-s' (Pascale and Athos)[11]

it is locked up in different compartments. The way we are structured means that there is very little cross-fertilization between departments and as a result the learning we acquire is not communicated effectively enough.' A restructuring process of SCF in 1995 may have gone some way to solving this commonly occurring problem.

Lack of time and other resources was also identified as a block to organizational learning by SCF managers. One of our colleagues explained: 'We struggle to find the odd hour, usually in [our] spare time, to learn but that is never going to work. To do it properly you need to put major resources behind doing it'. Organizational learning does require adequate resourcing, and particularly adequate time, devoted to it. Such an investment does two things. First, it creates opportunities for individuals, teams and groups to reflect on and extract lessons from their experience. Second, and perhaps more importantly, it gives a clear signal that learning is viewed by senior managers as a legitimate activity which can and must be prioritized by all members of the organization.

What can be done to strengthen identified weaknesses on the road to becoming a Learning Organization? The eight functions of organizational learning and the seven elements of the Organizational Development (OD) framework described above, when combined in a matrix, provide a useful tool for any voluntary organization to identify practical changes which would help it to build its organizational learning capability. By developing a self-assessment questionnaire, we have encouraged voluntary sector managers to assess their organization's learning capability. We then use each of the OD elements in turn to generate questions with them, the answers to which might suggest practical ways of addressing any identified blocks. For example, one voluntary organization we have worked with recognized that their dependence on a small number of key staff members made them very vulnerable if those individuals were to leave the organization. We encouraged them to look at each of the OD elements in turn and identify action they could take to reduce their vulnerability and to improve their learning capacity. Together, we came up with the following list of activities:

Strategy

Build organizational learning into the organization's strategy so that it becomes identified as a legitimate activity for all staff. Begin to define organizational strategy in terms of what the organization wishes to *avoid* (for example, over-dependence on particular projects or individuals) as well as what the organization wishes to achieve. Involve everyone in a 'bottom-up' approach to implementing the strategy and ensure that the strategic learning is regularly identified.

Structure

Build the organization around teams which are encouraged to meet regularly
to discuss their members' practice.

Systems

Ensure that all staff regularly write up their experience with a view to identifying and sharing lessons learned. Create management supervision and appraisal systems which encourage individuals to reflect on their experience and translate it into usable lessons for others. Build in opportunities for staff to give briefings to colleagues about the nature of their work and what others might learn from it.

Human resources

Broaden the responsibility for learning by providing opportunities for staff to 'learn how to learn', including critical thinking skills. Ensure that when staff leave the organization they are fully debriefed to avoid the loss of individual learning which would be of use to the organization. Create opportunities for staff to visit other parts of the organization and other organizations in order to benchmark good practice.

Culture

Ensure that staff are rewarded for the learning they contribute to the organization by using a range of methods, such as: creating opportunities to present their findings at conferences; providing support to publish their work; offering short sabbaticals to pursue specific pieces of research or writing. Avoid blaming individuals for reasonable errors as this creates defensiveness and deception; place the focus on learning from legitimate errors and not repeating them. Encourage the application of double-loop learning where procedures, policies and guidelines and their underlying assumptions are legitimate subjects for critical assessment.

Resourcing

Recognize that learning takes time. Make sure that all proposals for projects include adequate resourcing to enable learning to become a focal and not a peripheral part of the work.

Values

Encourage openness and reflection that accepts legitimate error and uncertainty so that individuals are not placed under excessive stress because they are afraid to speak out on issues. Encourage a sense of primary account-ability to the users of the organization so that individuals will see the point in strengthening the organization's capacity to respond to the needs of those users. Value diversity and encourage the constructive use of conflict and debate so that individuals do not feel they cannot say what they think or feel.

While some of these activities are not specific to retaining individual experience in an organization, they were all prompted by a concern about being over reliant on a small number of individuals who were viewed as the 'brains' of the organization. The list of activities provides a useful example of the range of ideas which can be generated using a systematic approach to planning organizational learning.

CONCLUSION

We have seen that voluntary sector organizations have some distinctive attributes and that there are particular benefits to be gained from developing as Learning Organizations. Organizational learning is an approach which can sit comfortably inside a value-based organization wishing to give high priority to participation, equal opportunities and quality delivery. The importance attached to accountability to both users and supporters makes it essential that voluntary organizations use their limited resources wisely. Organizational learning must, therefore, be at the heart of every voluntary organization if it is to take its accountability seriously.

By looking at the eight functions of the Learning Organization we have tried to describe some creative examples of how voluntary organizations are building learning into their organizations. In the areas where organizations identified blocks to learning, we have described the use of a tool to address these blocks and to strengthen the organizational learning capability of voluntary sector organizations.

We wish to acknowledge the commitment to learning expressed by the organizations mentioned in this chapter which allowed us to refer to their experiences. We would welcome dialogue with managers and practitioners both within and outside the voluntary sector on both the practical illustrations described here and the applicability of the organizational learning model in their own organizations.

REFERENCES

1 Garvin, David A. (1993), 'Building a learning organization', *Harvard Business Review*, July/August, pp.78–91.

2 Pearn, Michael, Roderick, Ceri and Mulrooney, Chris (1995), *Learning Organisations in Practice*, London: McGraw–Hill.

3 Morgan, Gareth (1986), *Images of Organisation*, London: Sage.

4 Gutch, Richard (1996), 'No pay, no say? No way', *The Guardian*, 13 March.

5 Posnett, John (1992), *Charity Trends: 15th Edition*, West Malling: Charities Aid Foundation.

6 *Ibid.*

7 Knight, Barry (1993), *Voluntary Action*, London: Centris, p. xvii.

8   Slim, Hugo (1993), 'Institutional Learning Review and Future Priorities', unpublished Save the Children paper.

9   Swieringa, Joop and Wierdsma, André (1992), *Becoming a Learning Organization*, Wokingham, England: Addison Wesley.

10 Mintzberg, Henry (1989), *Mintzberg on Management*, New York: Free Press.

11 Pascale, R.T. and Athos, A.G. (1981), *The Art of Japanese Management*, New York: Simon and Schuster.

15 Beyond Investors in People

Brian Reddy, Cheshire Fire Brigade

> Fire like all public services, needs periodically to review its approach to delivering its service to the public. Customer care a common aim within industry and commerce has an equal relevance in public life even though the commodity sold or purchased belongs to the public therefore the process is one of transfer or exchange of professional skills.

This is the first statement in Cheshire Fire Brigade's Chief Officer's publication *Fire and Future Prospects*, published in 1991.[1] It goes on to say:

> The basic need appears [to be] the bringing together of the skills of individuals in a way or culture, which enables each to contribute fully in decision making which is as near as possible to the point where the decision will have to be implemented.
>
> To do this requires a new structure which enables discussion and debate amongst groups of involved Officers. It also requires a change in culture to ensure accountability does not become a moving target with no individual holding true responsibility for decisions, or worse, avoiding a decision.

Was this a dream with no chance of coming into fruition?

The philosophy envisaged a new structure designed to provide a flexible management process which reconciled the needs of operational command, functional objectiveness and supportive management within a territorial environment, while ensuring quality of service. Six years on, Cheshire Fire Brigade has undergone changes to bring about a climate to implement this vision. The results of these changes and the processes that the brigade is still undergoing will be discussed in this chapter.

THE STRUCTURE OF THE FIRE SERVICE

The Fire Service in the United Kingdom was brought into being in 1948 by an Act of Parliament, The Fire Services Act 1947; it was, and still is, an all-encompassing Act. Following the Second World War, the Act returned the Fire

Service from being a national body to the care of local authorities. Following the Local Government Act 1974, the Fire Service was reformed yet again into 65 Authorities. Currently, the Local Government Commission is reviewing the structure of local government at county and district levels; it has already recommended the Welsh Fire Authorities be reduced from eight to three. Who knows how many Fire Authorities will remain when the review is completed in approximately 1999? The Fire Services Act 1947 has not changed in format except for certain minor amendments in 1959.

Bodies directly and indirectly influencing the management of brigades

There are three bodies whose influence pervades every aspect of the Fire Service organization and, therefore, influences the management of the Service at local brigade levels: (1) the Fire Services Act 1947 implemented the formation of the Central Fire Brigades Advisory Council (CFBAC). There are 41 representative places on the council including unions and Local Authority Associations. The Council deals with operational and technical matters; (2) the National Joint Council for Local Authority Fire Brigades (NJC) which deals with pay and conditions of service in the Fire Service. Pay up to and including the rank of Senior Divisional Officer is dealt with by this body; (3) the third body is the Fire Services Inspectorate.

The Central Fire Brigades Advisory Council

The Central Fire Brigades Advisory Council (CFBAC) was set up by the Fire Services Act 1947. The Council advises the Secretary of State on all aspects of the Fire Service. The CFBAC is made up of a Chairman (appointed by the Secretary of State) and representatives of 'the interests of fire authorities and of persons employed as members of fire brigades'. The Secretary of State can also appoint 'such other persons appearing to him to have special qualifications as he may determine'. The present membership of the CFBAC is:

The Association of Metropolitan Authorities (AMA);
The Chief and Assistant Chief Fire Officers Association (CACFOA);
The National Association of Fire Officers (NAFO);
The Fire Brigades Union (FBU);
The Department of the Environment (DofE);
The Home Office (HO);
Her Majesty's Inspector of Fire Services (HMI);
Special Nomination (Chief Fire Officer of London Fire and Civil Defence Authority).

The National Joint Council

The National Joint Council for Local Authority Fire Brigades (NJC) consists of   *183* representatives of the employers and recognized accredited representatives. Since the Fire Services Act 1959 the NJC has effectively determined conditions of service. Together with the Central Fire Brigades Advisory Council the NJC lays down the rules that govern the Service in the United Kingdom. The present membership of the NJC is listed below:

Number of Representatives

Association of County Councils	13
Association of Metropolitan Authorities	9
Confederation of Scottish Local Authorities	7
Northern Ireland	1
National Fire Officers Union	10
Fire Brigades Union	22

The Home Office Inspectorate

The Home Office Inspectorate was also established under the Fire Services Act 1947. The role of the Inspectorate is to advise the Home Secretary on fire matters and use their territorial inspectors and specialist inspectors in the case of fire prevention and technical matters to annually inspect the brigades for performance and report their findings to the Home Secretary. They also advise the Home Secretary on the functioning of Local Authority Fire Brigades and matters regarding the Fire Service, such as establishment levels. Their role also includes advice to brigades on up-to-date information, best practice and recommended minimum fire cover standards to be adopted nationally. The Home Office Inspectorate structure is shown in Figure 15.1.

PUBLIC SECTOR FIRE SERVICE AND MANAGERIALISM

'Managerialism' is an attempt to make something more efficient by better management. The vehicles most commonly used are a combination of proper management, accountable management, consumerism, marketing, and performance management, all of which, if adopted, bring a more business-like approach to the provision of public services, instead of the traditionally based professional values and ethos as pointed out by Isaac-Henry, Painter and Barnes.[2] If this definition of managerialism is accepted, then it seems prudent and obvious that the public sector should be subjected to it. The argument put forward by the Thatcher Government in the early-1980s was that reducing inputs of money and manpower will not only reduce costs directly but will push the public sector organizations (PSO) towards cutting out waste and irrelevance. Privatization has been a key concept of the government through the 1980s. By the 1990s over 50 per cent of the public sector had been placed in private hands with over 650 000 workers transferring to the private sector.[3] Managerialism is well suited to the private sector, where efficiency and effectiveness achieved by better management can be directly related to profit

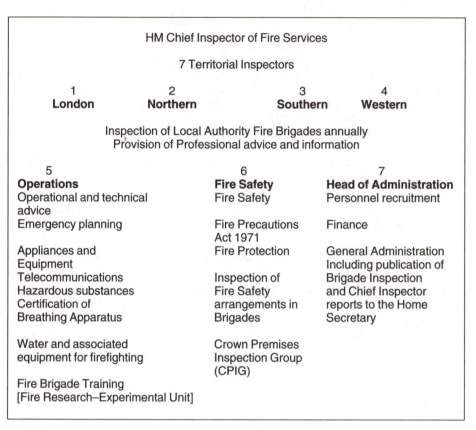

Figure 15.1   The structure of the Fire Service Inspectorate

and loss. A view often expressed is that private business practice offers a set of ready-made solutions to public sector management problems. Another view is that the contrasts in context and process between public and private are so great that any adoption of private sector practices is completely wrong.

Most management reformers like Tom Peters[4] and Isaac-Henry contend that the concept of managerialism offers a more logical, rational and sensible approach to improving public sector performance than existing administrative practice. Part of these reformers' theories assumes that there is no difference between running a Hospital or Fire Brigade and running a Factory or Travel Agent; indeed there are many differences, such as no profit or sales measurements to compare with profit-making organizations. This theory also includes the suggestion that 'professional managers', with academic qualifications in management, are the most suitable people to run everything, including public services. The drive to make the public sector more efficient by better management is nothing new; for example, Fulton[5] was most concerned that, given the size of the Civil Service (then over 730 000 civil servants), and the role it had to play, civil servants did not like the idea of being managers, preferring the role of policy advisers. Painter[6] identified three reasons why mistrust of *185* managers by professionals in the public sector runs deep:

> First, many decisions made in the public sector served professional rather than public interests and in the process bid up the cost of services.
>
> Second, management in the public sector was generally based on consensus and bargaining – the quintessence of incrementalism. Radical changes would be impossible to accomplish given that type of management ethos and style.
>
> Third, public sector management is thought to lack the toughness and the skills to implement the necessary changes.

Governments since the early-1980s encouraged the giving of responsibility to individual managers who possess the skills, status and power to manage and make decisions for the whole organization. This is the position to which a number of local authorities have moved; empowerment, accountability, devolved budgets, cost centres, and decentralization are now very much part of the vocabulary of the public sector. 'Accountable Management' is the term or title used to cover the breaking down of large bureaucratic organizations into smaller more manageable units with delegated power to individuals or groups. The drive towards accountable management in the public sector has been influenced by the statutory requirement on local authorities to put services out to Compulsory Competitive Tendering (CCT). This one initiative made public authorities separate operational matters from more strategic ones in order to see objectives and targets for the contracts, the latter being judged by performance criteria outlined within such contracts.

VALUE FOR MONEY

A major push for value for money (VFM) started during the de-industrialization years of the 1970s, which heralded the setting up of a number of spending control bodies. One was the Efficiency Unit set up in 1980. (This unit was important to the government of the day, taking a value for money approach if future savings were to be made.) Soon, there followed two further developments, the setting up of the Management Information Systems for Ministers (MINIS) and the Financial Management Initiative (FMI). Here, the foundation of accountable management was laid. The FMI was designed to provide managers in departments with clearly defined objectives, and to allocate clear responsibilities for resources and operations. In short, it was to help managers manage. This initiative was followed in the late-1980s by the Government's 'Next Steps Initiative', a further development of this process in its push for a value for money and performance culture in public sector organizations.

The successful introduction of modern management techniques and initiatives into any organization is dependent on the structure, culture, management style and the acceptance of change within that organization, these then are the building blocks of a Learning Organization.

BRIGADE STRUCTURES

The typical Fire Brigade structure is classically hierarchical and bureaucratic with its rigid rules and autocratic style. It has high values and ethos which have changed very little in 40 years. This system, introduced immediately after the war, has met Service requirements. The structure in most brigades followed a similar typical organization tree since their creation in 1948.

However, since 1985 there has been an increasing number of brigades changing to a flatter structure with shorter lines of communication, and away from the isolated organization. When a joint working party of the Central Fire Brigades Advisory Council (CFBAC) reviewed the rank structure in 1973 (the last time it was reviewed), they recommended abolishing the Deputy Chief Fire Officer rank. They also recommended an additional Senior Divisional Officer rank, leaving the Service with 12 ranks. Under the present system of operational fire management, as a fire spreads and more and more fire engines, and therefore firefighters, are called to it, so higher and higher ranking officers will attend. Tiny graduations in the 12-rank system, with a pecking order that must be respected, results in ineffective hand-over of the command and control of incidents. This confusion of multiple ranks and hand-over also created problems at the London Underground fire, at King's Cross in 1987, that claimed thirty lives (including the life of a firefighter). A reduction in the number of ranks at Divisional Officer level, from four to two, has been carried out in a number of brigades. The abolition of the Leading Firefighter rank has also been put forward by reviews into rank structure. Mr Robinson, the current Chief Fire Officer of the London Fire and Civil Defence Authority, suggests that a maximum of six ranks in the service would be the correct number to remove confusion, and facilitate the proper training of senior officers to equip them with the skills to competently provide the command and control to manage large fires.

Arguments can, and are, put forward for a flatter structure that improves the day-to-day management of the service. New, flatter structures are currently being introduced into a number of brigades. The reasons most commonly given for this movement are:

- improved communications;
- costs savings;
- devolved authority;
- empowerment;
- devolved responsibility.

However, the first of these is difficult to measure; certainly shorter lines of communication should in theory result in improved communications, but in practice the steps are fewer but much larger to span – this results in less people to pass the messages; the quality may be improved but the quantity is greatly reduced. It is interesting to note the trend which is equalizing the whole time establishments (the number of people funded) to actual strengths (the

187

number employed) in the UK Fire Brigades that has come about in recent years, coinciding with the push for value for money and flatter structures being introduced (see Figure 15.2).

The same arguments can be put for a reduced number of ranks to improve management and communications in the Service.

RANK STRUCTURES

As a result of organizational changes it is not possible to compare ambulance ranks with the other emergency services, therefore, the army has been used as the third comparison (see Table 15.1).

Ranks are only broadly comparable due to differing responsibilities. For instance, Chief Superintendent and Senior Divisional Officer ranks are sometimes Principal Officers appointed directly by their respective Authorities and are thus subject to regional variations.

However, it can be easily seen that the Fire Service has a smaller incremental scale compared to the police. They both have very similar types of command responsibility especially in emergency situations but the army has smaller incremental scales especially at the lower and middle ranks. This may be because of the differing requirements of a combat role. The large number of hand-over situations, when an emergency situation is developing, has been

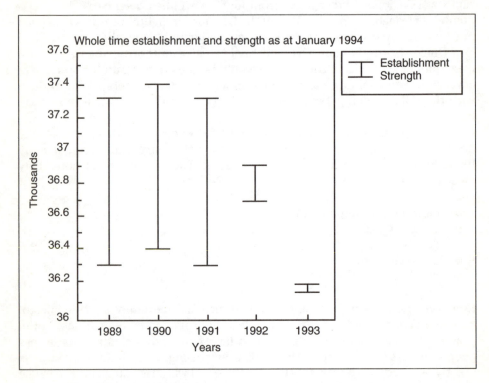

Figure 15.2   The narrowing gap

Table 15.1   Rank structure in three services

POLICE	FIRE	ARMY
Constable	Firefighter	Private
		Lance Corporal
	Leading Firefighter	Corporal
Sergeant	Sub Officer	Sergeant
		Staff Sergeant
		Regimental Sergeant Major
Inspector	Station Officer	Lieutenant
Chief Inspector	Assistant Divisional Officer	Captain
	Divisional Officer (3)	Major
	Divisional Officer (2)	Lieutenant Colonel
Superintendent	Divisional Officer (1)	
Chief Superintendent	Senior Divisional Officer	Brigadier
Deputy Assistant Chief Constable	Assistant Chief Officer	Major General
		Lieutenant General
Assistant Chief Constable	Deputy Chief Fire Officer	General
Chief Constable	Chief Fire Officer	Field Marshal
9 Ranks	**12 Ranks**	**15 Ranks**

proven at several incidents where firefighters have lost their lives to be a contributory factor to the problems experienced in successful command. The Army for instance, place a major emphasis on communications and reconnaissance, which may provide the answer as to why their large rank structure does not seem to impair communications during non-emergency actions. However when time is of the essence in emergency situations, shorter lines of communication have been seen to improve this area, which is recognized in the British Fire Service as being a problem one. There is no reason why the Fire Service should not take note of these findings and review the rank structure in the Fire Brigades, and the ranks be substantially reduced in number.

BRIGADE CULTURE

The Fire Service was, and still is, in many respects a very traditional, hierarchical, disciplinarian, closed and predominantly single-sex organization. The culture within it reflects, and to a large extent protects, those values and practices built up over three generations. Perhaps more than any other subject, culture is the one area that has provoked the most discussion and interest and is the most misunderstood reason for the resistance to change and the introduction of what seem perfectly legitimate managerial initiatives *189* being introduced quickly and smoothly into the service. Successful implementation revolves around changing attitudes to long-term beliefs and questioning values and practices that have developed over 50 years, since the existing Fire Service was set up in 1947.

Is there an ideal organizational culture?

It is suggested that excellent organizational cultures are those in which the people who work in such organizations share the following assumptions:

Equity

Relationships among members are seen as equitable – that is, they feel they can trust one another and see their personal, sectional and divisional interests as congruent with brigade and corporate interests. Excellent organizations share the value of 'productivity through people'. These organizations are able to motivate their employees by helping them 'shine' and feel like winners. Employees come to feel that the organization cares about them and will reward them and recognize them. Tom Peters[7] claims that the only way to achieve an 'excellent' corporate culture is to start with the assumption that excellence is an 'all-hands effort'. Thus, virtually all these successful organizations have a deep belief in the dignity, worth and creative potential of all their people.

Competency

Members of organizations develop unique competencies or skills and each individual sees how his or her work fits into the broader whole. If culture is to provide the glue that binds the organization together, it must somehow help the organization's participants define how they uniquely relate to one another; that is, the culture must clarify that participants can do better than anyone else. It requires very distinctive leadership individuals who delight in training others to perform more effectively than themselves. However, achieving this goal requires more than one person's vision. It may be that primarily one person articulates the dream, but people from all parts of the organization must interpret it and define how each person fits into the vision.

Adaptability

Ideal cultures develop unique competencies, for example, how work is to be done, what is acceptable and what is not acceptable. These ideal cultures can retain those competencies in changing situations.

The excellent culture, it is said, contains the seeds of its own change. Culture, if it is passed on as broad assumptions and values, rather than as rigid rules and practices, allows for flexibility. Given the motivation and general sense of the business that people have in excellent cultures, people are usually very willing to do whatever it takes to make the organization successful. If this includes adapting to a changing environment, this too can be built into a valued system. This should also assure people that risks and failures are part of the natural order of change; that is a no-blame culture. Without an acceptance of some failure, no one will try to learn anything new. Experimentation and learning can facilitate the adaptation and evolution of a cultural competence that can remain distinctive as well as keep up with the times.

The vision

As already referred to earlier, the Chief Officer of Cheshire Fire Brigade published *Fire and Future Prospects* in 1991. This document outlined his vision; the vision involved changing the management style to a more open, team approach, with a participative style of management and change of culture which revolved around changing attitudes, long-term beliefs, old practices and questioning values built up over 50 years. To implement the vision a number of mechanisms and tools were used, Total Quality Management (TQM) was practised and Quality Circles (QC) introduced. In these Quality Circles rank played little part in the decision-making processes. The government-backed initiative Investors In People (IIP) was becoming available at this time and proved one of the most important tools in achieving the vision's implementation.

To be successful I would suggest all organizations have to pay attention to at least six important areas.

- Management
- Planning
- Communications
- Responsibility
- Training
- Standards

Many line managers perceived the old practices as fundamental, reflecting the old beliefs and values.

Management – 'Do as I say not as I do.'
Planning – There was none; a reactive organization.
Communications – Knowledge is power so hold on to it. This encouraged rumours, if there are enough of them some will turn out to be true.
Responsibility – All are told what to do and when to do it.
Training – Repetitive, sometimes as a punishment. It was not seen as beneficial, just something that had to be done each day.
Standards – The Service did have standards; however, many were not measurable and were therefore left to an individual's interpretation.

To change a culture and influence the values in any organization takes a   *191* great deal of effort. Commitment must be from the top down. Management must believe in and sell the change to the whole workforce and get their commitment prior to any planned implementation. The timescale required to change a company or service industry, whether private or public sector, to a Learning Organization will vary immensely. In the Fire Service changes can be implemented very quickly. The disciplined nature of the Service assists in this, however, the Service is very traditional and resistance to change is very real and can be considerable. It may take a generation to accept the culture change, to become an established and accepted Learning Service Organization.

Just four years after the start of the culture change Cheshire Fire Brigade has restructured and has moved a long way down the road to changing its culture. It now has a defined training and development cycle for all its employees as follows:

the business plan;
personal interviews and development plans;
an annual skills audit and matrix;
an annual training audit;
Training and Development courses plan;
a comprehensive evaluation system for all Training and Development.

BENEFITS FROM THE CHANGES

The initiatives have turned our Training and Development on its head; from a top-down, 'we know best' approach, to a bottom-up, 'people come first' process which proceeds budget setting to meet these needs. This turning round and formalization of the process has resulted in addressing the issues. Whole sections were being ignored previously, they were treated as second-class citizens as far as Training and Development was concerned.

The results of all the activity and attention to detail are a 25 per cent increase in training courses being attended within the same budget parameters, and perhaps more important, the Training and Development being more focused where individuals and their line managers identify and agree the areas of Training and Development courses needed.

The changes are:

Management – People now have a better understanding of business and service objectives with a greater knowledge of opportunities, and constraints the business is under.
Planning – Employees at all levels are involved in planning and are encouraged to put forward ideas to improve service delivery.
Communications – People have opened up, become more trusting and communicating with each other to solve problems.
Responsibility – With this improved knowledge and involvement, staff are more ready to take on responsibility and the accountability that goes with it. Better decisions are being made with an increasing number of quality ideas coming forward.

Training – The appraisal process has brought together all levels of staff and assisted managers to understand subordinates' roles; this has helped clarify Training and Development needs.

Standards – Standards and targets are now defined and agreed. This has shown perhaps one of the greatest improvement areas resulting from the Investors in People initiative. A competency-based training system introduced an understanding by all employees of the levels of competency required, with defined standards and achievement levels.

Benefits accruing from an organizational learning approach can also be listed into three areas, individual, departmental and organizational. These benefits are being detected following the changes in the Fire Service and they are:

1   Individual:

    (a)   full utilization of potential;
    (b)   involvement in planning work and their future;
    (c)   provides a feeling of and actual achievement;
    (d)   provides a forum for recognition based on performance;
    (e)   makes the individual know what the job is;
    (f)   encourages self-management;
    (g)   appraises the manager;
    (h)   gives the individual a chance to air their views.

2   Departmental:

    (a)   improved communications and relationship with staff;
    (b)   greater understanding of subordinates' functions;
    (c)   provides a forum for ideas;
    (d)   aids long-term planning;
    (e)   increases subordinates' efficiency;
    (f)   clarifies roles.

3   Organizational:

    (a)   increased productivity and greater efficiency;
    (b)   higher quality of service outputs;
    (c)   greater flexibility in meeting customer needs;
    (d)   attracts higher-calibre employees;
    (e)   reduces staff turnover and absenteeism;
    (f)   greater motivation and commitment.

The Audit Commission published *In the Line of Fire* in 1994. This national report on the Fire Service was followed up in 1995 by an inspection of brigades. In 1995 Coopers and Lybrand, local authority auditors and management consultants, published a report on Cheshire Fire Brigade. The following two quotes from that report reflect our achievements to date, following a Learning Organization approach:

We were very impressed during the course of our work with the commitment and enthusiasm which was displayed by all those we met, and in particular with the open way which issues could be discussed and alternative views aired. We believe this is greatly enhanced by the new management structure and culture which has been introduced to the Brigade gradually over the past five years.

We have already commented that we believe the new management structure and open management style has enabled the Brigade to develop progressively and to pursue the objective of providing a quality service.

REFERENCES

1   Davis, D.T. (1991), *Fire and Future Prospects*, Cheshire Fire Brigade.

2   Isaac-Henry, K., Painter, C. and Barnes, C. (1991), *The management challenge in local government studies*, London: Chapman & Hall.

3   Figures quoted in *The Times*, 18 February 1989.

4   Peters, T. and Waterman, R. (1982), *In Search of Excellence*, New York: Harper and Row.

5   Fulton, J. (1969), *Great Britain and the Civil Service, The Civil Service, Volume 1*, Report of the Committee Cmnd 3638, London: HMSO.

6   Isaac-Henry, K. and Painter, C. (1993), *Management in the public sector: challenge and change*, London: Chapman & Hall.

7   Peters and Waterman, *In Search of Excellence*.

BIBLIOGRAPHY

Home Office (1989), *Future Fire Policy: A Consultative Document*, London: HMSO.

Reddy, B. (1994), *Where are we now?*, (unpublished dissertation), Preston: University of Central Lancashire.

16 Learning to change

Richard Wells, South Yorkshire Police

'*Quoi? Quand je dis: "Nicole, apportez-moi mes pantoufles, et me donnez mon bonnet de nuit", c'est de la prose?*': just as Monsieur Jourdain, in Molière's *Le Bourgeois Gentilhomme*, had sought to learn from his Master of Philosophy what 'prose' was, only to be bowled over by the discovery that he had been speaking it for 40 years, so too the South Yorkshire Police discovered, with some surprise, that what it had been doing for five years of cultural change marked it out as a Learning Organization.

Our outfit – 4 500 strong and with a £147 million budget – had battled through the rigours of the 1984 mining dispute. Officers had faced the daunting odds of thousands of physically robust and tough-minded miners, mobilized into active protest through fear of the decimation of their life-supporting industry and egged on to violence by political activists. The South Yorkshire officers often came from mining families themselves, and were determined to do no more than their duty, holding the political ring between employer and employee and keeping the Queen's Peace. Intervention by activists, by police forces from other parts of the country, and by central government put a radical spin on that task. Whatever the outcome of the dispute between owner and employee, government and trade union, the police task was successfully discharged.

Just five years later came the Hillsborough tragedy in which 97 innocent souls lost their lives in about the same number of seconds on the terraces of Sheffield Wednesday Football Club's ground. Some say that the 98th casualty was the reputation of the South Yorkshire Police. In the face of vituperative criticism from Merseyside, who had borne the brunt of the losses, from some quarters of the media and, though in the more restrained words of the judiciary, from Lord Justice Taylor, the organization battened down the hatches and determined to ride out the storm.

I had a different perspective. I had long admired the quiet strength and dignity of the South Yorkshire officers in their role in the 1984 dispute and knew that the police force with which I then served – London's Metropolitan

Police – was not blameless in the way we had sometimes trampled on the sensitivities of a territory with whose culture and way of life we had been unfamiliar. In my last post with the Met., I had been responsible for policing Wembley and had commanded the 1989 all-Merseyside Cup Final when the appalling behaviour of some of the fans at the time of the Hillsborough disaster had been repeated for all to see. When I was offered the Chief Constableship of South Yorkshire in June 1990, I knew that I was inheriting from a much admired predecessor a force of ability and pride which had momentarily lost its way.

CULTURAL CHANGE

I anticipated that cultural change would be necessary. The Police Service is, almost by definition, conservative in nature – usually reacting to circumstances and drawing eccentric behaviour inwards through the centrifugal force of the law. It need not be so, but it's often the way we are. Since confession is good for the soul, I think it's worth establishing now that, in 1990, I did not come to South Yorkshire planning to make the police a Learning Organization; a practitioner and pragmatist, I was never at the forefront of managerial theory and, as Learning Organization thinking developed in the late 1980s and early 1990s, I was a stranger to its creed. But I *did* come expecting the South Yorkshire Police to be an organization which could learn.

The traditional culture of the Police Service is white, male, conservative and reactionary. It was born into intense unpopularity in the early 1800s,[1] when even the name *police* grated harshly on the ears of a populace who had cherished its enmity with the French. Through tight discipline and a strongly enforced hierarchy of formal rank, it achieved a tight organizational grip on its members – many being soldiers of fortune returning from the Crimea, for whom drink and womanizing were reinforcements of life and survival. It dragged its reputation steadily upward, through bravery and devotion; it kept its behaviour free of criticism largely by rigid observance of rule and diktat.

When I joined in 1962, officers' houses (when they could afford them) were visited by senior ranks to see that they were 'suitable' and (an even greater intrusion) spouses were vetted! Armlets were still worn to indicate that a Constable was on duty and therefore not allowed to drink alcohol; it was an offence under the then Licensing Acts[2] for a licensee to serve a Constable with drink when the officer was on duty and, under Police Regulations, for the Constable to remove the armlet when on duty with intent to deceive a licensee. The City of London Police still sport their red and white striped armlets in a touching gesture to tradition.

This same traditional culture, which achieved ascendancy for the Service through tight grip, did not always distinguish between leading by firmness and controlling by fear. Even today, there are too many accounts (including, sadly, in South Yorkshire) which show that insensitivity or, worse, bullying exist in place of coaching. This, in turn, produces 'insurance' behaviour, with lightweight decisions pushed up what is seen as a vertical rank system to quite inappropriate levels, bringing a strong tendency to centralization and an atmosphere of mistrust. For example, the old culture is very happy to consign even small requests to paper. That paper is then pushed 'up' the organization, with intermediate grades annotating the progress of the file in a meaningless series of 'seen and noted' signatures. These add nothing to the communication process but insure the signatory against later repercussion that the file was not passed on. The focus was not on the worth of the process, the appropriate level or speed of the decision making, but on keeping one's backside intact. In a bid to end this, the South Yorkshire Police issued in 1992 a directive called, simply, 'Cutting Out the Middle Man' which urged all ranks and grades to consider, before committing a request to paper, whether paper was the best medium for the communication. If it was, then to consider who could best facilitate the request. The paper was then to be sent directly to that person, with intermediate points being used only if they were strictly necessary and would *add value* to the process. The new direction took some time to implement and those 'excluded' felt, for a while, at a loss to know what to do with the time earlier wasted on unnecessary paper-flow, and uncomfortable at the loss of control over what had always seemed important.

Another cultural belief whispers to us that the public are 'them' and inclined to bring bad news; we are the professionals and the more we keep our work secret, and tell the public what service they are entitled to, then the safer we will be. This can become institutionalized in our buildings: only the Police Service could have provided, in the author's day, an address of $26^{1}/_{2}$ Rosslyn Hill, NW3, to keep visitors to Hampstead guessing at where to find help. Once found (courtesy of the corrective influence of the traditional blue lamp), the old culture provided a cramped-counter, dark-varnished, beige-painted clinicity of reception to discourage lingering. Sometimes there were added, in bursts of wild creativity, posters to identify comprehensive breeds of missing dog or to educate in the prospective ravages of the Colorado Beetle. (The Metropolitan Police Service has now bought the half-house adjoining the old Police Station and the site now boasts the full number '26' for its address *and* a splendidly refurbished reception area.)

In the field, officers are endlessly brave, pragmatic and wise. Return them to their stations and the old culture seems to squeeze out the bravery and the creativity from them, leaving for managers a difficult mix of dry wit, scepticism and a cramped silence. The challenge, for any police leader, and teams of leaders, is to unlock the courage, the solutions and the wisdom, turning personnel outward from preoccupation with their own or the organization's needs to a point where they put the public first. Simple picture: wet High Street, constable on duty. Member of public wants to cross road and constable is about to help when senior officer appears on scene. Traditional culture: constable quickly forgets public need and organizational survival takes over – look after 'the gaffer'. The changes are broadly indicated at Figure 16.1. That was the dynamic direction but just how did we learn to do that?

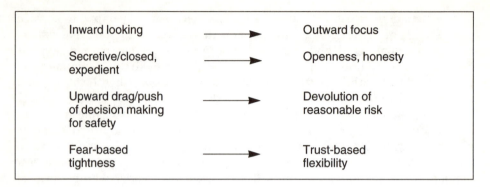

Figure 16.1   Planning change

SETTING SOME TARGETS

I have never been keen on revisionist writing of organizational history. It can make some marvellous silk purses of what have been real pig's ears of a job. For all that, there were broad elements of planning in what we intended to do. And here, I can lapse with relief into the protective comfort of the first person plural, since the Senior Command Team – the five Chief Officers – all gradually came to a consensus and shared in the proposed changes. If there were one thing to be done differently, it would be for me to have tapped earlier and more coherently into the strengths and shared vision of those four colleagues (it was a bit too much of a solo flight for too long). Between us we knew – although we did not always articulate in those early days – that there was a need for the culture to change and that the change should be led by a mission statement of sorts. The need for a 'mission' had occurred more by osmosis than by conscious learning. All of us had experienced, on different courses and in different readings, that a mission was 'a good thing'.[3]

On my arrival in Force, in preparation for meetings with the staff associations, I had prepared some eight pointers to the way in which I wanted to do business with people; the discussions produced a couple more and I used to chat about these ten points informally to officers at the time of their promotion. To my amazement, in one of many frequent early tours around the police area (a conscious part of two-way organizational learning), I found that a station had had these computerized (see Figure 16.2) under the heading 'The Chief Constable's "10-Point Plan"'. They did not deserve the dignity of the title but it made me realize that the organization was not only learning but willing to teach itself.

From that insight, the Senior Command Team was spurred on to giving greater certainty and framework to the process of forming the 'Plan'. We canvassed over 250 groups in the community about what should be our purpose as a Police Service, what our core values should be and how they would want us to do business with them. We did the same across the Force, additionally asking for crisp phrases which might become the Force motto,

South Yorkshire
POLICE
JUSTICE *with* COURAGE

CHIEF CONSTABLE'S '10-POINT PLAN'

1 Emphasis on public service
2 Staff care for customer care
3 Human face
4 Reasonableness of action
5 Communication of doubt upwards
6 Catching people doing right
7 Regular meetings to establish common ground
8 Do not waste any energy fighting each other
9 Honesty with courtesy
10 Allow individuality

Figure 16.2   The Chief Constable's '10-Point Plan'

Source: ©R.B. Wells

since, at the time, there was none.

It is important that the canvassing was *across the Force*. In learning to value our personnel, we came latterly to realize how damaging it was to work constantly with the model and language of a vertical hierarchy, which produced repeated verbal reinforcement of our front-line officers being at the *bottom* – not a place where their skills or courage deserve to be portrayed. We now try to work with a disk-shaped model (see Figure 16.3), using language like 'pushing out' or 'drawing in' information, with references to 'the centre' or 'the front-line', and emphasizing the strong interrelationship of roles and ranks, each with different but equal importance to the corporate goals.

The '10-Point Plan' document still reveals the old thinking in the use of the expression 'Communication of doubt upwards', which I had borrowed from contemporary accounts of 'Action Learning'.[4] To be truthful, it is still very common to hear 'up/down; top/bottom' references in our everyday discussions; the hierarchy – very necessary at times of operational crisis – constantly feeds the top–bottom metaphor.

Participation in the process of consultation over our 'mission' was patchy, though most were pleased to be asked. Others thought that mission statements were 'the gaffer's job' not theirs. We provided a blank sheet for 'spoof'   *199*

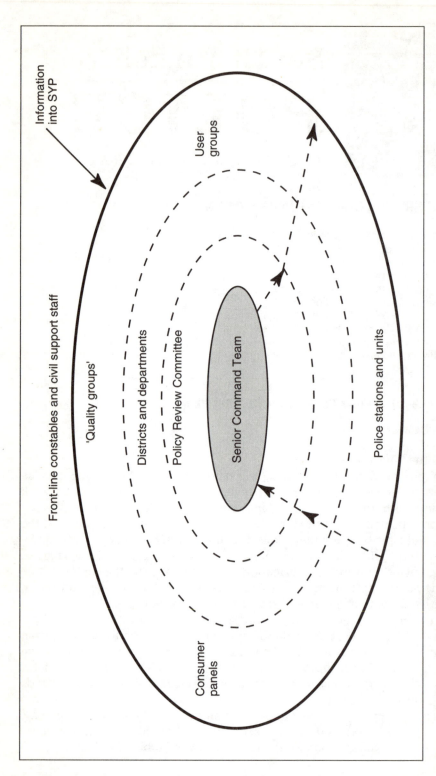

Figure 16.3 Interrelationships of roles and ranks

Source: © R.B. Wells

suggestions, knowing that the sceptical culture would throw them up anyway, and received some very amusing contributions that helped the toil of sifting the serious suggestions. A Sergeant from our choir contributed 'Justice with Courage' as a prospective motto (from his singing of Judas Maccabeus) and this has been adopted as part of our corporate design. Comedians thought that we might attract useful sponsorship with 'Justice with Watney's'.

All of the community and police suggestions were computerized, categorized and presented to the Senior Command Team in hard copy. We took ourselves away from our offices for two days – the organization has learnt that 'away days' achieve more in terms of both process and task – and first, pulled the material into continuous prose and then divided it into the bullet points of our 'statement of purpose and values' (see Figure 16.4). The internal process was shaped, at least in part, by national police directions of the time from which we were prepared to learn but by which we did not want to be restricted.

Also nationally popular at the time was the restructuring of police forces, now variously described as 'down-sizing', 'hollowing out' or 'delayering'. The Senior Command Team decided that cultural change should come first and structural change later. There were sound reasons for this. The earlier culture in the Force was still very 'tight' and traditional. Its strengths were high levels of integrity, physical courage and commitment. Its weaknesses lay in its surprising lack of self-assurance, its closedness and its strong sense of compliance with adult male authority. If not loosened by cultural change, these would militate against the consultative and participative processes needed to change the structure in such a way that there was a sense of investment in it by those who were later to make it work.

RHETORIC TO REALITY

The launch of the 'statement of purpose and values' was not an instant success. We took some steps to market its arrival by offering it back to the intermediate command ranks for amendment (only one change was suggested and that was adopted) and by asking the intermediate commanders to prepare, with their teams, plans for its broadcast and translation into action. Despite these precautions, it was greeted with considerable cynicism. I wrote a personal letter to each of the (then) 4 346 staff, topping-and-tailing each in ink with a first-name salutation and concluding greeting. The letter offered a clear and emphatic new deal: if officers and staff behaved lawfully, honestly and reasonably, they would be supported, even if they made mistakes. In exchange, they were asked to go out of their way, every day, to increase the constituency of those who would vote 'Yes' for the South Yorkshire Police.

Some doubtless greeted this with derision and mistrust; from others it met with apathy. A significant number took it seriously, although we were never quite sure what conscious links they made between it and their practical duties. A piece of in-house research established that the statement had achieved approximately 40 per cent penetration within 18 months and this aspect was to be further tested by research in spring 1996. The organization, as

THE SOUTH YORKSHIRE POLICE SERVICE

Statement of purpose and values

Our purpose

on behalf of the general public is:

- to uphold the Rule of Law
- to keep the Queen's Peace
- to prevent and detect crime
- to protect life and to help and reassure people in need.

Our values

In achieving our purpose, we must at all times strive to:

- act within the law, serving with integrity the ends of justice
- act fairly and reasonably, without fear or favour and without prejudice of any kind
- ensure that the rights of all citizens – especially the vulnerable – are safe-guarded, regardless of status, race, colour, religion, sex or social background
- be courageous in facing physical danger or moral challenge
- be honest, courteous and tactful in all that we do and say
- use persuasion, common sense and good humour wherever possible as an alternative to the exercise of force and, if force is finally necessary, to use only that which is necessary to accomplish our lawful duty.

Our way of working

In upholding these fundamental values, it will help us to be more effective in working together and with our communities if we:

- maintain the dignity of our office yet display humanity and compassion
- constantly practise high standards of personal and professional conduct
- remember that, although the office of constable carries power and authority, respect must be earned
- listen and try to understand the other person's point of view
- confront those who bully or exploit on behalf of those less than able to protect themselves
- act with a willingness to try new ways of working
- speak moderately, yet firmly and proudly, of what we do well
- admit our failings promptly and apologize for our mistakes
- show determination and resourcefulness in helping others.

'Justice with Courage'

Figure 16.4   Statement of purpose and values

a whole, learned to take it more seriously as senior officers linked the practical delivery of its values closely, and realistically, to promotion, career development and discipline, using it alternatively as a framework for questions on selection boards or by linking judgments in discipline tribunals (effectively court martial hearings) specifically to its precepts.

We learned, as a Senior Command Team, that in an action-oriented culture like ours, production of rhetoric can be both unproductive and counter-productive,[5] creating more diversion than unity, no matter how much effort goes into linking it to practice. Nevertheless, the 'Statement of Purpose and Values' is now widely accepted as a backdrop to our more open culture; it is not so much learned by heart as absorbed subliminally!

A sister document was unashamedly non-consultative: the Chief Constable's personal vision for the next five years was published simultaneously as 'Our Six-Hill Horizon' (see Figure 16.5) and, ironically, seemed to meet with very little opposition. We don't know why: perhaps – though unlikely, given the existing culture – its content was unexceptionable; perhaps the old culture of 'just tell us what to do and we'll do it' relished the absence of choice! The Senior Command Team tried consciously *not* to learn from the relative comfort afforded by this prescriptive mode – it was all too tempting. 'Our Six-Hill Horizon' has now reached its allotted five-year span. In an exercise in which the Senior Command Team sat down and considered its future strategy, and the role of 'Our Six-Hill Horizon' in it, it was decided that the document was still instructive and should remain, with some minor alterations to render it timeless in its relevance.

THE SOUTH YORKSHIRE POLICE SERVICE

Our Six-Hill Horizon

Within five years, or as soon as practicable, to have a South Yorkshire Police Service which:

1. is more open, relaxed and honest with itself and the public
2. is more aware of our environment, sensitive to change and is in a position to respond to change
3. is more clear about its role and identity and is obviously and justifiably proud of itself
4. is more closely in touch with its customers, puts them first and delivers what they want quickly, effectively and courteously
5. makes its decisions at the appropriate levels
6. is the envy of all other forces.

Figure 16.5   The 'Six-Hill Horizon'

Source: © R.B. Wells

CHANGING THE CENTRE OF GRAVITY

For the most part, however, the organization moved consciously towards greater consultation in policy making, and towards greater involvement of the user in our provision of equipment and in our communication.

In my early days in office, the first two meetings between the Chief Officers' team and the Chief Superintendents were largely sterile recitals of pre-circulated reports. These were read over at the meeting, comment being invited by the chairman – the Chief Constable. Little comment ensued and there was significant deference to the chair. A number of techniques of process and task were introduced to help the group to learn different values: the meetings were taken out of Headquarters and rotated around the territorial districts to give a sense of ownership, a method employed in an earlier command; emphasis was changed from rank to role (although it was not expressed in that way at the time; senior officers were stopped from interrupting junior officers in mid-flow). This sent a clear message that contributions from junior officers were valued as much as those from the more senior ranks; as Chief Constable, and as a new arrival to the organization, I was frequently and genuinely able to say that I did not understand a situation or a structure and would ask people closer to the 'sharp end' for their view. The organization has now learned to value these processes.

The idea of rotating the meetings outside HQ worked well in these early days, moving the centre of gravity towards the outlying districts who often felt neglected and the poor relation to HQ. Since they *were* often the poor relation, practical accommodation did not always meet theoretical requirements and, over time, we resorted more and more to the 'neutral' territory of our Sports and Social Club for such meetings. But the signal had been sent once and for all: people were no longer automatically summoned to the centre for meetings; the centre, with others, travelled out to meet its 'customers'.

Insisting that people could contribute uninterrupted – an expected courtesy in some quarters – made a marvellous contribution to breaking unnecessary reliance on hierarchy, freeing up young, creative (and sometimes rebellious) minds to enrich the discussion. Pheysey[6] writes compellingly in this context on distinctions between 'power cultures' and 'role cultures'. Some of these more enthusiastic and assertive junior contributors also had to be reminded themselves, on occasions, not to interrupt. Courtesy, it had to be pointed out, cut both ways.

As the freshness of vision clouded with increasing years in Force, we set great store by attracting other sources of this clarity of view: observers were invited to the Committee, from inside the Service and from beyond, whose frank views are canvassed, whether as a front-line officer or as a member of the public. The South Yorkshire Police constantly invites visitors, whether from government offices, the private sector or other forces. This is partly to soak up that 'outside' perspective (see Egan on 'identifying blind-spots')[7] but also to send a clear message to those working from our police stations: the Force is proud of itself. The invariable message to those visiting is: 'Turn left, look in any cupboard and talk to anyone you want'.

From what was called 'The Chief Superintendents' Meeting' (a misnomer – they were summoned but it was not *their* meeting) we have moved to a Strategy Group – the five Chief Officers, fed with sufficient information to determine the principal directions of the Force – and this interlinks with a Policy Review Committee. The Policy Review Committee now has a much expanded member-ship, reflecting role rather than rank and still inviting observers from the front-line as well as trades unions and staff associations. The observers are invariably asked to give an informed practitioner view to aid decision making. An interesting phenomenon – and performance indicator – is the gradual reduction of the informal gatherings which used to follow formal meetings, as members huddled together in interest groups to say the sort of things to each other that they should have said *at* the formal meetings. Exchanges are now more open and informal agenda more honestly expressed. Each Policy Review Committee meeting has, as its last agenda item, 'How Did We Do Today?' as a mechanism for learning about the way we do business together.

We have formed widespread user-groups to ensure that those who have to make use of clothing, vehicles and equipment are allowed a positive and influential say in its provision. Not listening to these views has been a resistant part of 'Headquarters culture', resulting in our providing kit which was not wanted or valued and which was, consequently, badly treated. The groups have provided a sense of ownership.

Whenever we can, we employ 'consumer panels' to test out our communication processes – trying draft words out on those who are going to have to convert policy into practice, to see if the words are comprehensible and the actions required practical.

IMPACT FROM BEYOND THE SERVICE

We are also learning from a whole range of outside advice. (Some of this we are unable to avoid.) The Home Secretary has a statutory duty in overseeing the provision of an effective Police Service to the community and quantitative benchmarks – centrally set key objectives in crime reduction – are set, now enshrined in statute law. Part of the same law requires Chief Constables to draw up a policing plan for their Police Authority who then, with greater or lesser amendment, adopt it. All Police Forces are learning to cope with these new fetters on the constitutional freedom to act within their own discretion as well as learning to manage those expanded freedoms, encouraged through devolution of greater financial accountability.

Not obligatory, but very much part of the contemporary police scene, is the access offered by consultants. As the world of policing has become more open to scrutiny and more attuned to the business world, droves of consul-tants beat upon Chief Constables' doors to offer incomparable bargains. These range from the 'one-self-taught-musician band' to the 'corporate-singing-and-dancing-ensemble'. We have learned, as organizations, when to afford our-selves this valuable advice and when to hold on to our watches and teach   *205* ourselves to tell the time. Discrimination is not easy in this context. Our own technique has been to avoid rushing at consultants, a feeling which comes easily to a 'parent/child' organization[8] inclined to rely on adult male authority figures. Cool questions are asked: have we the skills in house? Have we a software package which could help more easily? Could we write the software ourselves? Can the consultant deliver – what is the evidence from other clients? Will what is delivered last or will it decay without renewed consultancy fees? Is the consultant's track record in similar fields or is it an 'adapt and hope' contract?

In South Yorkshire – where you don't have to learn 'carefulness' with your money, it's in your mother's milk – we have stopped sending our police officers off to university to read law and send them off to read for Master's Degrees in Business Administration (MBAs) instead; we spend sensibly on corporate membership of the Sheffield Business School (SBS) and use wherever we can the available skills of our Police Authority members. Recently, for example, we used Professor Kevan Scholes[9] of the Sheffield Business School to facilitate a key seminar on forming the strategy for our restructuring of the Force. Locally produced seminars by the SBS are attended regularly by members of our various command strata, who then import the new knowledge back into the organization.

MBA achievers are strategically placed, as they approach the final throes of qualification, where they can use the requirement to produce a thesis in analysing a knotty police dilemma, briefing the organization as their bright – and tutored – minds come to grips with the issues involved.

Nevertheless, despite the emphasis on self-help, we do invest in the occasional use of carefully chosen facilitators to help us with both process and task issues, realizing that, as an organization, not only can we occasionally fail to see the wood for the trees but that we are sometimes in the wrong wood.[10]

One of the great benefits of turning our culture towards an outward-looking perspective has been the growth in partnership activity with the public, private and voluntary sectors. Collaborative work with Investors in People, National Vocational Qualification administrators, the European Foundation for Quality Management and the Prime Minister's Charter Mark award office has brought us a veritable raft of advice for one of the earlier, weaker parts of our learning – that of measuring progress in what we do in the qualitative domain. The traditional police culture was weaned on crime statistics, but those statistics – despite what politicians want you to believe – are notoriously unclear in what they reveal. The more of a 'snapshot' they are and the more they lump together unrelated categories of crime, the less meaning they have. Some useful insights *are* possible from single categories of crime. For example, when burglary figures are viewed with year-on-year rolling averages, they can display genuine trends as opposed to 'blips'.

To these quantitative statistics, the South Yorkshire Police have learned to add qualitative elements. We have commissioned two-yearly in-depth public research at the independent hands of Sheffield Hallam University into in-Force aspects of corporacy and morale, and external aspects of customer satisfaction.

INTERNAL REVIEWS

Aiding this process, the Force has invested strongly in its Corporate Development Department, which has functions of 'scoping' and boundary management, environmental scanning and policy analysis, as well as inspection and performance review. The corporate 'quality' initiative is housed within this department but should be learning and teaching itself out of a job; the ultimate goal is for the 'quality' theme to be an unconscious part of every employee's approach to work. Meanwhile, we try to recruit to this department a good mix of feet-on-the-ground practitioners as well as people with good intellect. Candidates are at their best when those two qualities combine.

Once again, externally and to distinguish the idea of learning from the idea of being taught, Her Majesty's Inspectorate of Constabulary constantly push for adoption of good practice as they tour our country's 43 Forces on both general and thematic inspections. The Inspectors are themselves a useful mix of former Chief Executives from the private sector and former Chief Constables.

OPENNESS FOR A 'SECRET SERVICE'

The battle for greater openness goes on as a lever in moving the organization towards customer awareness. There are, of course, necessarily secret areas of our work. If terrorists can choose the time, place and method of their attacks on society, we just cannot afford to give them the extra advantage of telling them details of our technology, deployments or techniques. But for the rest, our work can be much more open than we sometimes pretend.

A spirit of openness starts at home, with the way the organization treats its own personnel. Two interrelated and key elements have helped the South Yorkshire Police to feel more open with each other, so leading to greater transparency with the general public.

The first was the adoption of the 'away day' as the means of detaching members of staff from in-trays and telephones and, gradually, from their professional 'shells'. We learned to do this by trial and success and not altogether as a conscious process. The first stage was to hold essentially task-oriented sessions for senior managers at our Sports and Social Club. The setting was familiar and unthreatening as opposed to the work in hand which, at that time, was probably a mix of both the unfamiliar *and* the threatening.

In a culture which was happier with being told what to do and getting on with it, some conservative anxieties were stirred when members were asked to give over a whole day to three questions:

1   What do we do well; which we should continue?
2   What do we do badly; which we should stop?
3   What could we do completely differently in order to improve
    our service to the public?

The sessions brought mixed fortunes. There was strong support for a new approach; there were also rearguard actions to undermine it and those who supported it. There was apathy and self-doubt. We used junior ranking, trained facilitators to help the process and, though at first they were fearful of their task at the hands of prospectively unforgiving seniors, they went to work with refreshing openness yet diplomacy. Flip-charts for the first question yielded thin, hesitant answers. For the second, they were crammed with self-flagellation. The third set produced the seeds of excellent, creative ideas. The Senior Command Team learned much from the reticence of members handling the process of tackling this comparatively straightforward task.

The next stage was, therefore, to concentrate on the process itself. We removed ourselves from the Sports and Social Club to an outlying country house, wore much more relaxed clothing (though it was a matter of choice for all, some of whom still were happier with collar and tie), called in non-police facilitators and were essentially agenda-free: we were there to interreact. The results were electric. Free of task, members contributed freely, sometimes heatedly but genuinely, and supportive of each other.

Back at HQ, in uniform for formal Policy Review Committee meetings, a more relaxed and constructive atmosphere reigned amongst the same members who, interestingly, devised a small rectangular card bearing the name 'Bawtry' on it (the name of the country house), which was 'played' in the course of meetings if somebody's feelings were trampled on in our haste to crack on with the task. Even more interesting, although it was usually played by the person feeling bruised, it was also occasionally played *on behalf of others*. The holding up of the card was accepted as a way of stopping task to look at process. It was greeted usually with kindly laughter and rueful acknowledgement by offending players that they had erred.

From those early days, 'away days' have now spread through the organization and are an acknowledged way of dealing with improved processes of communication. One recent meeting with a task focus saw mixed ranks from superintendent to constable across two neighbouring districts meeting under the chairmanship of a very able sergeant – now, in a hierarchy-conscious outfit, that *is* learning.

The other commitment to openness came in the Senior Command Team declaration that nothing should be said or written about a member of staff which was not known to that person. It involved opening up personal records for scrutiny. This was preceded by much heart-searching for, although we knew it was the right moral step to take, we feared civil actions from people alleging loss of opportunity in their careers. The results, again, were almost magical. There was anger and some bitterness at what had clearly been dishonest treatment: for example, people had been told to their faces, some years previously, that they had done well but had narrowly missed selection on a promotion board. However, something very much more damning had been written covertly on their record. They had then waited with bated breath for their anticipated advancement, and waited, and waited. Yet, suddenly, those clouds of false expectation and mischief were behind us and we were in open, sunlit uplands. Even more fortunate, there were no civil actions; the act of opening the records was met with great generosity of spirit.

MEDIA RELATIONS AS A PART OF OPENNESS

Openness within the organization was a conscious end in itself but was also the route to greater openness with the public. This was reinforced by the repeated assertions, publicly, by members of the Senior Command Team that we were to make ourselves, as an organization, open and accessible in the interests of greater accountability. We adopted (and continue) a sustained media campaign in which we try to accept any opportunity to appear on radio, television or in the newspapers, explaining the way we want to do business.

This is supported by a policy statement that all members of the organization should feel free to speak to the media, changing the culture from a 'No, but sometimes you can...' to a 'Yes, but sometimes you can't...' attitude. This statementis supported by three-day in-house media courses, opened by the Chief Constable, and stressing the practical, as well as the ethical, value of openness. The courses are partly taught by local media reporters and editors, so reinforcing in the minds of local news outlets our serious commitment to the new direction.

STRUCTURAL CHANGE

Although the Senior Command Team had thought that the process of cultural change would take at least five years from 1990 to be sufficiently advanced to allow deep and genuine consultation on restructuring, the organization developed its own view! Some two-and-a-half years into the cultural change programme, front-line officers from Barnsley started to make clear representations that, in their opinion, the structure of the organization was impeding change. This coincided with government proposals to abolish two of the then existing ranks by name (though substituting an unhappy fudge of titles and salaries). Following these internal and external cues, the South Yorkshire Police set about a massive reorganization, incorporating delayering and rationalization of all functions.

The Policy Review Committee agreed to be guided by the following principles:

- No change would be just for change's sake.
- Recommendations were to be based on empirical findings not on whims or fads.
- Consultation was essential with those to be affected.
- People would be treated with dignity and compassion.
- It was to achieve greater effectiveness rather than cost-cutting.

Another new direction was to articulate the wish that 'districts were to come first'. This was to offset the strong cultural perception that if push came to *209* shove, Headquarters would always get the first choice, and the prime share, of personnel or equipment.

The 18-month long process got underway and there were moments of grave doubt as we generated piles of paper, and meetings of 40 or 50 staff after working hours and at week-ends. Sometimes we would make a decision in principle only to have to revisit it when we later realized that it was hooked into other, incompatible decisions, but the changing culture had, by then, legitimized the expression of doubt and the tolerance of some ambiguity. Reversing decisions was no longer seen as weakness but as good sense in the face of incontrovertible evidence.

We are now out of the process: the review is completed and the implementation is settling down, following a 'big bang' approach on one April day in 1995. Visiting Inspectors of Constabulary, comparing us with other forces undergoing similar activity across the country, reported informally that they had found 'exactly the same level of chaos but without the bitterness found elsewhere!'. My personal guess is that they did not survey our staff sufficiently widely, because there is undoubted bitterness in some quarters about the processes and some of the decisions. Although they were only a dozen or so, we knew there would be casualties and they lie strongly on our conscience.

Nevertheless, the processes involved, though arduous and sapping, showed a growing willingness in many key players to think and act corporately, taking their protective arm from around their own commands, ceding staff to those with greater need and putting the larger organization first.

There were some excellent lessons in communication, with the staff associations and trades unions playing an integrated and supportive role, obviously trying to spot common ground rather than gainable territory. The Force learned – through the appointment of a high-credibility senior practitioner to head up the Review and Implementation Team – the value of regular, easy-to-read, informal update bulletins.

BINNING AND BOTTLING

In all of this, there will inevitably be techniques and decisions that we will want to consign to the waste-bin and advances that we will wish we could bottle and sell.

If I were starting out all over again from 1990, I would probably do something enormously rational – take a sabbatical, get the Senior Command Team involved in all the reading, draw up a model, call in the consultants and work to a scheduled time-table, explaining to all personnel just what we were doing now and planned to do and when. It sounds glorious – and quite alien.

Elements for the bin:

- Solo flights, not taking senior partners into early, active confidence.
- Working without adequate management information.
- Failure to integrate departmental planning into a whole.

- Failure to integrate policy and practice.

Elements for bottling:

- Cultural change first, *followed by* structural change.
- Getting deep into process issues.
- Commitment to absolute honesty.
- Valuing the staff for worth as people not grades/ranks.
- Dealing with giving constructive feedback at an organizational level (how meetings fare, how policy is working out) as well as at a personal level.
- Rewarding the behaviours we want to encourage: honesty, openness, flexibility, assumption of responsibility, accountability.
- Drawing blame inwards towards seniority; pushing credit outwards.
- Working *with* existing culture even as you change it.
- Our home-grown formula, ICP – Issues/Cash/Priorities – to underpin formation of strategy.
- Drawing widely on knowledge and experience in-Force for help with policy formation.
- Tapping into external help as we battled with formulating strategy.
- Investment in staff and Information Technology for corporate performance review.
- Partnerships in learning with other organizations.
- Simple, humorous, easily read bulletins.

Of course, the learning goes on. Even as I write, we have just returned from a stormy 48-hour 'away day' where powerful emotions were stirred by a mismatch of perceptions, between the Senior Command Team and new members of the Policy Review Committee, about what the purpose was of the two days – was it emphasis on task or emphasis on process? Metaphorical fur flew. Afterwards, as people checked and found that they still had head and limbs intact and were still on agreeable terms with each other, the realization dawns on another segment of our organization that the expression of strong individual feelings is both legitimate and safe.

REFERENCES

1 Critchley, T.A. (1967), *A History of The Police in England and Wales, 1900–1966*, London: Constable.

2 Licensing Act 1872, Section 16(2).

3 Scholtes, Peter B. (1988), *The Team Handbook*, Joiner Associates.

4 Revans, Reg (1980), *Action Learning – New Techniques for Management*, Blond and Briggs.

5 Schein, Edgar H. (1988), *Organizational Culture and Leadership*, San Francisco: Jossey-Bass.

6 Pheysey, Diana C. (1993), *Organizational Cultures: Types and Transformations*, London: Routledge.

7 Egan, Gerard (1993), *Adding Value – Business Driven Management and Leadership*, Jossey Bass.

8 Berne, Eric (1966), *The Structures and Dynamics of Organizations and Groups*, New York: Grove Press.

9 Scholes, Kevan and Johnson, Gerry (1993), *Exploring Corporate Strategy*, New York: Prentice Hall.

10 Covey, Stephen R. (1992), *The Seven Habits of Highly Effective People*, London: Simon and Schuster.

17 The Learning Organization – the route to chaos or rejuvenation?

Bianka Mensah

When I was asked to write this chapter I thought very carefully about what it should be called. I thought about the organizations I had worked with during my 12-year career and realized that what had characterized them was the havoc caused by what was viewed as unwelcome change and the need to respond innovatively to that process in order to survive.

This innovation however, was often not planned in any meaningful way, and while it released the potential of those who seemed to have been trapped like flies within the web of these bureaucratic organizations, it turned the majority into rabbits standing in the middle of the road looking directly into the lights of an oncoming lorry knowing death was approaching and feeling unable to do anything to avert it. Others became saboteurs; feeling angered by the disordering of their world they turned to organizational disruption and crime to get back at those they felt had let them down. Some of those in positions of authority saw the opportunity for greater power and for a time stopped working for the organization. Their main motivation became the need to attain the best position before things settled down again. Little did they know that it would never completely settle down again.

This was chaos at the individual level. It is possible from my experience to say that as organizations have to continually meet the challenges of reinventing themselves, this kind of activity (that is, individual-level chaos) does diminish.

Organizations, stating the obvious, are only the sum of their parts, and variations of individual-level chaos were often then expressed at the macro level (corporately). This tended to take a number of forms. In the first instance what would become evident was an inability to take effective decisions at the most senior levels. This was followed by the organization looking inwards, blaming and scapegoating, unplanned delayering often resulting in the loss of skill necessary to facilitate the future development of the organization. Only then might there be what I will call rejuvenation.

The beginning of rejuvenation is usually signalled by the appearance of visionaries. There is usually one, but possibly more, visionaries in the organization who seem to suddenly come to the fore. These are not always the people at the top. Often, the truth of the matter is that these individuals have been sitting back watching the chaos, thinking and planning the change. They then present a strategy which takes account of where the organization has come from, its present position, where it could be going (as there is always more than one path), how to get there and more importantly how it can sustain itself through successive upheaval.

Such strategies often had the effect of bringing these organizations to life (unfortunately for some it was only for a short while), giving the working environment a new buzz. There was a new goal which was not just to survive; it was about recognizing that the organization was its people and could only develop and continue to progress as the people within it did. In addition, in the times in which we lived, organizations could not hope to fulfil all the expectations of the people that they employed; that it was, and is not, possible to provide them with security for the full breadth of their career(s). That innovation is not generated by making people feel comfortable but by challenging them. Furthermore, people need to have their minds open to what is possible and that this is not achieved through the routine of just doing but also by having the space to reflect on what they have done and how the knowledge acquired from reflection could be best used in the future; the mission was not only about the service but also about how that service would be delivered. We tend not to learn very much when things are going well. Often the learning that becomes most fundamental for us is achieved in situations of chaos.

The development of learning in these organizations was one of the strategies to continual rejuvenation; a way of working through chaos. Learning was used as a way of enhancing the ability of the people in these organizations to see chaos (or change) as a means of progression for the organization; to actively seek out change as a route to rejuvenation.

The organizations I have been generalizing about are in the main public sector. Later on in this chapter I will be using one of them as an example to give practical application to the generalized theory. From my experience these organizations did not make a conscious decision to become Learning Organizations, and in my view very few organizations generally do; they came to the process as a path out of crisis. It is often in the middle of chaos that learning, as a strategy, is developed.

Not everybody takes to it readily. Many 'traditionalists' see it as a soft option having less definition than the 'hard' programmes of redundancy and service redesign which may run in parallel to the development of learning in an organization, and did in all those I worked with. In addition, learning implies change at an individual level – a challenge to the way the individual has always done things. It may therefore be perceived as a threat to be overcome. To combat this, clear strategies of learning need to be developed to deal with potential saboteurs, those who would undermine their own learning and consequently that of the organization.

Learning should also be undertaken at different levels. It needs to be clear what you are seeking to achieve as much with the Chief Executive as with the cleaner who only comes in for two hours four times a week, and what may be applicable to staff may need to be adapted for senior managers. Faced with a matrix of variables of this order, it is not always possible to start at the same place with everyone. What is important is to work with all those involved to agree the process and its relevance to them.

THE ORGANIZATION AS A PHOENIX

The operating environment

To illustrate the theory outlined above I intend to use a case study taken from the world of Housing Associations. The 'movement', as it has been known until recently, has its roots in the voluntary not-for-profit sector, although it now prefers to be known as 'independent' (that is, from the normal constraints experienced by public sector bodies). It grew out of the need to address ever-increasing demands for more and better quality housing. Largely funded by public money it enjoyed, up to the late-1980s, relative growth in its numbers and areas of operation to the point where there are now just over 2 000 such organizations in the UK. As with any industry there are some large organizations within it, and the Association I will be referring to is one of these. Over the years the Association had received large sums of capital funding for its housing development programmes. It had also been classed amongst the innovative in this field with a tradition of developing new approaches to providing for households in housing need. With over 300 staff and a significant capital assets base, it should have been well placed to take advantage of the change that was to come.

The organization was formed around two operational activities, housing management and housing development. The former was further split into traditional housing provision and income, generating temporary housing provided to local authorities to house the statutory homeless who could not immediately be found suitable permanent accommodation. The purpose of housing development was mainly to add to the permanent stock of the Association which would be let mainly to people on the local authority waiting list.

Association A, as I shall call it, virtually doubled its housing stock and its staff numbers in the five-year period to 1990. Supported by the government and seen in many quarters as the answer to the increasing social problems of homelessness, Associations appeared to have a stable and secure future. In Association A there seemed to be the view that little would change and what did would not dramatically affect the way they were operating at the time.

In 1988 the government introduced a new Housing Act which was to spell chaos for most Associations. The early 1990s were lean years with falls in the *real* level of funding to Associations and an increasing threat of privatization. Associations fell out of favour with a government keen on controlling public expenditure and introducing more competition into the public sector.

The senior management of Association A, comfortable in the knowledge that it was amongst the top ten Associations with an unrivalled assets base, were slow to respond to the changes on the horizon. Its most lucrative market, the leasing of temporary accommodation for local authorities, began to feel the effects of increasing competition. Innovation seemed to have stopped. In the lean years of the early 1990s the organization was faced with cutting significant numbers of staff, having to reduce its development programme and the possibility of becoming stagnant.

Another area of difficulty was its management structure. This was characterized by an older and more traditional senior management with an inexperienced middle and front-line management where there had been promotion of professional expertise which had not been supported by the development of management skills. At the very top of the organization was a governing body made up of part-time lay professionals many of whom had been with the Association for between 10–15 years. The staff on the other hand, were young and dynamic, keen to see changes at the top which they believed would restore the Association to its position of being one of the most progressive in the movement.

Communication channels were rigidly downwards, although there was an active grapevine encouraged by the union. This further supported a 'them and us' culture which was developing as part of the growing fear in the Association.

During this time it appeared that the vision for the organization had been lost. This was evident in the way the organization began to submerge itself in its internal processes. There was growth in the importance of financial controls in response to concerns over the possibilities of fraud where large sums of public money were involved. There was also a greater emphasis on the management of resources which resulted in the closer scrutiny of budgets and cost-cutting exercises, particularly in support activities such as training. This is not to say that these measures are not important, but the manner in which they were undertaken meant there was a focus on negatives in the organization. As the level of tension within the organization increases the process of scapegoating and blaming begins, people become anxious and fearful and the internal communications grapevine usually works overtime and in a very negative way.

Seemingly unable to effectively respond to the *chaos* being generated around it, the Association began a process of creating *chaos* within itself. This would not necessarily have been a bad thing had it been a planned and managed process. This would have been one that challenged the current concepts within the organization; looked at its methods of operation and their relevance to the present environment; reflected and learned from what was happening. What the organization needed was something that would intervene and break the cycle of negative, inward-looking and scapegoating. This was recognized by a group of senior and middle managers keen to ensure the organization's survival and their own. They accepted that there was a need to change and also recognized that change would become a feature of the way their environment would operate in the future. Added to this was the initial recognition of their lack of skills to deal effectively with such an environment and more generally the lack of skills within the Association to effectively cope with constant chaos. These managers were to become the 'visionaries'.

Learning to survive

Change I see very much as a circle with learning at the very heart of the process. Once an organization has been through the difficult process of change for the first time and has consciously applied learning as a developmental tool subsequently, it should be possible to manage the process more appropriately each successive time.

Figure 17.1 represents the basic premise of this chapter. It aims to illustrate that it is possible to learn from the chaos that change generates, and also to use learning to create ordered chaos to rejuvenate the organization. In this context chaos should be a managed process. Some aspects of chaos could also be planned. This is possible if learning is established as a practice in the organization. For this to be the case it would need to be part of the culture or rather the way things are done in the organization.

With learning as part of the culture, managers should be in a position to predict, to a significant degree, the next phase of chaos (change) that will take place in their environment, both internally and externally. The result of this should be that the process of learning challenges managers and as I have said previously, opens their minds to what is possible. It should also provide a route to acquiring the necessary skills to develop themselves and their staff, and thereby the organization, through to rejuvenation.

Once this process is established it provides the link in a continuous cycle of chaos and rejuvenation. While not all change will be accounted for through this means, it should be possible to limit the effects of even unplanned change. The response to change should not be one of panic and negative reaction, but one of reflecting on what has been learned from previous episodes of chaos and how that could best be applied in the present. Even where events appear to be

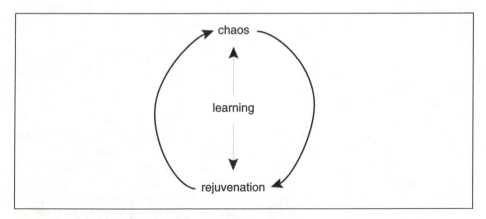

Figure 17.1   Chaos, learning and rejuvenation

distinctly different it should provide the means to develop more appropriate responses. Action is therefore proactive, positively inventive and measured.

The proof of the pudding

The problems with which the Association was faced were complex to resolve but it was crucial that the approach taken was relevant for all levels in the organization. One of the essential factors was the middle managers; their importance was that they had dual operational and strategic responsibilities. This duality also meant that they had the links both up and down the organization which would be essential in implementing any process and delivering the on-going benefits of change.

When I started with the organization change was already on the horizon. The Association was beginning to experience some of the difficulties I have outlined previously. It was helpful that some managers sensed that change would have to come and also that some form of intervention would be necessary to get the organization through what was viewed as the chaos that would occur. As the human resource specialist, I was keen to get a sense of how the organization was viewed by those in it. I spent the first three months talking with the senior managers, the middle and junior managers and as many of the staff as was possible. The story was a familiar one. There were already strains between the staff and the management group. The focus of the organization was inward, the main point of contention at the time being a revised disciplinary procedure.

There was also a widening gap in understanding between the middle and senior management group. The latter had the perception that the middle managers did not have the strong management skills necessary to *manage* the staff; the former thought the senior group were not capable of seeing the change agenda and could not deliver a prosperous and stable future for the organization.

An evaluation of the total organization was needed, and possible solutions assessed and discussed. It was important that all levels of management became part of that evaluation and bought into the solutions. As I was now part of this group I felt it more appropriate to commission an evaluation from an external body. The well-known large consultancy organizations would not have achieved what we needed and, it was felt, would only have alienated the groups involved. What was carried out was an exercise conducted by a single independent specialist with whom they could relate.

As part of the agreement to the evaluation taking place, the promise was made that it would not be possible to identify any particular manager from the overall assessment that would be given. Combined with the fact that this was the first time for a significant period that an intervention of this kind had been undertaken in the Association, it allowed those managers and directors involved in the process to be very frank about the problems as they saw them. The evaluation highlighted the existence of significant divisions both at directorial level and in some middle management areas. This was not surprising but what was concerning was the depth at which this worked against the effective operation of the Association. It also had ramifications for the effectiveness of any solutions.

A further concern arose with the issue of culture – the way the Association did things – it appeared that two cultures were being run in parallel. The first was that expressed by the senior (directorial group) managers and the second was based on the perception of the rest of the Association staff (including the remaining managers), about how things were actually done. What was clear was that certain things happened depending on which functional area you worked in.

The Association was effectively divided on functional lines. Traditional housing management which had been in mothballs for some time (but would witness a re-emergence); housing development, where the personality of the Director and his time in the organization had secured him a power base that was not effectively challenged and which had implications for the changes that were looming on the horizon; and the supposedly more commercial leasing operation which provided temporary accommodation. The latter's strength came from its ability to generate large revenue surpluses which had significantly boosted the Association's reserves and its ability to borrow on the financial market.

Working with the external development consultant, a series of meetings were held with all the senior managers. In addition, a questionnaire was sent out to a random sample of middle and junior managers. Another aspect of the exercise was the needs identification form which was sent out to staff so they could detail what skill- and knowledge-gap areas they felt they had. This had a broader remit than just addressing current training needs – an anonymous feedback sheet was attached which invited constructive comment from them on what they felt to be the problems in the Association.

Much of the information from this exercise confirmed what I have already detailed. It also highlighted that there was a considerable gap between the core of the organization (traditional housing management and development), and the commercial arm of the operation. This was at all levels. This was emphasized by the view at senior level that the Association lacked an internal corporate identity. However, though the senior managers subscribed to a need for such an identity, their actions appeared to actively work against its attainment. Evidence of this could be seen in the competition between functions. Furthermore, functional lines were strictly drawn with any attempts for cooperative work being seen as encroachment. Despite these tensions there was almost universal recognition that change would become a way of life and if the organization was not to become a fossil, some means had to be developed to ensure its ability to cope and prosper then and in the future.

The initial strategy was to pilot learning among the whole management group. It was hoped that by tackling this group first (the middle managers in particular), it would be possible to impact on the culture, values, vision and mission of the Association. The reasoning behind this was that, if it was to be successful, learning would have to become part of the culture; as much a *219* prized value (what the organization believes in) as its ability to be innovative; encapsulated in the vision (the perfect state the organization aims for), and clearly stated in its mission (what the organization does).

A management development strategy focusing initially on knowledge based learning was put in place. This was targeted at the middle- and junior-level managers. The programmes were modular in approach allowing the managers to pick out certain elements. Some modules however, were mandatory. These included one on the role of the manager as leader and facilitator, which did not only deal with competencies but also their understanding of the culture, values, vision and mission of the Association. The modular programme was later replaced by development groups which were groups of managers who regularly met to define their own learning needs and reflect on and share learning.

For staff there were knowledge-based programmes around personal and group development and detailing how to use team meetings as opportunities for learning. Other developmental opportunities were implemented such as secondment, using maternity vacancies and project work. A policy of job swapping was implemented that allowed two individuals to change roles for a period of six months. A programme of traineeships was established allowing staff the opportunity to gain skills and subsequent appointments in other areas of the Association. Self-development (that is, staff identifying development needs and opportunities and agreeing action plans with their managers) became key, particularly at a time of cost cutting. In certain instances (for example, the acquiring of non-work related qualifications) where the Association could not make a financial contribution, staff were given time off, interest-free loans and part loans (some of the loan would be reimbursed to the individual on successful completion of their course).

All of these programmes had varying degrees of success. Group development highlighted the need to empower the staff delivering the service. They needed more autonomy to make the decisions that would make the service more effective for our tenants. The difficulty in achieving this was how to enable managers to relinquish control in a hierarchical command structure.

The most successful of these programmes was the traineeship scheme. This scheme was far more structured, with identified critical success factors. A programme based on the Institute of Housing Professional Training Course was a core part of the approach taken. The Institute had agreed, in principle, to accredit the programme on this basis. They also were involved in the evaluation of the programme, a report of which went to the main Management Committee of the Association. The four staff who had been on the first programme were, on completion of the course, able to gain appointments in the areas they wished to work.

Secondment and job swapping were more experience based and relied heavily on the individual acquiring skills and knowledge by doing a job. Regular appraisal was built into the schemes and managers were required to provide evaluation reports at the end of the agreed period. Both had limited success because of the criteria laid down for matching individuals to particular jobs in the first place. There was also, understandably, a level of reluctance to release 'good' staff for these programmes.

The process then began to impact on other areas as the cultural influences began to take shape. The need for better communications came to the fore. This was not only internally but also with (what became known as) all our stakeholders, tenants, members, shareholders, etc. Internally we looked at ways to improve accessibility to the senior managers. One method that was implemented was a session with the Chief Executive on the junior management programme. There was also an investigation into the concept of continuous improvement at the service level and the application of the principles of Total Quality Management. There was the development of performance management systems and a move away from payment for length of service to payment for performance and achievement. The structure was reviewed to see how it could be set up to empower staff to better deliver the service.

I have left the details of the action around the senior management group to last perhaps because, with hindsight, I feel the problems encountered with this group were the first steps in the breakdown of the process. This group did not immediately recognize a need for development in themselves, but in the hierarchical structure of that time it was necessary that they were seen to be part of the process; paying lip service to it was not considered sufficient. The original strategy for the group had recommended team development work. The evaluation had shown that as individual directors they channelled considerable amounts of energy into protecting their areas of operation. It also found that this protectionism worked against the consensus management approach of the Chief Executive. Information appeared to be hoarded on the basis that knowledge was power. This was as much within the group as by the group itself. They operated on a need-to-know basis which generated an air of secrecy about everything they did. This served to alienate the middle managers, part of whose role was to straddle both this group and the one below.

It could be said that this limited the ability of the middle managers to be as effective as they could have been. A complaint, I have said before, which was levelled at them by the senior managers, particularly around issues of staff management.

The senior managers refused the opportunity of team development, opting instead for facilitation around more knowledge-based issues. They did, however, with one public voice support the process and highlighted their involvement in knowledge based events as a clear indication of the drive from the top. However, it often came to my attention that, behind the closed doors of one-to-one meetings with middle managers, their apparent support for the change was not always backed up.

DID IT WORK?

These new strategies worked up to a point. There were visible signs of people taking on the process. Managers began to actively request group skills training. As a result, a series of programmes were put on around human resource management issues. The set programmes in the management development programme were over subscribed. Requests were received for the establishment of self-development groups. Also, informal groups of managers began to meet on a regular basis to discuss Association-wide issues, exchange information and share experiences.

Front-line staff also became active in the process. They sought more involvement in the decision-making processes within the organization. As a result of this, when proposals for introducing performance management were being considered, extensive consultation took place directly with staff as well as with their representatives. Time was allocated on all in-house programmes for staff to be able to discuss issues in the Association. These would then be fed to the senior management team as part of a quarterly training briefing.

However, the air of secrecy at the top of the organization was still evident. In some ways this increased during this period, fostered by growing concern about the operation of the commercial housing management division.

In talking to staff about why they thought learning had been successful within the Association the most common response was that it seemed to offer a real and long-term solution which was not just about the Association but also about the development of the individual. People were beginning to recognize that the ability of the organization to fulfil all their career demands was limited. In addition there was some realization that there was something to the saying that you only got out of something what you put in. Furthermore, with the changing nature of work, they would need to be able to be flexible not only to meet the immediate needs of their present employment but any future jobs as well.

The changes in attitudes and the acceptance of learning resulted in an improvement in service, where the emphasis was now placed on stakeholder needs. This led to a number of initiatives being implemented. Better Information Technology systems, with networking capacity were introduced. There was evidence of increased responsiveness to tenants (both current and future) through forums, surveys and a faster turn-around of empty properties. The Association experienced a marked and on-going reduction in rent arrears which was achieved by setting targets in each area of the housing management operation, and better support and communication with tenants and benefit offices. For two years the reserves from our commercial housing management operation increased significantly allowing the Association to join a consortium that were able to borrow large sums from the financial market. A multidisciplinary team (the first ever project team) came together to develop a bid to tender for the management of a local authority's housing stock. The effectiveness of this approach was such that the Association won the bid.

Too many cooks?

There were problems rising to the surface as a result of the push for continuous improvement and greater empowerment. Some areas engaged with the process more than others and this resulted in uneven development. In addition, it became clear that there was a power struggle in progress at the top of the organization between the senior managers and the lay board of governors. This, in particular, diminished the focus of the senior management group to the process.

The whole organization was to become engaged in this power struggle following the sudden resignation of the Chief Executive. This was swiftly followed by the departure of the Director of the commercial housing management operation. These changes were poorly planned and pushed the organization, once again, into another unmanaged chaotic phase. During the following six months – fearing radical, negative change – a number of those who had championed the process left the organization.

The implementation of down-sizing now became a priority. The commercial operation was re-integrated into what was seen as the core activities of the Association resulting in the need for less front-line staff and less staff generally as the ripple effect of that decision took hold. After only three years, the process we were trying to establish was still too much in its infancy to survive the chaos taking place. It was not embedded well enough in the culture of the organization to be self-generating. In addition, I believe that the culture of the organization itself worked against the implementation of the process. The alienation and sense of mistrust which were part of the organization's cultural make-up lay under the surface of what we were trying to do, awaiting an opportune moment to re-emerge; the latter changes presented that opportunity. We clearly did not win the fight for hearts and minds, but this is something which cannot be achieved overnight and given another two or three years it would have been possible.

AT THE END OF THE DAY

A fundamental question is whether the fact that the process failed to become a *natural* part of the organization was a result of the environment in which it was expected to operate. Had it been a private sector organization in similar circumstances would the outcome have been any different? I would suggest not. No matter the environment, what is crucial to the success of any process is the stage of development of both the organization and the process that one is trying to establish, and what interventions occur and when. Both must be of sufficient maturity to survive any major upset. The organization must have sufficient history, resource and foresight to be able to limit the adverse impact of any unplanned change; and the process must have had sufficient time to have caught the imagination of those in the organization (won their hearts and minds) and be an established system. The whole organization must engage with the process and no one individual or group should feel that it is being 'done to them'. The latter could result in the development of sub-cultures and further affect how well the process becomes established.

Public/independent sector organizations should not be any different in approach than their private sector counterparts. In any event, any differences that might have existed are being eroded by the drive towards greater *223* competitiveness. However, I do believe that public sector organizations have one added dimension that may contribute to limiting the effectiveness of such processes. As the saying goes, 'he who pays the piper plays the tune' and the fact that they are funded out of the public purse makes them more susceptible to the political whims of incumbent governments. Consequently, it can often be seen that no sooner have they implemented one legislative change than another is issued. As a result, there is little, if any, time to see a process embedded before there is a need to change systems again or overlay one change process with another. This kind of yo-yoing can be contained if the visionaries and champions of the process have survived subsequent changes and are in a position to ensure its continued implementation. Often, as occurred in Association A, this is not the case. The effect of this is that the organization is catapulted back to the beginning. It is this stopping and starting that impacts on the effectiveness of the process.

We should nevertheless take heart from the successes that do exist in the public sector, particularly in local government and the health service. In these areas there is some evidence that political change is being more effectively managed and used to best advantage in the provision of better services which is our *raison d'être*.

BIBLIOGRAPHY

Burgoyne, John (1995), 'Feeding Minds to Grow the Business', *People Management*, September.

Dolan, Steve (1995), 'A Different Use of Natural Resources', *People Management*, October.

Handy, C. (1985), *Understanding Organizations*, Harmondsworth: Penguin Books.

Handy, C. (1992), *The Age of Unreason,* London: Arrow Books.

Mumford, A. (1989), *Management Development: Strategies for Action*, London: Institute of Personnel.

Peters, T. (1989), *Thriving on Chaos*, London: Pan Books.

Senge, P., Ross, R., Smith, B., Roberts, C. and Kleiner, A. (1994), *The Fifth Discipline Fieldbook: Strategies And Tools for Building a Learning Organization*, London: Nicholas Brealey Publishing.

Postscript: The future of the Learning Organization in the public services

Janice A Cook, Camden Social Services

There are currently numerous pressures on the public services:

> the battle with inflation and control of the Public Sector Borrowing Rate through public sector financing;
> the pressure to produce more for less;
> the associated attention to quantitative returns for output;
> the intervention of on-site and home-based Information Technology work styles;
> the impact of down-sizing and reductions in full-time employment;
> the impact of privatization principles, market-testing and Compulsory Competitive Tendering;
> the impact of equality of opportunity procedures.

These pressures will sharpen the need for Learning Organizations to engage in 'scoping' studies and in environmental scanning, with investment in resources deployed to policy analysis, performance measurement, assessment against plans by inspection and self-inspection methods. Links between long-distance forecasting, focused planning and Value for Money budgeting will be critical. Organizations will no longer be able to offer 'fiscal compliance' – meeting budget targets on time without verifiable regard for effectiveness.

All personnel – and particularly increased numbers of available graduates – will need an adjusted view of their relationship with their employer. As new Information Technology and the need for job-related training become evident, that training will become more intrusive into operations, more expensive to support and, in the end, will not be capable of being met by the organization alone. Staff will be required to develop self-reliance skills, taking active responsibility for their own learning, enhancement of their skills and personal development. This will often be in their own time and at their own expense and may clash with earlier, more dependent, cultures as well as with statutory

225

frameworks, such as the provision of overtime allowance. Learning Organizations will need to adjust to that development and support it through Distance Learning Packages, interactive video, video-conferencing, help-desks, hot-lines and peripatetic trouble-shooter teams and coaches.

Earlier assumed and informal 'psychological contracts' between employer and employee were based on a trade-off between talent offered and security assured. The demands placed upon the public sector, as described, will make employers require longer hours and harder work, with restricted opportunity for monetary reward (cash-limits) and career development (down-sizing).

Learning Organizations which invest in their people, care for them and give a qualitative return for their goodwill stand a better chance of survival – that is, resilience in the face of increased pressure – than those who grind their staff, as anonymous units, into quantitative returns alone through slavish progress-chasing. The return for goodwill may be met by simple attention to the atmosphere in which people work, allowing it to: celebrate difference; enjoy humour; thrive in teams; blend social and sporting contexts with working relationships; and, above all, provide regular and sincere recognition of good work under difficult circumstances.

CAN ORGANIZATIONS IN THE PUBLIC SERVICES BECOME LEARNING ORGANIZATIONS?

Maybe not

If a Learning Organization is taken to mean one which encourages training and development for its employees, the answer is likely to be 'yes'. Most public services have a tradition of providing and promoting these sorts of opportunities. In the face of changing technologies and the increasing supply of information, public service bodies are likely to want to ensure their employees have wider access to such information and are able to use it to good effect.

If, however, we switch our attention from the individual within an organization to the systems, structures and culture of the organization itself, we are likely to arrive at a different answer. Using Garvin's[1] definition of 'an organization skilled at creating, acquiring and transferring knowledge and at modifying its behaviour to reflect new knowledge and insights' throws into sharper relief the challenge to public service organizations. The sting in the tail of Garvin's formulation lies in the challenge to organizations to modify their behaviour to reflect the 'new knowledge and insights' which have been acquired. This is essentially a behavioural model. The extent to which behaviour is able to change depends largely on the constraints placed on change and on the inducements available. Frequently these are present within the same organization in varying degrees. They are manifested in different ways: through styles of management which may or may not be conducive to adaptation, and through pay and performance management systems which are designed to achieve certain ends without apparent regard for the often unintended constraints this imposes to the organization in 'modifying its behaviour'.

Despite attempts to re-create and present public service organizations as no different from their private sector counterparts, significant differences do exist. One of the most important of these differences is the Political control (with a capital 'P') to which they are subject. Hence, the application of management practice in private sector organizations, although subject to varying degrees of shareholder and boardroom control, can be quite different from the influences experienced by public service bodies; herein lies the uncertainty about their future as Learning Organizations since political control is unlikely to be relinquished in ways which would enable the sort of modification of behaviour which the Learning Organization applies.

Or maybe they can

The future of the Learning Organization in the public sector is assured and once an organization is on the road to becoming a Learning Organization the change becomes self-generating. Employees that have been empowered and who have accepted the responsibility, develop an attitude that is positive and become involved in the decision-making process and the implementation of those decisions. This change in attitude manifests itself in managers wishing to train the people they manage to eventually perform the job better than the existing job holder.

The modern public services have begun to realize that values and traditions have to be challenged and justified if they are to survive. Many of these values are shown in the most successful companies today. Values such as security of employment, an adequate pension scheme, respect of the individual and valued contribution of the individual to the organization's goal.

However, to survive as a Learning Organization, public services have to change. To change requires an understanding of the pressures from both internal and external environments. No healthy organization wants to die. The Learning Organization is the optimum way to achieve success and therefore the best chance of survival in what can be very hostile environments.

But why is it important to try?

The turbulence of the 1990s may abate, but the public sector will never return to the seemingly placid existence of the 1950s, 1960s and 1970s. For example, local government is no longer a monolithic service provider, but a key player in governance at the local level, operating in a plethora of partnership arrangements to provide satisfaction to a complex matrix of the population's needs.

The traditional structures and rules no longer apply, and attempts to hold on to them will only result in the organization drowning in a sea of inflexibility and red tape. Never before has it been more important for local authorities to develop the ability to learn from its interactions, and to put that learning to good use.

Substituting horizontal relationships for the traditional hierarchies is a key component of the local authority approaching the millennium. This can *227* happen only if a genuine commitment to creating an open culture which shares information exists. Partnerships and networks need to exist at all levels, both within and outside the organization. The local authority of the future will play a different role in different arenas: in some it will be leader, in others a facilitator, and in others the influencer, as well as the traditional provider of services.

The fluidity of these roles, and the ability to move smoothly between them, will require Council Officers and Elected Members to possess skills in multidisciplinary working, networking, advocating and managing contracts. The organizations will need to pay considerable attention to encouraging innovative ways of exploiting knowledge and skill, and to breaking down traditional barriers between departments as well as between the Council and other agencies.

Local authorities are still the primary agencies for providing for, and transforming the quality of life of, residents. Alone of all bodies, they consider the whole community, and they are democratically elected, able to provide an element of accountability which cannot be replicated by quangos, business or most voluntary agencies. If they are able to achieve the kind of flexibility possessed by Learning Organizations, they will be able to provide high-quality local leadership which reflects local needs and strategies.

All public services, or not-for-profit organizations, have a significant role in contemporary society. As we have repeatedly pointed out, there is no reason why these organizations should not become exemplars of good practice, allowing the private sector to learn from them.

The services provided by the organizations described in this book will have impacted on every single person who reads it, and on every person in the UK to varying degrees. Whether better health, freedom from crime, fire prevention or accident rescue, education, physical or emotional support, the list is almost endless: it is hard to imagine a more important challenge.

IN CONCLUSION

It could be argued that there are wider issues to be taken into account when considering the future of Learning Organizations in our society, and some interesting questions come to light in this thinking:

Is the Learning Organization the most evolved form of organization, or are ethics and morality significant in the next stage?

Can a negative, exploitive organization become a better exploiter by using Learning Organization technology?

By developing towards becoming a Learning Organization, what do organizations offer the common good, for example, what about pollution, relief of poverty, health issues, quality of life, etc?

Does learning, in so far as it embraces all the workforce, inevitably lead to greater worker/employee empowerment? Does industrial democracy beckon?

The Learning Organization has the potential to become an embracing, commonly understood concept, which can group a range of organizational activities and give them meaning and priority. The ethos of the Learning Organization is one which fits readily to the aspirations of many public service organizations and, it could be argued, is needed to maximize and target limited resources. We are unlikely to see the emergence of kite marks of 'an approved Learning Organization'; however we may see the introduction of the term more widely in the public services. The danger could be that it becomes too wide a label; a meaningless set of words rather than a committed, focused and integrated part of an organization's way of operating. In the current training world, with more emphasis on outputs, targets and quantifiable gains, the positive and inclusive opportunities presented by the idea of a Learning Organization could be seen to be out of fashion. We hope not!

REFERENCE

1 Garvin, David A. (1993), 'Building a learning organization', *Harvard Business Review*, July/August.

Index

Diary of a Change Agent

Tony Page

Tony Page is a 40-something management consultant, wrestling with the conflicting demands of a growing business and a growing family. For three years he kept a diary to which he confided his hopes and fears, his triumphs and setbacks. With painful honesty he analysed his working and business relationships as he strove to add value to his clients' businesses and to improve his own abilities.

The diary captures a unique personal journey and by including further commentary, analysis and exercises Tony Page both challenges the reader and emphaizes the human component in managing change.

Tony Page's book:

- introduces diary-keeping as a method for continuous professional and personal learning
- demonstrates ways of gaining control over personal performance
- shows how to conduct conversations that empower other people to change and learn
- provides an example and a direction for leaders who want to 'walk the talk'
- uncovers why corporate change programmes fail and how to mobilise people in an organization.

This honest account will have immediate appeal for anyone serious about business performance improvement, change and learning.

Gower

The Empowerment Manual

Terry Wilson

Most thinking managers would probably claim some knowledge of empowerment - the underlying philosophy, the potential benefits, perhaps some of the techniques involved. But how do you turn that knowledge into action that will match the specific needs of your own organization and the people who work in it? How do you measure their readiness to embark on an empowerment programme? How do you choose the best starting point and the most appropriate policies?

Terry Wilson's manual is based on his experience helping many organizations to empower their staff - and it can help you to do the same. Part I will enable you to decide on the most suitable type of programme and the best way to introduce it into your company or unit. Part II contains a series of activities through which you can assess your existing level of empowerment and then develop a detailed scheme for increasing it. The final Part tells the true story of how a successful company adopted empowerment to help it achieve its business goals. Throughout the text you will find questionnaires, checklists, exercises and action plans designed to help you map out the best way forward.

If you're serious about empowerment, but need a guiding hand to support planning and implementation in your organization, this *Manual* is for you.

Gower

The Facilitation of Groups

Dale Hunter, Anne Bailey and Bill Taylor

Group synergy is a source of power that has scarcely been tapped. Facilitation offers a way of unlocking that power. This book reveals the secrets of the art of facilitation and shows how to use it to initiate group empowerment.

Developing facilitation skills means first fully understanding the facilitator role: that of a guide helping a group or individual towards a conclusion, without steering the decision. To become an effective group facilitator you need to understand the principles of self-facilitation and the facilitation of individuals, as well as that of a group.

The authors, all experienced facilitators, begin by fully explaining the skills required and the benefits to be derived. The Toolkit which follows includes practical activities, designs and processes, and includes a model facilitation training programme.

This combination of personal experience and practical advice will have wide appeal for facilitators, trainers and group members.

Gower

New Leadership for Women and Men

Building an Inclusive Organization

Michael Simmons

What are the key attributes of successful leaders in today's organization? The answer to this question is of course hotly debated. But Michael Simmons' ground-breaking book is the first to place the development of a new leadership for women and men at the heart of the argument. In particular, it is the first to focus on the benefits of helping leaders to overcome the negative effects of gender conditioning on the quality of their leadership.

The author proposes that leaders must transform their organizations by learning how to manage a turbulent environment, increase productivity and quality, and build an 'inclusive organization'. Achieving these aims requires that *everyone* is involved in planning the future direction of the enterprise and contributes to its continual improvement. But gender conditioning leads many managers to put up barriers to the full involvement of all their people. Transformation means reaching beyond equality to an organization where boundaries and limitations are not placed upon anyone. It needs a new kind of leadership capable of harnessing the intelligence, creativity and initiative of people at all levels, especially those who have traditionally been excluded.

This timely book provides much more than a searching analysis of women and men's leadership. Using real-life examples and case studies, it sets out strategies, programmes and techniques for improving organizational performance, and describes in detail the type of training needed. In short, it is a book designed to inspire not just thought but action.

Gower

Practical NLP for Managers

Ian McDermott and Joseph O'Connor

It is almost a truism to say that your success as a manager depends on the quality of your communication.

NLP (Neuro-Linguistic Programming) is based on the study of excellence and provides the most powerful tools currently available for improving communication skills. There are many books setting out the relevant techniques; this is the first to show them at work in a practical management setting. The authors, both of them experienced NLP trainers, look in turn at each of the key elements in the management process and show how NLP can help. They explain:

- how to capture other people's attention and trust
- how to motivate
- how to use language (including body language) to maximum effect
- how to handle staff appraisals
- how to develop a consistent set of organizational values.

Practical NLP for Managers is a powerful communication skills tool for every manager who wants to improve their powers of persuasion and leadership.

Gower

A Real-Life Guide to Organizational Change

George Blair and Sandy Meadows

'Management ideas may change with fashion, but the underlying concepts do not lose their validity. We offer you prepared food for thought for your organizational microwave, rather than exotic dishes that are very difficult to copy.'

George Blair and Sandy Meadows - themselves battle-hardened veterans of the change process - take a refreshingly different approach to most of the new books, videos, seminars and gurus emerging to tell managers how to cope with change. They encourage the reader to start from the reality of his or her own organization and have the courage to design the programme that will work in real life.

Drawing both on proven systems and their own extensive experience, they chart the way forward from strategy to implementation. With the aid of checklists, illustrations and case studies, they show how to diagnose existing problems, how to construct the appropriate plans and how to deal with the politics. They examine the various options, including empowerment, TQM and re-engineering, set out the criteria for selecting the best mix for your own circumstances and then explain the techniques involved in implementation. Unlike many other books on change, they pay due attention to the need for a reward strategy to support the aims of the change programme.

This accessible and often humorous book is firmly grounded in reality, and will be a welcome relief for managers trying to assimilate accepted 'best practice' in change management into their real working lives.

Gower

The Zen of Groups

A Handbook for People Meeting with a Purpose

Dale Hunter, Anne Bailey and Bill Taylor

Increasingly the work of organizations is being carried out by groups rather than individuals. Moreover, all of us belong to groups throughout our lives - families, school, community, education and recreation groups. This book is designed to help you become a more effective member of the group and to show how the effectiveness of the group itself can be greatly increased. It offers insight into what makes groups work powerfully, and teaches through practical advice and numerous exercises.

The Zen of Groups is in two sections. The first nine chapters explain how groups function and put forward a number of ways for improving their performance. Throughout the text, 'Thinking Points' ask a series of questions designed to challenge the reader's assumptions. The second section consists of a 'toolkit' containing 95 techniques and exercises for developing group effectiveness. The exercises are indexed under eighteen headings, ranging from *Tools for generating ideas* to *Tools for ending and evaluation* to enable the reader to select the most appropriate.

The Zen of Groups is written in an informal style, and based on the authors' experience of working with a wide range of groups over many years. It will be of immense value to facilitators and group members alike.

Gower